THE

JURISPRUDENT

PHYSICIAN

THE JURISPRUDENT PHYSICIAN

A Physician's Guide to Legal Process and Malpractice Litigation

MARGARET DEAN, B.S.N., J.D.

LEGIS ✦ PRESS

Phoenix, Arizona

LEGIS ✦ PRESS
3646 E. Ray Road, Suite B16-52
Phoenix, Arizona 85044

ISBN 0-9670004-0-8

Library of Congress Catalog Card Number: 99-71509

Printed in the United States of America

With greatest appreciation, this is dedicated to –

my husband, Kevin, and to my children, Sean, James, Robert, Erin, and Thomas

– without whose inspiration, patience, and support this would not have been possible.

CONTENTS

INTRODUCTION

This book was developed as a result of experience with physicians in a variety of settings – formal, informal, litigation, non-litigation, educational, and social. Regardless of the setting it seemed to be a universal experience of physicians that they had unanswered questions about the workings of the legal system – and no reference to easily resort to. Some had a general interest in the legal system; others sought very specific information about particular aspects of legal practice or procedure that affected them directly on a day-to-day basis. It seems that apart from a meager assortment of scattered papers or talks on a few topics of their interest, on the whole, the education of physicians lacked a comprehensive exposure to important legal aspects of their chosen profession.

For most practitioners, the task of learning and understanding their legal obligations and roles is accomplished through on the job training. Such a "trial and error" approach can be unnecessarily nerve-racking at best and financially or professionally risky at worst. This book was developed to serve the vital interest physicians have in understanding the practical interactions between medicine and law. It gives physicians what they need – an overview of the law as it applies to their day-to-day practice. Whether you read it from cover to cover, or peruse a section here and there, it will help you understand "the system" – your responsibilities, and your rights.

The title for this book – *The Jurisprudent Physician* – is a play on words. It comes from the word *jurisprudence*, which is a Latin term referring to the philosophy or science of law. The title phrase aptly captures the spirit of this publication, which is aimed at helping the practitioner to ply his medical trade "prudently" with respect to the law.

The medical student – the resident – the newly established practitioner – and the veteran physician will all find immense value in reading this book. It can be read cover to cover for general interest, or for specific reference to particular topics within selected chapters. Medical schools will find that *The Jurisprudent Physician* offers them an excellent means to present students with a practical exposure to real world medical practice. Professional liability insurers will recognize the benefits this book provides to their physician-insureds. And physicians who find themselves on the wrong end of a medical malpractice case will better understand the process that will sweep them along in the litigation current. For many physicians, the information provided herein may mean the difference between being swept under by the current and keeping their heads afloat.

It is true that information and understanding are power – and that anxiety and fear of the unknown can be mentally crippling. No physician should face a simple records request, a deposition, or a medical malpractice lawsuit without having a resource to turn to for guidance. When it comes to conducting yourself in a legal context, ignorance is not bliss; it is misery, or worse. Use the information on these pages to help you understand what the legal system expects of you, why those expectations exist, and how you can meet those expectations reasonably and comfortably. The information presented will be of benefit to you because it will (1) assist and guide you when you voluntarily participate in the legal system; and (2) minimize the likelihood that you will be an involuntary participant in the system.

In all honesty, several frustrations must be confessed in connection with this writing. Taking the minor one first – gender references must be dealt with in any work of this sort. I found it least awkward to use male and female pronouns in an alternate rather than either/or (he/she) fashion. In nearly every instance of gender reference, either may be used. No slight is intended toward either sex by my use of singular gender reference. Frustration number 2, the more significant one, originates in the fact that this book strives more to present concepts than black letter law. To that end, I found it necessary to modify statements, perhaps ad nauseum, with qualifiers such as "generally", "typically", "usually", etc. Hopefully, this will not be wearisome for the reader and will instead serve as reminder that the intricacies of state and federal laws are sometimes distinctions *with* a difference.

Just as material is presented in many law school courses, this book is geared toward introducing basic medical-legal concepts that are important for every physician to know. With an understanding of legal principles and concepts in mind, when jurisdiction specific rules, regulations, and laws arise, they can be referenced as needed.

To serve the general needs of practicing physicians this book is general in presentation throughout, except for illustrative examples. As a practical matter, its value would be lost if specific legal situations or needs were presented in detail. Because laws may, and often do, vary from state to state, it would be a task of monumental proportions to attempt to present the specific laws of each state. That's what code books, case reports, and treatises are for. And more than likely, more than a few laws would be out of date by the time of publication. Besides, the purpose of this book is not to repeat the laws written in the cases and codes of each state; it is to present and explain in conceptual form, the legal relationships and obligations physicians encounter in their practices.

As the reader is reminded throughout the book, any physician who has a legal question or problem that relates to the specific law of his or her jurisdiction should consult a qualified professional — attorney, claim specialist, risk manager, professional liability carrier, or accountant.

The direction of this book was very much influenced by the questions that have been asked of me by physicians over the course of years in practice. If a particular matter presented seems trite to you, assume that it was done so for the benefit of unlearned or inexperienced brethren. Although this book may not be all things to all physicians, it is broad in scope and contents by design. As a practical reference and guide for physicians exposed in some manner to legal processes or to litigation – whether theirs or others, it is my hope that this book will be of benefit to many. If only to evoke reactions such as "Oh, I didn't know that", "Now I understand", "I ought to do this differently", or "This legal stuff isn't as intimidating as I thought", the writing of this book will have been worth it. As embodied in the Hippocratic Oath, the medical covenant is one of profundity – and one certainly worthy of enlightened pursuit.

SECTION ONE

LEGAL OVERVIEW: A PRIMER ON LAWS, COURTS, AND LAWYERS

1

ORIGIN AND DEVELOPMENT OF AMERICAN LAW

WE THE PEOPLE, of the United States, in order to form a more perfect union, establish justice, insure domestic tranquility, provide for the common defense, promote the general welfare, and secure the blessings of liberty to ourselves, and our posterity, do ordain and establish this Constitution for the United States of America.

Preamble to the United States Constitution, 1787

The aim of this chapter is to provide a brief sketch of the origin and development of American jurisprudence. This starting point will provide a framework and foundation to help understand legal processes that physicians become involved with.

It is recognized that some physicians might have a true pedagogical interest in things legal; others simply seek a practical working knowledge of the legal aspects of their everyday practice. Regardless of which category you fall into, this overview of the origin and development of Amercian law is designed to help you recall what was probably once presented to some extent in classes taken years ago -- Civics, American History, or even Business Law. This rather condensed refresher course will perhaps serve to dust some cobwebs off the shelves of your memory.

U. S. Constitution – Origins of the "Law of the Land"

Taking their cue from the principles, ideas, and concerns expressed in the "Unanimous Declaration of the Thirteen United States of America" (the proper name of the Declaration of Independence), and following 12 years of government under the Articles of Confederation, the founding fathers realized there was a need to change the form of government of our young nation.

The Articles of Confederation had been designed to, and did in fact, preserve great autonomy for the individual states, but the result was a rather weak and ineffective national government. In fact, under the Articles of Confederation, each state was its own sovereign and the "united" in United States of America really meant little more than membership in a loose association of independent states. It was accepted by most at the time that the Articles did not work well for the fledging country.

Although there was agreement among leaders about the need for change, there was disagreement about how it should be achieved. Many believed that the only way to *legally* change the form of government was to amend the Articles of Confederation. Others, who ultimately prevailed, were in favor of a stronger national government and wanted to draft an entirely new document that would create a federal government and reserve power to that federal government. In order to meet and craft such a document, representatives of the original states met at what we refer to as the Constitutional Convention.

Twelve states (except Rhode Island) elected 74 delegates (including George Washington from Virginia) to the original Constitutional Convention in 1787. Thirty-three of the delegates were lawyers. Only 55 delegates actually attended the Convention, and of those, just 39 delegates signed the Constitution. The final form of the Constitution was the result of heated debate and compromise. Once the Constitution was signed, by its own terms, it required ratification by nine of the states. By 1790, all thirteen of the original states had ratified the Constitution.

One of the most important clauses of the Constitution to emerge from the convention debate was a declaration known as "the Supremacy Clause". In this clause, the Constitution was declared to be the supreme law of the land. The importance of this clause is that it required an understanding among and concession by the states that the national government created by the Constitution was the most powerful. This was a departure from government under the Articles of Confederation. It meant that state governments lost the right to secede from the union, either as individual states or groups of states. Of course, we know that this clause of the Constitution was tested eighty years later when the southern states determined to quit the Union. We also know from the outcome of the Civil War that the Constitution indeed was proven to be the law of the land.

Outline of the Constitution

The United States Constitution is the fundamental "law of the land" that provides the framework for our national government and the principles under which our nation operates. As is well known, the Constitution provides for a tripartite government consisting of the executive branch (President), the legislative branch (Congress), and the judicial branch (Supreme Court). Perhaps less well known, or appreciated, are some of the concerns, goals, and fears of the framers of this document.

Granting, defining, and limiting power among the three branches of federal government involved recognition of the need for power, the dangers of excessive power, and a method for balancing and checking power. Scholars, students, and others have written extensively in essays, textbooks, and commentaries on the development, goals, accomplishments, and limitations of the Constitution. It is probably sufficient for purposes here to recognize that it is the blueprint for our system of national government. It is also worthy to note that the relationships among the national government, the states, and the people, were significant issues of concern and conflict to the original framers, and will always be so to interpreters of the Constitution.

The original Constitution consists of seven articles. The various articles give the national sovereignty authority to exercise only the enumerated powers given to it. In theory, powers that are not expressly enumerated are reserved to state sovereignties. As to those powers granted, the federal government is given supreme authority. When a conflict arises between state and national law, the federal law controls.

In the event that you have an interest in reading through all or portions of the Constitution, it may be helpful to have an outline of its structure. Figure 1-1 provides a topical outline of the original articles.

The Bill of Rights

The first ten amendments to the Constitution are collectively referred to as the Bill of Rights. These amendments were proposed by the first Congress that assembled under the newly adopted Constitution. They were ratified in 1791. The amendments relate primarily to the protection of individual rights. Among these rights are: the right of free speech; protection from unreasonable searches and seizures; the protection from self-incrimination and double jeopardy in criminal trials; the right to a jury trial in criminal cases; the right to a speedy trial by an impartial jury in criminal cases; and the right to a jury trial in civil cases.

It is interesting to note that for the four years preceding adoption of the Bill of Rights, under the original Constitution there were no guarantees of freedom of speech, freedom of the press, or freedom of religion – all of which are contained in the First Amendment.

We the people . . .

Article I - relates to the manner in which Congress is chosen and lists its powers.

Article II - sets forth the manner of electing the President and lists duties and powers of the office.

Article III - establishes the Supreme Court and sets forth the duties of the federal judicial system.

Article IV - guarantees that each state will give full faith and credit to the laws and court decisions of other states, and that citizens of one state will be treated like citizens within the states to which they travel; controls the admission of new states to the Union.

Article V - sets forth the manner by which to amend the Constitution.

Article VI - declares the Constitution to be the supreme law of the land.

Article VII - sets forth the original rules for ratification of the Constitution.

Figure 1-1: Topics of U.S. Constitution by Articles

Constitutional Amendments XI - XXVI

In addition to the Bill of Rights, the first ten amendments, there are sixteen more amendments that have been passed at various times as the need for additional protections and clarifications arose.

Of interest, the 13th, 14th, and 15th amendments are known as the *RECONSTRUCTION* amendments. They were passed after the Civil War in order to end slavery and guarantee important rights to black citizens, including the right to vote. Six of the last eleven amendments (16th through the 26th) deal with elections and voting; two relate to the prohibition of intoxicating liquors (instituted by the 18th Amendment and repealed by the 21st Amendment).

Ready for a quiz? Here is a test of your constitutional scholarship.

- Did you know that you cannot be denied the right to vote by reason of failure to pay your taxes? (See the 24th Amendment).

- For how long has the two-term limit applied to the office of the president? Since 1951. (See the 22nd Amendment).

- When were women guaranteed the right to vote? In 1920. (See the 19th Amendment).

- For how long was the use of intoxicating liquors prohibited? Thirteen years. Prohibition was instituted in 1920 by the 18th Amendment and repealed in 1933 by the 21st Amendment.

A review of the Amendments impresses upon us the fact that the Supreme Law of the Land continues to be a work in progress.

Other Laws of the Land

Having said that the United States Constitution is the supreme law of the land, it is important to keep in mind that there are many other sources and types of laws. Each state has its own type of constitution document. Moreover, counties and cities often have charter documents. In addition to these framework type documents, we citizens are bound to observe the laws, statutes, ordinances, and regulations promulgated by Congress, state legislatures, county boards, and city councils. If that is not enough, there is yet more law to obey! This other type of law is referred to as "common law" or case law. Common law is developed by courts on a case by case basis, but often governs those connected with subsequent cases. Here is an outline of these other types of laws.

Constitutions and Charters

Each state has its own constitution or charter document that sets out the framework for its form of government. This would be the supreme law of the state. Similarly, counties and cities typically have charter type documents that establish the limits of their powers and functions. Although instruments such as state constitutions and county or city charters are important documents, the citizenry rarely have reason to directly encounter law of this form. Much more often we are familiar with "code" law, such as traffic laws.

Statutes, Codes, and Ordinances

Generally speaking, federal statutes are enacted by Congress, state statutes are enacted by state legislatures, ordinances are enacted by county and city governments, and regulations are promulgated by agencies. All of these types of *enacted law* may be referred to as statutory law. Essentially, statutory laws either proscribe certain conduct, activities, or behaviors, or they mandate certain conduct, activities, or behaviors.

As an example of statutory law, think of the traffic laws that each state legislature enacts to control vehicular transportation within the state. As another example of codified law, think of the federal tax code. These are laws enacted by governing bodies, whether they be federal, state, county, city, or municipal. All such laws are "written in the books" and are subject to amendment or repeal by the enacting body. Typically, statutes, codes, and ordinances are set forth in collections of books, often referred to as codes.

Caselaw or Common Law

Case law is a type of law that is developed by judges on a case-by-case basis ➥ as issues arise during the course of litigated cases. Case law typically results from a ruling or decision on a particular issue presented by the facts of a particular case. The issue for the court may be one of interpreting a particular statute, deciding whether a particular statute applies to the facts presented, or deciding an issue to which no statute applies.

Although there are exceptions, generally speaking, the holding or opinion of the court will control and be the "law" of the case in which it is issued. However, many court rulings and decisions can also have far-reaching impacts on subsequently filed cases. This is especially true when a court decision represents the interpretation of a widely applied legal concept, statute, rule, or regulation. Whether a case ruling on a concept, statute, rule, or regulation will actually apply to a subsequent case will depend on the facts of each individual case. If it does, any subsequent case involving that legal concept, statute, rule or regulation will be subject to the earlier court interpretation.

The primary way to locate case law is to read the written opinions of appellate courts that have decided various issues. Fortunately, there are indexing conventions developed by legal publishing companies that "key" topics, concepts, and issues for easier reference.

Citing Case Law and Statutes

Whenever a case is referred to, either in support of a particular proposition or argument, or as one that might be read for interest, the official case name and its citation or "cite" will be given. A case citation is important because it indicates exactly where the case can be located, read, and retrieved. A state case citation consists of the official case name, the number of the state reporter volume and the page of the volume on which the case appears. The state cite is nearly always accompanied by a citation to a regional reporter volume in similar format.

Citation to a Colorado state court case would appear as:

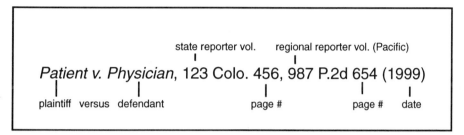

This particular Colorado case could be located by looking either in the official state of Colorado Reporter volume or the official regional Pacific Reporter volume, second series, ("P.2d") at the designated pages. Each reported state case is reported in both a state reporter and a regional reporter.

State statutes are codified in series of code books broken down into "titles". As an example, Arizona's statutes are collected in a series referred to as ARIZONA REVISED STATUTES. Statutes are identified and referred to in Arizona as follows.

ARIZ.REV.STAT. §12-561 or A.R.S. § 12-561

To look up this particular statute, you would go to title 12, which is "Courts and Civil Proceedings", and look up the statute numbered 561, pertaining to the definition of medical malpractice actions.

For those who have an interest in looking up state statutes, keep in mind that the statute books in each state will be called by slightly varied names, but overall the coding is similar from state to state. Uniform statutory citations have not yet arrived. Appendix 1 contains a state-by-state listing of statutory cite refereces. Of course, access to the statute books can be readily obtained at law libraries, most commonly maintained by county courts and law schools. Computerized legal research is becoming more popular for lawyers and non-lawyers alike.

Which Law Controls?

We know that the United States Constitution is the supreme law of the land, but is there a hierarchy of laws beyond that? The answer is yes. Essentially, the laws of each state sovereignty control within that state. That is, the statutes and case law of one state are controlling within that state, but not others. There are exceptions to this rule that arise in situations where there are irregularities concerning the domicile of the parties and the location of the events in question.

In practice, when a court is called upon to decide particular issues, it looks first to the law of the state in which it presides. When there is no applicable statute or case law in one jurisdiction, the lawyers and judges *may* look to other jurisdictions to see how a particular issue was handled by other courts, but an inquiring court is not bound to follow the statutes or case law of another state.

In the event that specific statutory and case authority are absent in state law, it is often the case that a law school professor or student has written a scholarly article or essay relating to the topic being researched. It is uncommon to come upon an issue that no case, court, or legal scholar has ever discussed, written, or pondered. Even so, a judge would not be bound by anything other than the actual law of his own state.

To illustrate these points, consider as an example an Alabama appellate court that has issued a decision on patient informed consent. The holding of the court would control in Alabama, but would not control the judges in the state of Missouri who were faced with a similar issue. Although the Missouri judges may consider the Alabama decision as *persuasive*, they would not be bound to follow the Alabama decision.

Once again, there are exceptions that relate to conflict of laws and choice of law issues, but those are too complex to detail for purposes here.

Refinement of Laws

As is evident from the manner in which the United States Constitution came to be, the laws of the land are not static. To some, the "law" may be personified as a living, breathing embodiment of societal norms that grows as the society grows, and that adapts to the changes in society. To others it is helpful to envision a law as a block of raw stone that is rounded and smoothed with each court interpretation of its meaning. The point of both metaphors is to demonstrate that laws often go through a process of refinement either to reflect changes in the culture, or to clarify their meaning and application.

What we mean by the term "the law" is the body of enacted rules, regulations, and statutes, and the court cases and appellate decisions in which they are applied and interpreted. The laws under which disputes in our society are avoided and resolved are often dynamic rules that, for better or worse, adapt to changes in our society.

One reason for the refinement process is that although legislative bodies attempt to draft legislation in clear terms, and courts strive to clearly state their holdings, they sometimes fail. Certain phrases or even single words in a statute or case may be subject to different interpretations. Each time an appellate court is asked to review and decide the meaning of the words or phrases in a statute, a rough spot on our metaphorical block of marble stone is chiseled away.

Ideally, raw marble is refined and improved (made clearer) with each stroke of the sculptor's chisel. However, even the most carefully carved stones sometimes lose their usefulness and are abandoned – just as outdated laws are sometimes repealed. As an example, remember the 18th Constitutional Amendment instituting prohibition, and the 21st Amendment that repealed it (the ultimate in revision!) thirteen years later in 1933.

Scholars have debated, and will continue to debate whether laws, such as the United States Constitution, are over-interpreted or stretched far beyond the "original intent" of the framers. It is likely that the debates will continue, and regardless of what one thinks *should* happen, it is a fact that, as with the times, laws change.

Distinction between Criminal and Civil Cases

Criminal cases and civil cases are alike in that both involve a search for the truth – that is, an effort to find out what really happened. Yet, they are very different in purpose. In one type of case, the aim is to enforce the laws of the government, while in the other is to resolve disputes between private citizens.

A criminal case is an action brought by a governmental entity (city, county, state, or federal) against a citizen for breaking the law of the governmental entity. Generally, violations of federal statutes are prosecuted in federal courts; violations of state laws are prosecuted in state courts; and violations of city ordinances are prosecuted in municipal courts. In criminal cases the plaintiff or complainant bringing the action is the governmental entity. The caption of the case names the governmental entity prosecuting the case, i.e., *State v. Jones.*

Civil cases are lawsuits between private parties (citizens), including corporations and governmental entities, to resolve their private legal disputes. The city, state, and federal governments provide forums for the resolution of such citizen disputes. In civil suits, however, the government is not seeking enforcement and penalties for lawbreakers. (There are instances in which governmental entities are parties in civil cases either as plaintiffs or defendants.) Civil cases typically have private party names in the caption, i.e., *Jones v. Smith.*

Medical malpractice cases are civil cases in which typically the plaintiff is an allegedly injured patient; the defendant is a healthcare provider – a hospital, a physician, or both.

Next

Having laid a foundation for understanding the origin of our federal and state court systems, the next chapter takes a closer look at the organizations of these court systems. Join in on the journey of a case as it makes its way from trial court through state courts of appeal.

FAQ:

1. Are medical malpractice cases always civil cases?

Yes. Medical negligence cases, those brought by patients against health care providers, are civil cases. However, physicians may also be involved in other types of cases such as those involving licensing or professional practice issues. These are typically handled in administrative proceedings.

2. If I treat out of state patients in my home state and one of them sues me for medical malpractice, can I be sued in another state?

In most instances, you could not be sued in the home state of an out of state patient. The patient could bring suit against you in the state where you provided the treatment. The answer to this question becomes more complicated if you advertise your services in other states and sometimes treat patients in other states. It would depend on the nature and extent of your advertising and out of state practice.

3. If I am licensed to practice medicine in more than one state, and practice in more than one state, which states' laws apply to me?

The laws of each state will control your practice within that state. If the laws vary, the legal obligations and protections that apply to you may vary.

2

A Look at Federal and State Court Systems

Section 1. The Judicial Power of the United States, shall be vested in one supreme Court, and in such inferior Courts as the Congress may from time to time ordain and establish.

U.S. Constitution, Art. III.

One of the purposes of this book is to inform physicians about medical malpractice cases – how, why, and where they are brought. The intent of this chapter is to provide a basic outline of our federal and state court systems. The majority of medical malpractice actions are filed in state courts rather than federal courts. You might wonder, what is the distinction between federal and state court, and why are medical malpractice cases usually filed in state court? What happens to cases on appeal? Read on, this chapter is for you.

The Federal Court System

As you will recall from Chapter 1, when the Constitution was drafted and adopted, it created a national, or federal government that had not existed previously. Although the states had their own governments, which included court systems, there were no federal courts because there was no real federal government. In creating the model for federal government, the architects of the Constitution called for a tripartite form of government that included a judiciary in addition to the executive and legislative branches. In simplest terms, the United States Supreme Court and inferior federal courts are creatures of the Constitution, provided for in Article III of the Constitution.

According to the Constitution, the federal court is to consist of the Supreme Court and "such inferior courts as the Congress may from time to time ordain and establish." U.S. Const. art III, § 1. Currently, the federal court system is comprised of 94 district courts or trial courts, and 12 courts of appeal in addition to the Supreme Court. In addition, there are bankruptcy courts in each district that are staffed by bankruptcy judges.

Figure 2-1 represents a diagrammatic view of the federal appellate courts and the state jurisdictions they serve.

In addition to the twelve circuit courts (which also handle tax appeals), there are courts of appeal for the Federal Circuit (including patent and trademark appeals, merit system appeals, International Trade Commission appeals, and Board of Contract Appeals), and the Armed Forces.

The jurisdiction of federal courts extends primarily to federal matters and to those raised between citizens of different states. Although there is some overlap in jurisdiction with state courts, for the most part state and federal courts handle distinctly different matters. The jurisdictional scope of the federal courts is generally set forth in the Constitution in Article III. In the event that there are state and federal laws that appear to conflict, generally federal law is said to "pre-empt" state law and will be applied by the court.

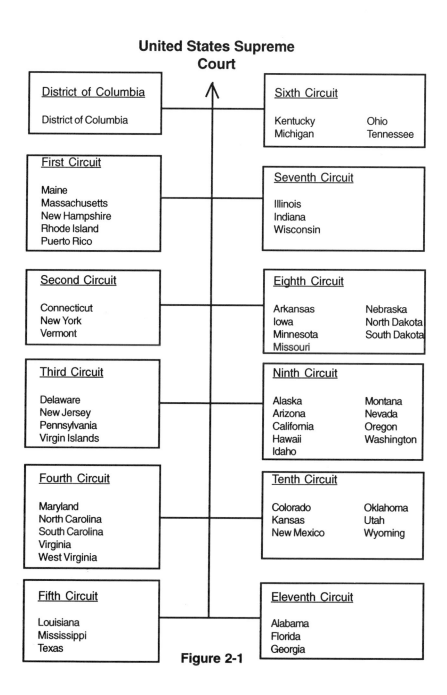

Figure 2-1

Jurisdiction of the Federal Courts

As provided for in the Constitution, the federal courts have jurisdiction in five basic types of cases. They are:

(1)   cases in which the United States is a party

(2)   cases involving foreign officials

(3)   civil cases with parties from different states involving more than $10,000

(4)   cases involving the United States Constitution and federal laws

(5)   federal specialty areas involving patents, copyrights, or bankruptcies

As might be expected, these categories of cases involve primarily federal matters and issues, rather than distinctly intrastate parties and matters.

State courts and federal courts share jurisdiction in categories (3) and (4), but state courts have sole or exclusive jurisdiction in cases involving state law. Only state court decisions that involve federal law or the U.S. Constitution may be appealed in federal court.

With this understanding, it is fairly easy to see why relatively few medical malpractice cases end up in federal court. Malpractice cases usually do not involve federal laws or the federal government. More often, the medical malpractice plaintiff and physician live in the same state, and constitutional issues are rarely raised in medical malpractice cases.

An exception to this generality arises when medical care has been provided in a federal hospital, such as a military or veteran's hospital. In cases involving the federal government as a tort (medical negligence) defendant, special laws apply. These special laws are collectively referred to as the Federal Tort Claims Act. The Act governs such things as how claims are to brought, what claims may be brought, the amount of damages permitted to be recovered, and the amount of attorney's fees that may be recovered.

State Court Systems

Most state court systems are set up with tiers of trial courts and appellate courts that have limited jurisdiction over special types of cases. The names of the courts vary from state to state, but most states have a limited jurisdiction level, a major trial court level, and an appellate level.

The limited jurisdiction courts include justice of the peace courts, traffic courts, and municipal courts. These courts handle traffic and parking offenses, minor criminal offenses, preliminary hearings for more serious criminal matters, and small claims.

At the next level are the general jurisdiction trial courts where wide ranges of civil and criminal cases are tried. This is the major trial court level and is often referred to as superior court or state district court. It is at this level that most medical negligence actions are brought. These trial courts often handle appeals from the lower courts as well. Courts of this level are usually administered at the county level.

In addition to trial courts, each state has an appellate court level consisting of at least a "supreme court" (New York's trial court level is referred as "Supreme Court"), and in most instances, an intermediary appellate court level. The primary function of an appellate court is to review proceedings in lower courts to determine whether matters have been processed fairly. If there has been some irregularity or error in the trial court and a new trial is therefore required, the case will be remanded back to the trial court for further proceedings. Trials are only conducted in trial courts; not in courts of appeal. Appellate courts review trial court proceedings to determine whether the proceedings have been conducted in a manner that is fair to both parties.

Figure 2-2 shows a typical state court system. As you can see, state matters are "tried" in the limited and general jurisdiction trial courts. Typically, there are then one or two levels of appellate courts – an intermediate appellate court and a supreme court.

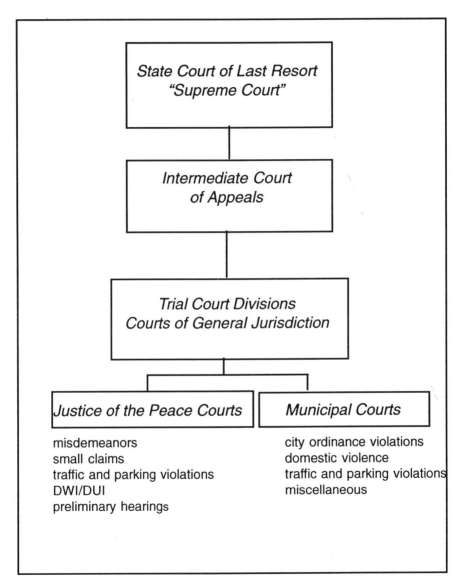

Figure 2-2: State Court System

A Trip Through State Court

If your have ever noticed or heard about civil cases that seemed to go on in court for years and years, you might have wondered how a case could proceed that long. There are a number of factors that determine the length of time a case is in litigation. Case complexity and protracted pre-trial disputes are just two examples. Or it could be that a case has made its way through the trial court, appellate courts, and back again – a journey that could indeed take years or even decades. To help understand how this can happen, let's follow a hypothetical case through a state court system.

Trial Court

Since most medical malpractice cases are brought at the superior court (trial court) level, that will serve as a starting point for our illustrative journey. The case we will follow is a medical negligence case that begins when the plaintiff, an injured patient files a Complaint in county superior court against two physicians and a hospital alleging failure to obtain informed consent and fraud.

The period of time from the filing of the Complaint to the start of the trial varies from jurisdiction to jurisdiction, but for purposes of our example we will use an approximate figure of 2 years. During this time the parties gather evidence, take depositions, and prepare for trial.

The length of a medical malpractice trial could be anywhere from one or two days (rarely that short) to several months, depending on the number of defendants and the complexity of the issues raised. Most commonly, medical malpractice cases take several weeks to try.

During the course of a typical trial there are literally scores of decisions and rulings on various issues that are made by the trial judge. These could include decisions about whether certain claims or defenses should be allowed, whether certain witnesses should testify, whether witnesses' testimony should be limited, whether certain exhibits should be admitted, and whether the conduct of the attorneys is proper. In theory, each ruling of the judge can provide the basis for a party to claim error in the proceedings. It is upon such error that a party may make an appeal.

In our hypothetical case, at the end of a several week trial the jury may find for the patient-plaintiff on some or all of the claims brought, or for the defendant doctor(s) and or hospital. Once post trial motions have been briefed, argued, and ruled upon, the time for filing an appeal begins to run. This stage of the process could take several months. At this point, our case has been in litigation for nearly 3 years. We then move on to the appellate stage.

Court of Appeals

Any or all of the parties who have lost on a ruling, and who have exhausted their remedies in the trial court, may file an appeal on the basis that the trial judge: (1) misapplied the law; (2) failed to follow rules of procedure; or (3) in some other way prevented the party from receiving a fair trial. It is possible that one, two, or all three parties in our case might want to file an appeal. Now for obvious reasons a party would not want to appeal decisions on issues or claims on which he has prevailed. However, when multiple claims are brought and defended it is possible for a party to lose on one claim and win on the other. Thus, a case involving two claims where one is lost and the other won might result in appeals by both sides who each lost on one claim.

Let's say in our case that the jury found for the patient on her claim that the defendant doctors failed to obtain informed consent, but found for the doctors and hospital on the claim of fraud. The patient files an appeal on the fraud claim; the doctors file an appeal on the informed consent claim. The bringing of an appeal usually involves obtaining a partial trial transcript, transferring the trial record to the court of appeals, and researching and drafting appellate briefs. It may take 6 months or more to accomplish these tasks. Then, the parties wait, wait, and wait some more. It is not unusual in most states to wait from six months to a year before having an appeal set for oral argument before the court of appeals.

Oral argument in the court of appeals is important because it gives the appellate judges (typically a panel of 3) the opportunity to hear the positions advanced by each party and allows the judges to question the lawyers about strengths or weaknesses of the appeal. Once the judges have heard oral argument, they will then meet, confer, research, and ultimately reach a decision.

Keep in mind that the court of appeals judges decide the appeal issues based only on review of the written record of the trial, review of the law, written briefs of the parties, and oral presentations by the parties' lawyers. Appellate judges do not conduct trials or hear from any live witnesses.

In many appeals, the decision of the appellate judges comes in the form of a written document called an "opinion". Appellate opinions often set forth a recitation of pertinent facts, a review of pertinent law (statutes and cases), the court's ruling, and reasoning for the ruling. When appeals raise a number of issues or raise complex issues that require in depth analysis, opinions can be quite lengthy – 30 to 50 pages (or more!). In some courts, it may take well over a year after oral arguments before appellate opinions are issued. By this point on our trip through the courts our medical malpractice case might be nearly 5 years old.

Ultimately, the appellate opinion will state whether the trial court ruling or outcome is *affirmed*, meaning upheld, or whether it is *reversed*. A case that is reversed may then be *remanded*, or sent back to the trial court for a complete or partial re-trial consistent with the appellate holding. In our hypothetical malpractice case, let us say that the patient lost her appeal on the issue of fraud and that the doctors won their appeal on the informed consent issue. As it stands at this point, the fraud claim is out of the case, but the parties need to return to the trial court for a re-trial of the informed consent claim. That's that – or is it? No, it isn't. If either party is dissatisfied with the intermediate appellate ruling, he or she can file another appeal to the court of last resort – the state's supreme court.

State Supreme Court

In civil cases, appeals to the state supreme court are discretionary. That means that the case may or may not be accepted for review by the supreme court. In order to find out whether the court will accept review, the parties file written briefs arguing the importance of further review by the higher court. If the court accepts review it may ask for additional briefing, review the record, and decide the case with or without oral arguments by counsel.

The court may do one of three things:

- refuse to accept review, in which case the appellate decision stands
- accept the case and agree with the lower court of appeals, either adopting its decision or issuing its own opinion
- accept review of the case and reverse the court of appeals, explaining why in its own decision.

If our hypothetical medical malpractice case petition for review were to be accepted, the case could be "in the supreme court" for another couple of years. When all is said and done, the final outcome of the supreme court review could be to send the case back to the trial court for a re-trial of the informed consent claim. Scheduling the case for re-trial would involve an additional wait. By this time, about 6 or 7 years have likely passed and we are right back where we started — in trial court. Although one might think the "trip" to be almost over, it might not be. The parties still have the right to appeal from the second trial if there is an irregularity in any of those proceedings. It could be off to the court of appeals again.

This hypothetical trip through the courts is certainly possible, but a trip of this length would be the exception rather than the rule in most medical negligence cases. One of the reasons that most cases don't go 'round and 'round the system is that court administrations often assist the parties by urging them out of the "system". Here are some methods that are gaining in popularity.

Alternative Dispute Resolution

Many state court systems have encouraged the development of alternative dispute resolution (ADR) systems that are designed to keep cases out of the traditional court litigation process. The most common forms of ADR are mediation and arbitration. ADR is not suitable for every case, but more and more parties are seeing the benefits of alternate methods of resolving civil disputes.

Here are some general observations about ADR:

- ADR is thought to work well for "smaller" cases in which the amount of money involved is relatively minor.

- ADR can be a very cost-effective way to resolve "large" cases because the costs to process a case can be more easily controlled.

- If the parties agree, procedural and evidentiary rules can be relaxed to permit less formal and therefore less expensive presentation of a party's case.

- The parties have greater control over the scheduling of intermediate and final litigation events.

Mediation

Mediation is a form of ADR that involves having the parties mutually agree to a resolution or settlement of their case. Mediation is typically conducted by a neutral third person who meets with the parties, jointly and separately, to explore their respective positions. The mediator may point out to a party a weakness in the case that may have been overlooked or ignored in order to help the party reach a realistic assessment of the value of a claim.

A mediator can theoretically be anyone agreed upon by the parties. Most often he or she is a skillful lawyer or retired judge who has an understanding of the psychology of negotiation, good people skills, and experience in getting parties to compromise and resolve their differences.

Arbitration

Arbitration differs from mediation in that an arbitrator is a neutral third person who actually decides the outcome of the case. Arbitrators are also likely to be retired judges or lawyers who have an interest in serving as arbitrators. The role of an arbitrator is that of a fact finder, similar to a judge or jury, who hears an abbreviated, and more informal, presentation of evidence and then decides which side prevails.

In some jurisdictions, it is mandatory that smaller value civil cases go through an arbitration process. Arbitrators are randomly appointed by the court from a list of practicing lawyers in the community. Court appointed arbitrators typically provide their service on a pro bono basis. Parties that are dissatisfied with the outcome of the arbitration process may appeal. The appeal may consist of a full-fledged jury trial in superior court.

Because disputes can be resolved more quickly via arbitration, in a case of any size or type, the parties may agree to split the cost of hiring a mediator or arbitrator in an effort to have their case decided outside of formal litigation. Court systems very much encourages parties to pursue ADR even in cases where it is not mandated.

One of the attractions of private arbitration is that parties have great flexibility in structuring the "rules of the game", as long as they are consistent with notions of fairness and justice. For instance, in order to achieve finality and certainty, parties that wish to, may stipulate that the arbitrator's finding is binding and non-appealable. This is one way to avoid a potentially arduous and costly journey through the trial and appellate court system. It is likely that litigants in all types of cases will increasingly appreciate the benefits of using ADR methods to resolve their disputes.

Next

Have you wondered about partners and associates, billable hours and contingency fees, how judges are selected, or how medical malpractice lawyers learn their trade? The next chapter sets the record straight regarding myths, misconceptions, and mysteries of lawyers and lawyering.

F.A.Q:

1. Have any medical malpractice cases ever gone to the United States Supreme Court on appeal?

Yes. There have been a handful of medical malpractice cases appealed to the U.S. Supreme Court. As an example, see *Fein v. Permanente Medical Group,* 474 U.S. 892, 106 S.Ct. 214 (1985). The Supreme Court was asked to review the constitutionality of a California statute that capped non-economic damages (pain, suffering, disfigurement, impairment, inconvenience, and other non-pecuniary losses) in medical malpractice cases at $250,000. The medical malpractice plaintiff was awarded $1,287,783 by a jury, including $500;00 for non-economic damages. The trial judge applied the statute and cut the non-economic damage award to $250,000. The plaintiff then challenged the constitutionality of the statute, urging that it violated Due Process and Equal Protection guarantees of the U.S. Constitution. A majority of the U.S. Supreme Court decided that the case did not present a federal question and declined to decide the issue. A dissenting justice disagreed and thought the issue should have been decided by the court.

2. May a case brought in state case be appealed in the federal court?

Most cases brought in state court can only be appealed within the state court system. The highest appellate court in each state is the supreme law of the land with respect to that state's law. However, if federal rights or responsibilities are raised in a state case, appeals on those issues may be brought in the federal court system.

3. If a case goes through mediation successfully, what is the outcome referred to?

Settlement. In successful mediation, the parties agree to resolve disputes by settling their claims rather than litigating their claims.

4. If I agree to go through arbitration but don't like the award of the arbitrator, can I appeal the outcome?

It depends on the type of arbitration. In court ordered arbitrations, the parties are provided with a right to appeal. The appeal usually consists of a jury trial "de novo", meaning a new start in the trial court. In private arbitrations, the parties may negotiate the "appealability" of an arbitrator's award.

✦   ✦   ✦   ✦

3

WHAT DOCTORS SHOULD KNOW ABOUT LAWYERS

A lawyer is a representative of clients, an officer of the legal system and a public citizen having special responsibility for the quality of justice.

Preamble to the Model Rules of Professional Conduct of the American Bar Association

The education, training, and work of lawyers parallel in some ways the professional development and education of physicians, but in some ways there are vast differences. Lawyers go through educational and practical rites of passage – "do or die" semester finals, tryouts for law review, moot court, the bar exam, first trials, specialty certifications, etc.— that often seem enigmatic or arcane to the uninitiated. The intent of this chapter is to unveil some of the inscrutable aspects of lawyers and "lawyering" — a goal that goes hand in hand with making physicians' exposure to the law less intimidating.

Undergraduate Education of Lawyers

The undergraduate education of lawyers is quite varied. There are no standard undergraduate curriculum requirements for application to law school. As a result, it is not unusual to have a mix of law students with backgrounds in disciplines as varied as the types of undergraduate degrees offered. However, there tend to be some undergraduate degrees that are seen more commonly among applicants, including political science, business, and English degrees. In recent decades law schools have seen increased applications from students with graduate degrees, including an occasional physician!

Law School Applicants

Acceptance into law school is based primarily on a matrix of grade point average and score on the Law School Admissions Test ("LSAT"). Each law school determines what GPA and LSAT scores are minimum requirements for consideration.

Law School Curriculum

The standard law school curriculum is a three-year full time program. First year law school is quite demanding emotionally and intellectually based on the volume and nature of subjects introduced, the learning methods employed, and the evaluation and testing processes used. In addition, the "culture" at most schools encourages a Darwinian atmosphere of survival of the fittest, which makes for added tension. Perhaps it is no surprise that those students who are equipped with a competitive drive thrive in such an environment.

The typical first year curriculum includes such subjects as real property, torts, legal research and writing, criminal law, civil procedure, and evidence. These are typically required courses and there is usually no opportunity for electives until second and third years. In most schools subjects are taught using case studies and the Socratic method of asking questions rather than straight lecturing.

The Socratic method of teaching derives from the manner in which Socrates taught his students – he would ask a series of questions of his students that led them to find out for themselves what he wanted them to know or learn. This method of teaching, employed by a skillful professor, can prove to be a challenging, and sometimes humbling, experience for an uninitiated first year student. Law professors often use this method (some better than others), or a variation thereof, to teach principles of law to first and second year students.

For those students who sailed through their undergraduate work as a nameless face in the back row of an auditorium sized classroom, participation in learning via the highly interactive Socratic method can be a nerve-racking experience.

Although there is a fairly standard curriculum for first and second year students, most law schools offer a variety of electives that allow students to focus on particular areas of interest. These might include such areas as trial practice, oral advocacy, legal research and writing, environmental law, tax law, Indian law, probate law, torts, criminal law, family law, commercial law, insurance law or corporate law.

The Bar Exam

The bar exam is the licensing test given by each state that must be passed in order to practice law in that state. Although most third year students are jubilant about completing law school, they are also keenly aware of the "ultimate test" that awaits them. For many students, test preparation is a full-time job and even though they have just put three years of law school behind them, vast majorities enroll in "bar review courses". Bar review courses usually run three hours a day, four to five days a week, for about six weeks. A variety of "experts" provide intensive reviews of the many subjects covered on the bar exam, practice tests are given, and test-taking tips are provided.

The bar exam components vary somewhat from state to state, but typically include three parts:

- a multi-state professional responsibility exam, covering legal ethics

- a multi-state bar exam - a 1 day nationally standardized objective test on uniform legal principles and concepts

- each state's essay exam, covering a variety of subjects including laws specific to each jurisdiction

In most states the two-day bar exam is administered twice a year – in February and July. Scores are typically reported about six weeks later. Those who pass a state's bar exam and meet "character and fitness" standards are then admitted to practice law in that state.

State Bar Associations

In each state, the admission of new lawyers and practice of law are regulated by state bar associations. The state bar association is responsible for processing applications to practice law (including "character evaluations"), administering the bar licensing exam, regulating advertising, conducting disciplinary functions, providing specialization certification and regulation, tracking annual continuing legal education requirements, and providing continuing legal education seminars and courses. Membership in a state bar association is mandatory in nearly all states and requires the payment of annual dues. Included within the regulatory function is the power to suspend from the practice, or permanently disbar, lawyers who have violated the state's code of professional ethics, or in some way acted "unprofessionally".

For those with an etymological interest, use of the term "bar" comes from the English court system. There, the bar is the partition or rail beyond which members of the public and barristers cannot pass. Only solicitors, as officers of the court, are admitted beyond the bar.

Other Professional Associations

In addition to the various states' bar associations that have official regulatory functions, there are numerous other professional groups or bar associations for various groups of lawyers with common interests. The American Bar Association is a non-mandatory nationwide association of lawyers that offers a broad range of services to the profession at large. It also has many "sections" that are of interest to lawyers in various specialties. The American Trial Lawyers Association is a national organization of trial lawyers who primarily represent injured victims (plaintiffs). Most states have local chapters of ATLA. Defense Research Institute is a national organization for trial lawyers who represent primarily civil defendants. These are just a few examples of the many professional associations for lawyers.

Among other activities, professional associations often compile databases of information on certain types of cases, expert witnesses, and research. These national associations are very efficient at gathering and supplying information and resources to their members in the various states.

The American Inns of Court is a national organization modeled after the British Inns of Court. Local chapters, or Inns, are comprised of three types of members: masters (accomplished senior attorneys, judges or law professors), barristers (accomplished junior level attorneys), and pupils (newly admitted attorneys or third year law students). Within an Inn, groups are formed by matching two or three masters together with two or three barristers and pupils. Following a school-year schedule, the Inn generally meets as a whole once a month, at which time one of the groups presents a topic to the Inn. The presentation of a topic may take the form of a skit, a lecture, a guest lecture, a game, or any one of a variety of other types of production. The value of the organization comes principally from the fact that the Inns are very devoted to improving the professionalism of their members.

Most states, counties, and larger cities also have a variety of specialty bar associations that provide networks of resources, information, support, and other services to those with common interests.

Legal Training

Unlike in the medical profession, there is no standardized training program for new lawyers. For most, it is on-the-job training and learn-by-doing. Some law firms have semi-formal in-house training programs, but for most new graduates, the methods by which they learn how to "practice" law are as varied as the jobs they find.

For most new lawyers who begin their careers with private law firms, initial work assignments may be limited to research and writing projects. In litigation firms, young associates gradually take on more responsibility for depositions, court hearings, and eventually, trials. In some firms this training period may take years; in other firms a lawyer may be permitted to handle his or her first trial within a year's time.

In many ways, becoming a "trial lawyer" is a sink or swim proposition. Not every law school graduate is cut out for trial work and after a year or two in the litigation trenches, those who are not will often self-select out of litigation. Lawyers who are sincerely committed to learning or improving their trial skills may attend multi-day trial colleges. These usually consist of intense how-to training sessions on handling all aspects of a trial. After presentations by accomplished trial attorneys, attendees are often videotaped and critiqued on their mock performances of the various trial skills.

For some law school graduates finding a job means sending out resumes, pounding the pavement, interviewing, and waiting. For others it is a matter of hanging a shingle and waiting for the first client to walk through the door. One of the most valuable benefits of obtaining a law degree is the variety of professional work that graduates find or fashion for themselves.

Continuing Legal Education

Most state bars have mandatory annual requirements for lawyers to obtain continuing legal education. As a result, a broad range of legal seminars is offered by many private and public bar associations and by professional seminar presenters. Because new developments, trends, and changes in the law are common, there is never a shortage of topics to be updated on. Lawyers who have had particular success in a given area are generally not reluctant to share their "secrets to success" with fellow lawyers and therefore the supply of speakers and presenters is usually ample.

Specialty Certifications

In many states, state bar associations offer certifications for attorneys who specialize in particular areas of practice. Certification is based on demonstration of both quantity and quality of practice in a given area of law. In a number of states, lawyers who specialize in medical malpractice law have obtained certification as specialists in personal injury and wrongful death litigation. To achieve a certification of this type a state bar may require that an attorney have been the lead attorney in twenty major trials involving personal injury or wrongful death claims, and that he successfully pass a written essay exam on substantive and procedural law. Re-certification may be required every three to five years.

Ethical Obligations of Lawyers

The professional conduct of lawyers is governed by formal rules of professional conduct, which in most jurisdictions are adaptations of the American Bar Association's Model Rules of Professional Conduct. These comprehensive codes and rules are considered to be minimum ethical standards for the practice of law. Violations of ethical rules subject attorneys to disciplinary action. Penalties meted out for infractions can include censure, fines, temporary suspension from the practice, or permanent disbarment.

As stated by the ABA Model Rules, is important for attorneys to remember the nature of their practice:

> A lawyer's responsibilities as a representative of clients, and officer of the legal system and a public citizen are usually harmonious. Thus, when an opposing party is well represented, a lawyer can be a zealous advocate on behalf of a client and at the same time assume that justice is being done. So also, a lawyer can be sure that preserving client confidences ordinarily serves the public interest because people are more likely to seek legal advice, and thereby heed their legal obligations, when they know their communication will be private. In the nature of law practice, however, conflicting responsibilities are encountered. Virtually all difficult ethical problems arise from conflict between a lawyer's responsibilities to clients, to the legal system and to the lawyer's own interest in remaining an upright person while earning a satisfactory living. The Rules of Professional Conduct prescribe terms for resolving such conflicts. . . .

Rule 42. Arizona Rules of Professional Conduct, Preamble excerpt.

As with the medical profession, the legal profession is largely self-policing. State bar associations are the professional equivalents of state medical examiner boards. Just as with physicians, lawyers who violate ethical standards of practice are subject to review, sanction, suspension, and even disbarment.

Types of Practice

There are a number of ways to categorize the different types of legal practice. One way to broadly categorize practice types would be to look at public (government lawyers) and private practice lawyers. Public lawyers are those who are employed by federal, state, county, and city governments to represent their interests and those of their departments and agencies. This includes criminal prosecutors who work for the United States Department of Justice, state attorney general offices, county prosecutors and city prosecutors. Federal and state governments employ significant numbers of lawyers. In some states, the attorney general's office is the largest "firm" in the state.

Another way to view types of practice would be to look at civil practice and criminal practice. Criminal practice encompasses both prosecutors and criminal defense lawyers. Prosecutors represent the government (federal, state, county or city) in bringing charges against those (defendants) who have violated a criminal statute (federal, state, county or city). Defendants are represented by lawyers of their own choosing if they can afford one, or by government provided lawyers if they cannot afford one.

Civil practice is a broad category that includes a wide variety of non-criminal matters. Because the practice of law is so broad, most attorneys specialize in one or two related areas of practice. Some examples of practice types include family law (divorce, adoption, pre-nuptial agreements), corporate law, commercial transactions, probate (wills, trusts, guardianships, conservatorships), environmental law, insurance law, personal injury law, tax law, workers compensation law, and real estate law.

Law Firms

The number of lawyers who practice their trade in the private law firm setting is significant. A "firm" is a group of lawyers who practice together either as partners, associates, or corporations. Most lawyers who specialize in medical malpractice cases, whether for representing plaintiffs or defendant physicians, do so as associates or partners in a law firm. Here are some characteristics of law firms.

Size

Law firm size can range from the sole practitioner, who may or may not be a specialist, to the multi-national firms that employ hundreds of lawyers in different states and foreign countries. What is considered "small", "mid-sized" or "large" varies from location to location. In New York City, a twenty-lawyer firm would be considered small. Yet in a small mid-western locality that could well be the largest firm in town.

The resources made available through technology now make it possible for sole practitioners and smaller sized firms to very effectively "compete" against much larger firms. In some ways, smaller firms find that they are better able to adapt to and take advantage of the ever-advancing technologies.

Associates and Partners

The business and organizational structures of law firms vary depending on their size and practice area. However, in most firms lawyers begin practicing as "associates", which means they are employees of the firm. After four to five years, capable lawyers advance to become "senior associates" or "junior partners". Continued and further demonstration of skill or the ability to attract clients to the firm, or a combination of both, usually entitles a lawyer to become considered for "partnership" at a firm. Partners are generally "owners" who have a financial investment in a firm and who are responsible for the management and practice of the firm.

Specialty Lawyers, Departments, and Firms

As with our society in general, the age of specialization is certainly in full swing in the legal profession. Not only do individual lawyers have specialty practices; it is also common to see divisions of law firms and entire firms that practice within a given specialty. For instance, a firm of ten lawyers may specialize in plaintiff's personal injury law while another firm with fifteen lawyers may do nothing but personal injury defense.

It may be of interest to know that medical malpractice lawyers (both plaintiff and defense) are usually considered to be sub-specialists within the practice of personal injury law. The reason for the sub-specialization is that when compared to ordinary personal injury cases, medical malpractice cases are usually governed by different laws and rules. This means that in addition to acquiring familiarity with medical terminology, procedures, and practices, the medical malpractice lawyer must know special substantive law and procedural rules.

Methods of Compensation

The manner in which lawyers are paid for their work depends on the type of work they do. Here are the most common methods.

Salary

Lawyers who are "employed" by governments, agencies, and corporations are generally paid on a straight salary basis. Salaried lawyers who are employed by non-governmental entities, such as by corporations, may also be subject to bonus incentives that are made available to other employees.

Contingency Fee

A contingency fee arrangement is one in which a lawyer is compensated by taking a percentage of the recovery obtained for the client. Such fees are "contingent" because they are paid only when and if there is a recovery. If a lawyer works on a case for several years, takes the case to trial, and loses the case, the lawyer is paid nothing for his time on the case.

The origin of the American contingent fee is traced to the mid-19th century. Prior to that time, the English rule was generally followed. In colonial America and through the first 100 years of our country's independence, it was illegal for attorneys and others to assist in the pleading of another's claim for promise of a reward. To do so was considered to be champerty, which was often punishable by imprisonment and fines.

By the middle of the 19th century Americans - jurists, politicians, and citizens – discarded the ways of the English and came to appreciate the merits of contingency fees – oft described as the "poorman's key to the court house".

CONTINGENCY FEE AGREEMENT

1) Lawyer agrees to represent client in connection with medical malpractice claim arising out of surgery performed by Dr. Dolittle on mm/dd/yy.

2) Client agrees to cooperate with lawyer and understands that lawyer and her firm do not make any guarantees regarding the outcome of litigation.

3) Client agrees to pay Lawyer 40% of any recovery, whether by settlement or trial. If the case proceeds to appeal or retrial, the contingency fee will be re-negotiated by Lawyer and Client.

4) By law, Client is responsible for costs of the litigation regardless of whether there is a recovery. Costs include items such as filing fees, deposition fees, copying charges, facsimile charges, telephone charges, electronic research charges, and travel costs. Lawyer will advance the payment of costs, which will ultimately be deducted from Client's recovery, if any. At any time Lawyer may request that Client pay for cost incurred in the litigation.

5) Client may discharge Lawyer at any time. In such event, Lawyer has right to reimbursement for costs incurred and a quantum meruit claim based on work performed.

6) Lawyer may terminate representation of Client in the event that Client refuses to cooperate or requires that Lawyer act against her best judgment or unethically.

Dated_____   Client_____

                               Lawyer_____

Figure 3-1: Sample Contingency Fee

Billable Hourly Rate

Many lawyers, primarily those that do defense work, bill clients based on the amount of time spent on a case. A given lawyer usually performs all work on a given case at a set hourly rate. Hourly rates could be as low as $75 an hour or as high as $300+ an hour. A lawyer's hourly rate is usually a function of the type of work done, the experience of the lawyer, and the reputation of the lawyer's firm. On cases that involve the work of several lawyers of varying skill and experience it is not uncommon to have each lawyer "billed out" at a separate rate.

Unlike in contingency fee work, lawyers who bill by the hour are always compensated for the time they spend performing work for a client. As with contingency fee representation, clients are usually responsible for "costs" incurred in connection with their case. Costs are amounts actually spent to process the case. They are distinct from attorneys' fees.

Different Fees for Different Lawyers

The way in which a lawyer charges his clients depends in large part upon the type of work he does. In medical malpractice cases, plaintiff's lawyers are paid one way, and defense lawyers another. Here is a look at how and why two lawyers working on different sides of the same case would be paid in different ways.

Contingency Fees for Plaintiff's Lawyers

Most lawyers who accept medical malpractice cases do so on a contingency fee basis. That means that the lawyer will carefully evaluate whether the case appears to have merit. If it does not, the potential client will be turned away. Usually the plaintiff's lawyer will have the facts of the case reviewed by a qualified physician. If the reviewing physician opines that the case has merit, and there are no procedural impediments (i.e., the statute of limitations has expired), the lawyer will likely accept the case.

Once the decision to take a case has been reached, the lawyer and client sign a contingency fee agreement that sets forth the details of the agreement. Provisions commonly seen in a contingent fee contract are set forth in Figure 3-1. The terms shown are simplified sample provisions – actual terms might vary based on the complexity of a case and statutory requirements for fee agreements.

From the lawyer's perspective, there are obvious risks in working on contingency fee cases. Since the lawyer's fee is a percentage of the client's recovery, in every case the lawyer takes a risk of not being paid at all if there is no recovery for the client. This feature of contingency fee work provides plaintiff's lawyers with a strong incentive to carefully select cases. Although it is popular to think that some lawyers will take just about any case on a contingency fee basis, as a practical matter, the thought of working on a case for possibly hundreds of hours without getting paid is adequate inducement for most to refrain from filing frivolous lawsuits.

Contingency Fee Debate

It seems there has always been an exercise in debate about whether contingency fee based litigation is desirable. Here are the basic arguments for and against.

Those who favor contingency fees take the position that such a fee structure "opens the door to the court house" by removing financial barriers for injured victims who otherwise could not afford to pay for legal representation. It is thought that this in turn leads to a safer society because those who are negligent are held responsible, which then results in economic pressure for people, institutions, and manufacturers to correct careless practices, dangerous conditions, and defective products. Those who are against contingency fees contend that the courthouse doors are thrown so wide open that the system becomes clogged with increasing numbers of cases, including those of questionable merit.

Taking a side in this theoretical debate seems to depend on one's view of whether and how access to the court should be limited. As a practical matter however the debate has been resolved. In our system of democracy a higher value has been placed on providing access to the court system. Note that even with the open door policy, there are still mechanisms in place to discourage and sanction the filing of frivolous litigation. Stated bluntly, lawyers don't like to work for "nothing".

Billable Hours for Defense Lawyers

Medical malpractice defense lawyers, in contrast to plaintiff's lawyers, are paid regardless of the outcome of the case. Win or lose, they are paid based on the time spent on a case.

Because most medical malpractice defendants are covered by insurance for professional liability, their defense lawyers are selected by and paid by their medical malpractice insurance carrier. The hourly rate for the malpractice defense lawyer is negotiated by the insurance company, rather than by the defendant doctor. Hourly rates for malpractice defense lawyers are at the higher end of the hourly rate scale because medical malpractice law is a specialty practice area.

Lawyer Profitability

Having looked at how plaintiff and defense lawyers are compensated, and why it differs, here is a more qualitative look at lawyer compensation.

Plaintiff's Lawyers

In law firms that handle primarily plaintiffs' personal injury cases, including medical malpractice claims, individual lawyers usually receive a base salary. In most plaintiff firms, a significant portion of a lawyer's annual income comes in the form of bonuses. Bonuses are paid to a firm's lawyers depending on the profitability of the firm over a given period of time (quarterly, semi-annually, or annually).

Profitability of a plaintiff's firm is essentially a function of two things – the number of cases brought into the firm; and the amount of contingency fees collected on cases. Some lawyers are better at bringing cases into the firm; those who are not "rainmakers" may excel at obtaining favorable settlements or large jury verdicts.

Since plaintiff's lawyers are paid based on the outcome of the case, regardless of the time spent, there is a built-in incentive for plaintiff's lawyers to handle and resolve meritorious cases efficiently, whether by settlement or trial. The less time and money required on a case, the better.

Defense Lawyers

In defense firms, including those that handle medical malpractice claims, lawyers are also judged on their profitability. For the defense attorney profitability is mostly a function of the number of hours billed to clients. The more hours worked and billed, the more income generated for the firm. In many defense firms (those that do primarily defense work), advancement in the firm from associate to partner depends in great part upon meeting annual billing quotas. There may be an express or implicit annual billable hour requirement in order to be on the firm's "partnership track". At times it has not been uncommon for defense firms to set annual billable hour requirements of 2000 to 2200 hours. Basic arithmetic reveals the extent to which some lawyers are expected to, and willing to, work on a weekly basis.

Those defense attorneys who meet and exceed their law firm's billable hour expectations are likely to be rewarded with bonuses, advancement in the firm, or both.

Lawyer Advertising

Advertising by lawyers has been, and continues to be, a controversial subject that has polarized lawyers of all practice types within the profession. There are those lawyers who find it to be disgraceful, unprofessional, and dishonorable. Many blame lawyer advertising for the low esteem regarded the profession in recent decades. Those in support of lawyer advertising claim that it is the use of a legitimate means to promote business and provide information to the public.

The constructive debate over lawyer advertising has been silenced and is now merely rhetorical. This is because of a United States Supreme Court case holding that a lawyer's right to advertise is protected under the First Amendment as a category of free speech.

Case Illustration

In Bates v. Arizona State Bar, 433 U.S. 350 (1977), two Arizona attorneys placed a newspaper advertisement for their "legal clinic". The ad stated that they were offering "legal services at very reasonable fees" and actually listed fees for certain services such as uncontested divorces, uncontested adoptions, simple personal bankruptcies, and changes of name.

The Arizona Supreme Court upheld the conclusion of a bar committee that the attorneys had violated Arizona's lawyer disciplinary rule, which forbade lawyer advertising. The advertising lawyers challenged the state supreme court decision in the U.S. Supreme Court, arguing that Arizona's ban on attorney advertising violated First Amendment rights to free speech. The U.S. Supreme Court held that the advertisement in question, as commercial speech that served individual and societal interests in informed and reliable decisionmaking, was entitled to First Amendment protection.

It was noted by the Supreme Court noted that:
- the case did not involve in-person solicitation
- lawyer advertising would not undermine true professionalism

•lawyer advertising is not inherently misleading

•advertising is a traditional free market mechanism that may benefit the administration of justice

•advertising may serve to reduce the cost of legal services to the consumer

•attorneys who are inclined to cut costs, will do so regardless of the rules on advertising

In many states, bar associations have promulgated regulations in an effort to at least limit the types of claims and content of lawyer advertising. They often require that advertisements (print, radio, and television) be dignified, avoid puffery and fantastic claims, not mislead the public in any way, and explain the basis for fees and costs.

Research – the Staple of Legal Work

Although the substance of legal practice varies from specialty to specialty, there is one aspect of practice that is common to all – legal research. Legal research and writing are taught in virtually every law school's first year curriculum because no matter what form of practice a lawyer eventually pursues, he will need to perform and rely on research.

Legal researching is one of the least glamorous, but most important aspects of legal practice. Poorly done research can have disastrous consequences for a lawyer and client. A lawyer who has missed finding a relevant statute or case risks losing a motion, a claim, or an entire case. A client whose lawyer has performed incomplete research could suffer staggering financial losses.

Very few, if any, popular "lawyer" books, shows, and movies accurately portray the importance or extent of research in a lawyer's work. In fact, for every brief written, and oral argument made, chances are good that a lawyer or even a team of lawyers has spent hours researching "the law" on a particular point or issue.

For every issue or question presented by a client or case, a lawyer must first find out what the law is — that is, whether there are statutes or cases that answer or address the question raised. If so, the statutes and or cases must be analyzed to see how the issue has been dealt with. In many instances, a lawyer researching a particular issue may find that there are a number of cases that deal differently with the same issue, depending on the particular facts of each case. The task will then become one of analyzing the cases to see why they were decided differently. Usually the factual distinctions explain the different outcomes.

It might seem to be a Goliath-sized endeavor for a lawyer to search for cases or laws buried in stacks of ten pound books. It actually would be, were it not for the indexing systems used by legal publishing companies. There are official and non-official legal publishing companies that publish the court decisions and laws of each and every jurisdiction. All statutes and published cases that interpret them are "keyed" according to points of law and procedure, and then cross-referenced with other pertinent statutes and cases.

Not all cases are "reported". The body of reported cases typically consists of appellate decisions that involve issues of interest beyond the actual case in which they were decided. In contrast, statutes and regulations are always written and reported in some fashion.

The combination of good indexing and technology now allow for immediate access to tremendous volumes of legal resources. What once involved hours or even days spent going through volumes of hard-bound books to trace the history of a particular issue can now be done in a fraction of the time sitting at one's computer without ever opening a book. Even so, at times there are research projects that involve good old-fashioned bookwork. And, indexes and computers still cannot perform the lawyer's job of creating the right "search".

Judges

A section on lawyers would not be complete without briefly discussing those who become judges. The focus here will be on state court trial judges, rather than on federal judges.

Each state is different with respect to the way in which its superior court (trial) judges are selected. In some states judges are elected, in other states they are nominated by committees or commissions and selected by the governor. Some states use both methods depending on the county. The latter method is referred to as merit selection. Each method has its advantages.

Proponents of elected judges are of the belief that the electorate should directly select the judges in their communities. This usually means that judicial candidates choose a party affiliation, campaign, and otherwise go after the popular vote. Detractors of judicial elections tend to view such campaigns as too political – it is undignified for judicial candidates to proclaim a party affiliation, campaign on issues, and seek votes. There is also concern in judicial elections that a candidate's actual qualifications may matter less than the amount the candidate spends on a campaign. Moreover, it is feared that a judge running for re-election may be tempted to decide cases or issues based on voter popularity rather than strictly on the merits.

Merit selection judges are those who have been nominated by a committee made up of individuals from the legal and local community. Usually, the committee is required to submit a certain number of nominees from the major political parties to a high-level state official, typically, the governor. The governor then interviews the finalists and selects, or appoints the trial judge. (This same procedure is also followed for appellate judge appointments.)

In order to recognize the "will of the people", merit selected judges are often subject to retention votes in general elections. This means that voters are asked whether each individual judge should be retained on the bench.

It is rare for a merit-selected judge to be removed in this manner, but in those situations where the general public has concern about a particular judge, this approach allows for participation in the process.

Even though the merit selection method does not involve public campaigns and elections, it is not entirely free of politics either. The nature of the politics involved is simply different. Generally speaking, however, the quality of judges selected under the merit system is quite high.

The ethical conduct of judges, whether elected or appointed, is governed by a code of judicial ethics. The provisions of such codes are directed at ensuring that a judge's conduct and work are free from the appearances of impropriety and partiality. All who appear before judges must be assured of fair and impartial treatment, a key protection of our democracy.

Who's Who?

There are a number of national, state, and local attorney positions that for the most part are government posts. Here are descriptions of the more commonly encountered positions.

United States Attorney General

The U.S. Attorney General is a cabinet level position for the nation's number one lawyer, akin to the Surgeon General. The President appoints the Attorney General. This lawyer heads the Justice Department, which is generally responsible for advising and representing the federal government and its agencies.

State Attorney General

Each state has an attorney general who is either elected or appointed to the position. It is the responsibility of the attorney general to serve as the state's lawyer. This service is typically accomplished by use of a number of assistant attorneys who work under the direction of the attorney general.

United States District Attorney

District Attorney, or "D.A" is the term applied to the federal prosecutor who represents the United States government in each federal judicial district. Those lawyers who work under the direction of the district attorney are referred to as assistant U.S. attorneys.

District Attorney

In states where the judicial territories are divided into districts, the state's prosecuting officer in each district is referred to as the district attorney. It would be the equivalent of the county attorney in states whose judicial districts correspond to counties.

County Attorney

The county attorney is the state's lead prosecuting attorney in each county. The county attorney represents the county government in legal matters and is responsible for representing the state and county governments in criminal cases.

City Attorney

The city attorney, as the name suggests, is the head attorney for the city who represents the city and its departments in prosecuting criminals, providing legal advice, and legal representation in civil matters.

Public Defender

Public defenders are criminal defense lawyers who represent defendants who cannot afford to pay for their own representation. Defense attorneys are appointed to represent indigent criminal defendants.

Prosecuting Attorney

The term "prosecuting attorney" is a generic reference to lawyers who represent the government – federal, state, county, or city – in prosecuting claims against criminal defendants. Thus, the U.S. attorney general, district attorneys, county attorneys, and city attorneys all serve as prosecuting attorneys when they represent their respective governments in pursuing criminal charges. However, when these same attorneys represent their governments in civil matters, they are not acting as prosecuting attorneys.

Next

The next section of the book covers legal aspects of medical practice that are encountered in nearly all types of medical practice. The first chapter of this section looks at the licensing, regulation, and discipline of physicians.

FAQ:

1. Is law school as grueling as it is often portrayed in books and movies?

For some individuals, and at certain law schools, the "law school experience" is truly an ordeal to be endured. There are those who "drop out" because they find the law school environment to be overwhelmingly demanding. Yet other students thrive in the competetive atmosphere. Some lawyers look back on their law school experience as the worst time of their lives. Others will fondly remember their time in law school as the most intellectually demanding, but pedagogically fulfilling experience of their lives. Thus, the answer, being "yes" for some and "no" for others, is in the mind of the questioned.

2. Is preparing for and taking the bar exam really a big deal?

Yes. It would be a rare find to encounter an honest answer to the contrary.

3. Who makes more money - plaintiff lawyers or defense lawyers?

It depends on the lawyer, the firm, and the practice. Keep in mind also that many lawyers do both types of work.

4. Do you have to be a lawyer to be a judge?

In some jurisdictions, justices of the peace are not required to have a law degree. In general jurisdiction trial courts, the judges are requried to be lawyers with a specified number of years in practice before joining the bench.

SECTION TWO

LEGAL ASPECTS OF MEDICAL PRACTICE

4

PHYSICIAN LICENSING, REGULATION, AND DISCIPLINE

I will practice my profession with conscience and with dignity; ... My colleagues will be my brothers; ... I will maintain by all the means in my power, the honor and the noble traditions of the medical profession; ...

Hippocratic Oath, Geneva Declaration, 1948

In the medical profession, as in many professions, the responsibility of licensing and disciplining members falls largely on fellow physicians, who with the authority of government oversee entrance into and practice in the profession. The rationale for imposing such regulatory oversight is the fact that each state has a strong public policy interest in protecting members of the public from unqualified physicians and unsafe practices.

Regulatory Boards

In each state, boards of medical examiners typically govern licensing, regulation, and discipline of medical practitioners. There are separate boards for allopathic and osteopathic physicians. The boards are creatures of statutes through which legislators define, set, and limit the duties and powers of the board.

Purpose of Regulatory Boards

The fundamental purpose of a licensing board is to grant licenses only to those who are competent to safely practice medicine within a given state. As such, boards can require applicants and practicing physicians to submit evidence, either written or oral, to satisfy board members that they are adequately informed regarding an applicant's ability to practice medicine.

Medical Board Members

Either by statute or rule, such things as the board's composition, appointment of members, terms of members, compensation of members, and the board's powers and duties are set forth.

Membership on most boards is not limited exclusively to physicians. Usually boards are comprised to include several members of the public. Public members are often health-related professionals, such as members of a state board of nursing. Most states call for geographic diversity on a county or regional basis.

The manner in which physicians and lay members are selected to be board members varies from state to state. In many states, official appointment to the board is made by the governor, usually from a list of names submitted by the state medical association.

Many states have a residency requirement of five years and require that board members remain active in practice during their term of appointment. The typical term is five years.

Board members' appointments may be terminated for a number of reasons, including attendance failures, extended absence from the state, retirement from practice, neglect of duty, incompetence, or unprofessional conduct.

Board members are often compensated on a per diem basis for each day spent in actual service in the business of the board and for related expenses.

Because medical boards deal with granting and regulating licenses, which is a governmental regulatory function, state legislatures have granted to board members personal immunity from lawsuits. Such immunity attaches for members' good faith actions that relate to board activities. The practical effect of this immunity means that a board member could not be sued by a disgruntled applicant whose application was rejected, or by a physician who has been duly disciplined or censured by the board.

Accountability of the board is usually monitored by means of an annual report to the governor setting forth a summary of licensing and disciplinary activities each year.

Medical Board Powers

The specific powers and duties of medical boards are generally spelled out by state legislatures. Standard types of powers and duties include such things as:

- reviewing credentials and physical or mental abilities of applicants whose professional records may not meet the requirements for licensure

- ordering and evaluating physical, psychological, psychiatric and competency testing of candidates or licensed physicians as necessary

- initiating investigations into whether a doctor has engaged in unprofessional conduct or is physically or mentally incompetent to safely practice medicine

- developing and recommending professional standards

- disciplining and rehabilitating physicians

- exchanging information with licensing and disciplinary boards and medical associations of other states, jurisdictions, and foreign countries

- preparing and distributing educational materials

- adopting rules and regulations regarding the qualifications of doctors

- establishing fees and penalties

The Practice of Medicine is a Privilege

It is clear from a review of various states' statutes and case law that the practice of medicine is considered to be a privilege, and not a right. It is a privilege granted and controlled by each state's legislature. This means that only those who meet state licensing requirements are granted the privilege to practice. Moreover, the failure to comply with ongoing practice requirements can result in subsequent temporary or permanent loss of the privilege.

Here is the law of Texas on this subject:

The legislature makes the following declarations:

(1) the practice of medicine is a privilege and not a natural right of individuals and as a matter of public policy it is considered necessary to protect the public interest through the specific formulation of this Act to regulate the granting of that privilege and its subsequent use and control; . . .

Vernon's Ann. Texas Civ.St.Art. 4495b

Basic Licensure Requirements

Requirements for licensure do not vary significantly from state to state. The substantive requisites are all designed to ensure that minimum standard levels of education and training have been achieved. In most states, the basic requirements for granting a license to practice medicine are met by showing:

1. graduation from an *approved* school of medicine, or one of equivalent quality

2. successful completion of an approved twelve month hospital internship, residency, or clinical fellowship program

3. physical and mental capability to safely practice medicine

4. a professional record showing that an applicant has not committed any act, or engaged in any conduct that would result in disciplinary action

5. a professional record indicating that an applicant's license in another state, territory, district, or country has not been revoked, refused, suspended or restricted in a way that relates to the ability to safely and competently practice medicine

6. payment of fees as required by each state board

7. completion of a required application process

Licensing Leeway

Most states have enacted statutes that permit licensing boards to consider mitigating circumstances if there is some deficiency in an applicant's background or application, such as past disciplinary action. In such cases, a board can investigate and determine whether certain conduct has been corrected, monitored, and resolved. If there is a deficiency in an application a state board will provide a written statement of the deficiency. Boards may then request that the applicant attend a hearing.

In situations involving applicants who have graduated from *unapproved* schools of medicine, most boards have additional requirements such as:

- demonstration of the ability to read, write, speak, understand, and be understood in the English language

- possession of a standard certificate issued by the educational council for foreign medical graduates, completion of a fifth pathway program, or completion of thirty-six months as a full time assistant professor at an approved school of medicine

- successful completion of an approved twenty-four month hospital internship, residency or clinical fellowship program in addition to the basic twelve month requirement

Licensure and Board Exams

Once basic eligibility requirements have been met, applicants are granted licensure upon completion of parts one, two and three of the national board examination. Typically, part one of the boards is taken during second year of medical school; part two is taken during the fourth year of medical school; and part three is taken sometime after successful completion of six months of an approved hospital internship. In many states, in lieu of an internship, applicants who serve as full-time assistant professors in board approved in-state medical schools are also eligible to take part three of the examination.

Training Permits

Training permits are granted to those who are participating in accredited internships, residency programs and clinical fellowship training programs.

The permit only allows the holder to practice in the supervised setting of a training program.

Inactive Licenses

Holders of active licenses may request an inactive license. Typically, boards will then waive the annual license fee and continuing medical education requirements. The holder of an inactive license cannot practice medicine or maintain a drug enforcement administration controlled substances registration without special registration. Conversion from inactive to active licensure usually involves payment of the annual renewal fee and presentation of some evidence that the holder has medical knowledge and can physically and mentally safely practice medicine. The quantity and quality of evidence required to satisfy a board will often vary depending in great part on the duration of and reason for the inactive license status.

Continuing Medical Education

Continuing medical education requirements vary from state to state, but characteristically involve the imposition of an hourly requirement set by the board, for which written documentation must be submitted each year.

Regulating "Unprofessional Conduct"

Because a primary duty of medical boards is to safeguard the public, one of the most critical responsibilities a medical board is charged with is to identify and investigate instances of "unprofessional conduct". Recognizing that the term by itself is somewhat vague, most state legislatures have enacted statutes that specifically list and define the types of physician conduct that constitute "unprofessional conduct". Here are activities commonly listed in statutes:

- intentionally violating a patient's confidential or privileged communication

- false, fraudulent, deceptive or misleading advertising

- prescribing controlled substances to members of a physician's immediate family

- failing to maintain adequate patient records

- signing prescription forms which are blank, undated, or pre-dated

- making false or fraudulent statements in connection with applications for privileges

- representing that an incurable disease can be permanently cured by a secret method, procedure, treatment, medicine or device if such is not the case

- charging or collecting a clearly excessive fee

- sexual intimacies with a patient

- using experimental forms of treatment or diagnosis without adequate informed consent from a patient

- obtaining or attempting to obtain or renew a license to practice medicine by fraud or misrepresentation

- failing to provide proper supervision of licensed, certified or registered health care providers employed by a physician

- refusing to submit a body fluid examination as required by the board pursuant to an investigation of alleged substance abuse

- failing to report to the board in writing any evidence that an other physician or physician assistant is or may be medically incompetent, guilty of unprofessional conduct or mentally or physically unable to safely practice or assist in the practice of medicine

If a medical board investigates and determines that a physician has acted in a manner that has been statutorily defined as "unprofessional", the physician will then be subject to further action by the board. The further action will likely consist of efforts to correct unprofessional conduct and punish the offending physician.

> **Case Illustration**
> In *Nethken v. State*, 56 Ariz. 15, 104 P.2d 159 (1940), a doctor who was licensed as a naturopath diagnosed a lump on a patient's foot as cancer. In order to treat the cancer, he applied electricity to the foot to "burn out the lump" by using a diathermy machine, typically used by surgeons. The naturopath was convicted in court of practicing medicine without a license. The court sentenced the seventy-six year old defendant doctor to one to three years in prison even though the jury recommended extreme leniency because of the doctor's old age. It appears from the case that the doctor also posed as a doctor who specialized in treating tuberculosis and cancer.

Reporting Unprofessional Conduct

Board investigation into allegations of unprofessional conduct may occur on the board's own initiative or as a result of a complaint brought by a colleague, patient, or anyone in a position to suspect physician misconduct.

It is important to keep in mind that a physician who fails to report that another physician – *is or may be* guilty of unprofessional conduct, – *is or may be* medically incompetent, or – *is or may be* mentally or physically unable to safely practice medicine – may himself guilty of unprofessional conduct. This means that if you know or suspect that a partner, colleague, or professional acquaintance is compromised in his ability to safely practice medicine, you have an affirmative obligation to make a report to the regulatory board. A failure to report could render you guilty of unprofessional conduct. Physicians, you are your brothers' (and sisters') keepers! (It may be of some comfort to know that lawyers are subject to the same type of reporting obligation.)

Hospitals also have an obligation to report to boards concerning a physician's fitness for medical practice. Whenever a doctor's privileges at a health care institution are denied, revoked, suspended, supervised, or limited, the institution may have a reporting obligation. Hospitals are often required to report to boards if the conduct on which the privilege action was based shows that a doctor:

- *is or may be* guilty of unprofessional conduct

- *is or may be* medically incompetent

- *is or may be* mentally or physically unable to safely practice medicine

If any of these findings apply, in most instances the chief executive officer of the institution is required to inform the board of the action regarding the physician's privileges. A report including a statement of the reasons for the action, along with patient chart numbers that led to the action, are typically required as well.

By statute, a person who reports or provides information to a board in good faith is not subject to an action for civil damages. Note that for the protection to attach, a reporting individual must be acting in good faith. This means that an individual making groundless complaints for the sole purpose of harassment would not have statutory immunity and might still be vulnerable to an action for defamation.

Even though statutory protections exist, as a practical matter physicians may find it is difficult to "rat" on a colleague. Perhaps the better way to view one's obligation in this context is to keep in mind the potentially greater good of preventing serious harm to a patient, and ultimately, to the colleague.

Board Investigations of Unprofessional Conduct

Either upon receipt of a complaint, or its own initiative, a board will perform an investigation of some degree, depending on the reliability and seriousness of the concern raised. Some investigations are straightforward and simple; others are complex and time intensive. Although an investigation may take one of several forms, in all instances the physician in question is notified of a complaint and the board's investigation.

When a licensing board conducts an investigation, if indicated, it has the power to issue subpoenas to compel the appearance and testimony of witnesses. It may also demand the production of documents for examination or copying. Usually, any person who appears before the board has the right to be represented by counsel.

Once a board conducts an investigation into allegations of incompetence or unprofessional conduct, it has a number of options. Generally, a board may do any of the following:

- determine that the issue raised is without merit and dismiss the matter

- determine that the matter does not require direct action against the doctor's license, but is serious enough to file a *letter of concern* or a *letter of reprimand*

- enter into a voluntary consent agreement with a doctor to limit or restrict the doctor's practice and/ or assist in providing rehabilitation

- request an informal interview with the doctor to determine whether further action is necessary; it may then dismiss, file a letter of concern, file a letter of reprimand, or find possible grounds for revoking or suspending a doctor's license; if so, it will file a formal complaint and set a hearing

- conduct a hearing and issue a decree of censure, which is an official action against the doctor's license

- require a doctor to make restitution to a patient or patients for violations of rules of professional conduct

- set terms and conditions of probation, including suspension, restrictions on practice, restitution to patients, education or rehabilitation

- enter into a formal agreement with a doctor to restrict or limit his practice in order to rehabilitate the doctor

- impose civil penalties of anywhere from several hundred to several thousand dollars for each violation of the rules of professional conduct

Legal Representation

If you ever find yourself involved with a licensing board in connection with an allegation of unprofessional conduct or medical incompetence, it is strongly recommended that you seek legal counsel to protect your rights and interests. What may be at stake is the ability to practice your chosen profession. Remember that what the state giveth — your medical license to practice — the state can taketh away.

There are lawyers who specialize in representing physicians in licensing and proceedings so be sure to consult with experienced counsel.

Next

The relationship between physician and patient has special legal significance. After reading the next chapter you will understand why and when the relationship you have with your patients is fiduciary in nature, confidential, and privileged.

FAQs:

1. Is "unprofessional conduct" the same thing as medical malpractice?

No. A board's finding of unprofessional conduct is not the same as a civil jury's finding of malpractice. Each is a separate finding by a separate fact finding body. However, it is not uncommon for the facts that support a board complaint to also support a medical negligence complaint in court. Interestingly, it is possible for a board to find unprofessional conduct and a jury to return a finding of no medical negligence on the same facts, and vice versa.

2. Can a board's investigation and findings be used in a medical malpractice case against a doctor?

The answer depends on what it is that is to be "used". In most instances the factual information considered by a medical board may also be used in a medical malpractice case as long as it is not privileged information to begin with. Internal reports and memoranda generated by a board that reflect its deliberations are normally protected from discovery in a medical malpractice case. If a board reviews records of other patients in connection with its investigation, the names and identities of those patients are confidential and cannot be made available to the public. The board's ultimate findings, orders, and actions are generally discoverable in a medical malpractice action.

3. Do members of the public have access to board files on each doctor?

Some portions of files are accessible to members of the public. "Letters of concern" or "reprimand" are public documents. The existence of previous complaints against a doctor is public information. As patients become more consumer-oriented, they are more likely to make inquiries of state licensing boards. (Computer technology will make access to this information easier than ever before.)

Lawyers representing plaintiffs in medical malpractice cases are certain to get copies of a defendant doctor's file. This will typically include copies of the application for licensure, copies of any complaints, results of board investigations, any letters of concern or reprimand, and consent agreements or board actions to limit or restrict a doctor's license. If you are defendant in a medical malpractice case, whether justified or not, it is wise to have your attorney get a copy of your licensing file so you won't be caught off-guard by the plaintiff's lawyer.

4. Is a doctor who is "guilty" of unprofessional conduct guilty of a crime?

No. Determination of guilt or innocence of a crime takes place in a court of law through a criminal court proceeding. However, many states have statutes that proscribe certain conduct relating to licensure. For instance, the practice of medicine without a license, obtaining a license by fraud or deceit, or impersonating a board member to issue a license to another, are classified as felonies in many states. By contrast, the determination of whether a physician has acted "unprofessionally" takes place in an administrative setting before a board of medical examiners. A physician who is found to have acted unprofessionally has not necessarily committed a criminal act, but may have.

5. If I think or know that another doctor did something "unprofessional" do I really have to report it?

Technically speaking, yes. If you don't, and it somehow becomes apparent that you did know of another's unprofessional conduct, in most states, you may then be found to be guilty of unprofessional conduct yourself. Remember that the term "unprofessional conduct" is usually defined in state statutes or board regulations. It would be a good idea to review these statutes before deciding whether you are obligated to report on another.

6. Are peer reveiw physicians totally protected from actions brought by disgruntled physicians?

No. Peer reviewing physicians must be acting for proper purposes or they may lose statutory immunity from suit. For an interesting case involving this issue see the United States Supreme Court's opinion in *Patrick v. Burget*, 486 U.S. 94, 108 S.Ct. 1658 (1998). The facts of the case are as follows. The petitioner was a general and vascular surgeon who became employed by a private group-medical practice clinic ("Clinic") in a northwestern town of 10,000 residents. There was one hospital in the town and the surgeon was a member of its medical staff as well. One year after becoming employed at the Clinic, its partners invited the surgeon to join them as a partner. The surgeon declined the offer and instead started his own practice in competition with the surgical practice of the Clinic.

Once the surgeon established his practice, the Clinic physicians consistently refused to have any professional dealings with him. He received no referrals, even during times when there was no general surgeon on staff at the Clinic. Rather than refer patients to the surgeon, Clinic physicians referred patients to other surgeons located as far as 50 miles away. Clinic physicians also refused to assist the surgeon with his practice - they declined to provide consultations, refused to provide backup coverage, and then complained about the surgeon's hospital practice. Ultimately, the complaints brought by Clinic physicians were referred to the State Board of Medical Examiners. It was a Clinic physician who chaired the BOME committee that investigated the matters. The BOME committee issued a letter of reprimand, but it was retracted when the surgeon sought judicial review of the BOME proceedings.

A couple of years later, at the request of a Clinic physician, the hospital executive committee initiated a review of the surgeon's hospital privileges, and ultimately voted to terminate his privileges. The surgeon requested a hearing and demanded that the executive committee, chaired by a Clinic physician, testify as to their personal bias against him. The committee members refused to do so, and the surgeon resigned from the hospital staff rather than risk a termination of his privileges.

While the hospital peer-review proceedings were going on, the surgeon filed suit against the partners of the Clinic, alleging that they violated the Sherman Act. The surgeon asserted that the Clinic partners initiated and participated in hospital peer review proceedings in order to reduce competition from him rather than to improve patient care. The jury found in favor of the surgeon and awarded $650,000 on the two antitrust claims brought. As required by law, the district court trebled the damages awarded.

On appeal by the Clinic partners, the Court of Appeals for the Ninth Circuit reversed. It found that although there was substantial evidence that the Clinic partners had acted in bad faith in the peer review process (the court characterized the conduct of the Clinic physicians as "shabby, unprincipled and unprofessional"), and even if they had used the process to disadvantage a competitor rather than to improve patient care, their conduct was immune from antitrust scrutiny. 484 U.S. at 98

The U.S. Supreme Court accepted review of the case and reversed the judgment of the Court of Appeals. It held that the immunity applied by the Court of Appeals (state-action doctrine) did not protect the peer review activities in this case from the application of federal antitrust laws. The Supreme Court noted that Congress could, but has not yet, excepted medical peer review from the reach of the antitrust laws.

✦   ✦   ✦   ✦

5

PHYSICIAN AND PATIENT - A "PRIVILEGED RELATIONSHIP

The health of my patient will be my first consideration

I will respect the secrets which are confided in me

I will not permit considerations of religion, nationality or race, party politics or social standing to intervene between my duty and my patient . .

Hippocratic Oath, Geneva Declaration, 1948

Legislatures have recognized as a matter of public policy, and consistent with societal values, that there are certain social and business relationships that are worthy of special protection. In addition to protections associated with the physician-patient relationship, legislatures also protect certain other relationships, such as those between attorney and client, priest and penitent, and husband and wife. This chapter outlines the nature and purpose of physician-patient confidentiality, the statutory privilege, and practical implications of physicians' relationships with their patients.

Public Policy of Physician-Patient Confidentiality

The public policy interest in protecting the physician-patient relationship is based on recognition of the value of a healthy citizenry. Statutory protection is given to the relationship because patients are more likely to receive optimal health care and treatment if there is full and frank disclosure and discussion of medical histories, complaints, symptoms, and treatments with physicians. If patients feared that such personal information was not confidential, they would tend to misreport or under-report health conditions. As a result, health conditions would more likely be mistreated or untreated, causing a general decline in overall health of the populace.

The physician-patient relationship is often characterized as being a fiduciary relationship — that is, one in which the patient places trust in the physician, and because of the physician's special education and training he is obligated to act in good faith at all times in matters concerning his patient. Due to a physician's special education, training, skill, and knowledge, it would be easy, yet unfair, and undesirable for him to put his interests above those of his patient. He must not do anything to take advantage of his trusting patient. The oft-heard rule of caveat emptor does not apply to physicians and their patients.

Case Illustration

In *Moore v. Regents of the Univ. of Cal.*, 51 Cal. 3d 120, 793 P.2d 479, (1990), the blood of a patient/plaintiff had unique characteristics that could provide scientific and commercial advantage to those who had access to it. The patient's physician recommended to the patient that he have his spleen removed. However, the physician did not tell the patient of his plan to use portions of the spleen and post-operative blood samples for research that had no relationship to the patient's needed medical care. After surgery, the patient found out and brought suit against the physician. The physician argued that the claim should have been dismissed. The court disagreed and said that the physician had a fiduciary duty to inform the patient of his personal research and economic interests that were unrelated to the

> patient's health. The patient had a right to know of the personal inter-
> ests of the physician that might affect the physician's professional
> judgment with respect to the patient. The court allowed the case to
> proceed against the physician for breach of the fiduciary duty to dis-
> close facts material to informed consent.

You may not have thought about the fact that each time you see a new or established patient, you are required by law to treat the relationship as one in which the patient has certain privileges or protections. You, as a physician, are legally obligated to protect those certain rights of your patient.

Privilege Statutes

In furtherance of the public policy interest in protecting the confidentiality of physician-patient communications, state statutes have been enacted to establish a physician-patient privilege. A typical civil privilege states:

> In a civil action, a physician or surgeon shall not, without the consent of his patient, or the conservator or guardian of the patient, be examined as to any communication made by his patient with reference to any physical, or mental disease or disorder or supposed physical or mental disease or disorder, or as to any such knowledge obtained by personal examination of the patient.

A privilege statute such as the sample above is what is known as an evidentiary privilege, protecting confidential communication from disclosure in a civil case or courtroom. There are numerous other federal and state statutes and regulations, as well as professional standards that protect the confidentiality of physician-patient communications in other contexts.

According to the American Medical Records Association:

> The information contained in the health record belongs to the patient, and the patient is entitled to the protected right of in-

formation. All patient care information shall be regarded as confidential and available only to authorized users.

Most professional regulation statutes provide that a physician's unauthorized disclosure of patient information is "unprofessional conduct", unless the disclosure is required by law.

Case Illustration

In *Ryan v. Board of Registration of Medicine*, 388 Mass. 1013, 447 N.E.2d 662 (1983) the court upheld the medical board's censure of a physician because the "physician violated good and acceptable medical practice when he released to the press information concerning a patient's medical condition." 388 Mass. at 1014, 447 N.E.2d at 663

Privilege Particulars

The law on physician-patient confidentiality is well developed. In most every jurisdiction, courts have interpreted nearly every phrase of the privilege statutes. As a result, there are some standard comments that may be made about the law of the physician-patient privilege.

- A patient may waive the privilege of confidentiality.

- A parent may waive the privilege on behalf of minor children.

- Medical information obtained for treatment purposes is protected.

- Medical information obtained through court-ordered assessments is not protected.

- Results of diagnostic tests are confidential.

- The privilege belongs to the patient and cannot be used to shield a physician.

- Even though the privilege belongs to the patient, a physician is required to assert the privilege on behalf of a patient who is not present.

- Even though privilege statutes technically only create an evidentiary privilege, meaning a physician is privileged from being questioned about his patients in a civil or criminal action, courts generally interpret the statutes to provide patient confidentiality as the general rule, whether or not in the context of a legal action.

- In some instances a court may order that patient records be disclosed without violating confidentiality as long as names or other identifying information are blocked out. Courts often permit this in an effort to balance the public policy interest in discovery of relevant evidence.

- Federal and state regulations provide for confidentiality of medical records: held by federal agencies, in Medicare participant hospitals, of home health services, of human subject research, of departments of health services, of departments of developmental disabilities, of depart ments of economic security, and of all communicable diseases.

Case Illustration

In *Rittenhouse v. Superior Court (Bd. of Trustees)*, 235 Cal.App.3d 1584, 1 Cal.Rptr.2d 595 (1991) the court held that the physician-patient privilege survives the death of the patient. Stanford University sought the disclosure of a deceased man's medical records in an effort to prove that he suffered from a mental disability and could not have been the intended beneficiary of a holographic will. Stanford would have been the beneficiary of the estate if it could prove the bequest to man invalid. The court upheld the privilege and denied Stanford access to the records. In its decision, the court noted that the "obvious objective of the physician-patient privilege is to foster open communication between patients and their healthcare provid-

> ers. Without assurances that their revelations would be safe from public exposure, persons in need of care would often be discouraged from the open and complete disclosure of private information which is essential to effective treatment. (citations omitted) Stanford argues that when the patient is no longer alive, that policy is not served by preserving the shield of confidentiality. We disagree.
>
> The possibility of posthumous exposure of sensitive, highly personal, and sometimes embarrassing information about one's physical or mental condition, information which often involves surviving family members or other individuals with whom the patient has had contacts, would hinder the free communication between patient and professional which the privilege is designed to encourage. We read section 993, subdivision (c) and the Law Revision Commission Comment thereto as affirming the continued viability of the physician patient-privilege after the death of the patient and granting the personal representative the same right to claim or waive the privilege as any other holder.
>
> 235 Cal.App. 3d at 1590, 1 Cal.Rpter.2d at 598-9.

Special Considerations

Two areas of special concern arise with patients whose medical history or condition involves drug and alcohol treatment, or HIV or other communicable diseases. Medical records involving these types of information are protected from disclosure by federal statutes and regulations. As an example, by regulation all information obtained from patients for the purpose of diagnosis, treatment or referral in federally assisted drug or alcohol abuse programs is absolutely confidential. Even implicit and negative disclosures are prohibited.

In the case of communicable diseases including HIV status, special rules also apply. Generally, no one may disclose or be compelled to disclose confidential HIV or other communicable disease information that is obtained in the course of providing health services. Again, physicians should take care to avoid making implicit or negative disclosures.

Exceptions to Confidentiality

Having said that physicians should be very conscientious about protecting confidential patient information, be aware that not all information in a patient's medical record is confidential. Here are some examples of instances when certain persons or entities may have access to otherwise confidential information, and under what circumstances.

- Generally and technically speaking, non-medical information is not confidential. Even so, it is not recommended that physicians give out biographical or demographic information about their patients.

- Certain government agencies have statutory access to certain records without patient consent. For instance, the U.S. Department of Justice may use medical records to investigate Medicare or Medicaid fraud, tax fraud, or to help locate fugitives. This agency has access to otherwise confidential information based on "supervising interests of society". *Horne v. Patton,* 291 Ala. 701, 287 So.2d 824, 830 (1973).

- State licensing boards that are investigating licensing issues are entitled to patient records.

- Interestingly, but not surprisingly, patients who raise the insanity defense in murder prosecutions automatically waive the right to patient confidentiality.

- In situations involving psychiatric patients who present a threat of serious harm to others, physicians may disclose information without patient consent.

As one can see, the privilege of confidentiality is not absolute and may be outweighed when competing interests, such as public safety arise.

Affirmative Duties to Disclose

There are instances in which, notwithstanding patient confidentiality, a physician has a statutory and affirmative obligation to report certain information to governmental authorities. Statutes vary from state to state, but typically the following types of information are to be reported:

- Any evidence of child abuse or neglect (to police and child protective services)

- Any evidence of sexual activity involving a minor (to police and child protective services)

- A reasonable belief that abuse or neglect of an incapacitated or vulnerable adult has occurred (to police or protective services)

- Treatment of gunshot, knife or other non-accidental wounds (to police or sheriff)

- Contagious diseases and death from contagious disease (to state or local health department)

- Patients who have tested positive for syphilis, hepatitis or AIDS (to the patient)

- Injuries arising out of or in the scope or course of a patient's employment (to worker's compensation agency and employer's worker's compensation carrier)

It is also interesting to note that the principle of confidentiality cannot be used by a health care provider as a shield against liability for negligence.

Case Illustration

In *Emmett v. Eastern Dispensary & Casualty Hosp.*, 396 F.2d 931 (D.C. Cir. 1967), the son of a deceased man sought copies of his father's records for the purpose of investigating a medical malpractice/wrongful death claim against a hospital. The hospital refused to provide the records claiming that they were confidential and could not be released. The son alleged that the hospital 'willfully and wrongfully withheld' the decedent's medical records 'for the purpose of preventing' him 'from obtaining any information regarding the circumstances of' the death.

In considering the extent of the hospital's obligation, the court said: [T]his duty of disclosure, we hold, extends after the patient's death to his next of kin. [footnote omitted] To be sure, medical professionals can and should vigilantly safeguard the patient's secrets from unauthorized scrutiny. [footnote omitted] They may, prudently and conscientiously, take such precautions, including suitable identification, as may be necessary to enable determination of the propriety of a requested revelation, and we would consider qualifiedly privileged any divulgence reasonably made to one apparently entitled to it. [footnote omitted] But we could not justify a refusal to yield the information to a qualified recipient, whether or not it stems from the dictates of self-protection. 396 F.2d at 936

* * * * * *

Decedent's son and only child had so vital an identification with any cause of action potentially arising upon his father's negligently caused demise as would enable him to waive the physician-patient privilege as to pertinent medical data where there was no personal representative to act in his behalf so that the assertion of the physician-patient privilege did not defeat son's right to inspect decedent's medical report or establish physician's and hospital's duty to preserve confidentiality of records against all save decedent's legal representative. 396 F.2d at 936

Duty to Disclose – the "Tarasoff Rule"

One of the most notorious of exceptions to a physician's obligation to protect confidentiality, and one worthy of special comment, relates to physicians whose patients present a known threat of harm to third persons. In such instances, the physician has a legal duty to divulge otherwise confidential patient information.

There is a landmark case in which this legal duty was recognized. The case is *Tarasoff v. Regents of Univ. of Cal.*, 17 Cal.3d 425, 131 Cal. Rptr. 14, 551 P.2d 334 (1976). The California Supreme Court opinion consists of 100+ pages, in which a divided court analyzed the legal, medical, public policy and practical ramifications of an important exception to patient confidentiality. Because of the thoroughness and significance of the decision, the text of the opinion is both interesting and instructive. Rather than providing a summary of the facts, analysis, and decision, actual excerpts from the case are presented.

Case Illustration

"Plaintiffs' first cause of action, entitled 'Failure to Detain a Dangerous Patient,' alleges that on August 20, 1969, Poddar was a voluntary outpatient receiving therapy at Cowell Memorial Hospital. Poddar informed Moore, his therapist, that he was going to kill an unnamed girl, readily identifiable as Tatiana, when she returned home from spending the summer in Brazil. Moore, with the concurrence of Dr. Gold, who had initially examined Poddar, and Dr. Yandell, Assistant to the director of the department of psychiatry, decided that Poddar should be committed for observation in a mental hospital. Moore orally notified Officers Atkinson and Teel of the campus police that he would request commitment. He then sent a letter to Police Chief William Beall requesting the assistance of the police department in securing Poddar's confinement. Officers Atkinson, Brownrigg, and Halleran took Poddar into custody, but, satisfied that Poddar was rational, released him on his promise to stay away from Tatiana. Powelson, director of the department of psychiatry at Cowell Memorial Hospital, then asked the police to return Moore's letter, directed that all copies of the letter and notes that Moore had taken as therapist be destroyed, and 'ordered no action to place Prosenjit Poddar in 72-hour treatment and evaluation facility.' Plaintiffs' second cause of action, entitled 'Failure to Warn On a Dangerous Patient,'incorporates the allegations of the first cause of action, but adds the assertion that defendants negligently permitted Poddar to be released from police custody without 'notifying the parents of Tatiana Tarasoff that their daughter was in grave danger from Posenjit Poddar.' Poddar persuaded Tatiana's brother to share an apartment with him near Tatiana's residence; shortly after her return from Brazil, Poddar went to her residence and killed her. 17 Cal.3d at 432-3, 551P.2d at 343

Although plaintiffs' pleadings assert no special relation between Tatiana and defendant therapists, they establish as between Poddar and defendant therapists the special relation that arises between a patient and his doctor or psychotherapist. [Footnote 6 omitted] Such a relationship may support affirmative duties for the benefit of third persons. Thus, for example, a hospital must exercise reasonable care to control the behavior of a patient which may endanger other persons. [Footnote 7 omitted] A doctor must also warn a patient if the patient's condition or medication renders certain conduct, such as driving a car, dangerous to others. [Footnote 8 omitted] 17 Cal.3d at 436, 551 P.2d at 343-4

The role of the psychiatrist, who is indeed a practitioner of medicine, and that of the psychologist who performs an allied function, are like that of the physician who must conform to the standards of the profession and who must often make diagnoses and predictions based upon such evaluations. Thus the judgment of the therapist in diagnosing emotional disorders and in predicting whether a patient presents a serious danger of violence is comparable to the judgment which doctors and professionals must regularly render under accepted rules of responsibility. We recognize the difficulty that a therapist encounters in attempting to forecast whether a patient presents a serious danger of violence. Obviously we do not require that the therapist, in making that determination, render a perfect performance; the therapist need only exercise 'that reasonable degree of skill, knowledge, and care ordinarily possessed and exercised by members of (that professional specialty) under similar circumstances.' (cites omitted) Within the broad range of reasonable practice and treatment in which professional opinion and judgment may differ, the therapist is free to exercise his or her own best judgment without liability; proof, aided by hindsight, that he or she judged wrongly is insufficient to establish negligence. In the instant case, however, the pleadings do not raise any question as to failure of defendant therapists to predict that Poddar presented a serious danger of violence. On the contrary, the present complaints allege that defendant therapists did in fact predict that Poddar would kill, but were negligent in failing to warn. 17 Cal.3d at 438, 551 P.2d at 345

We realize that the open and confidential character of psychotherapeutic dialogue encourages patients to express threats of violence, few of which are ever executed. Certainly a therapist should not be encouraged routinely to reveal such threats; such disclosures could seriously disrupt the patient's relationship with his therapist and with the persons threatened. To the contrary, the therapist's obligations to his patient require that he not disclose a confidence unless such disclosure is necessary to avert danger to others, and even then that he do so discreetly, and in a fashion that would preserve the privacy of his patient to the fullest extent compatible with the prevention of the threatened danger. (See Fleming & Maximov, The Patient or His Victim: The Therapist's Dilemma (1974) 62 Cal.L.Rev. 1025, 1065—1066.) [Footnote 14 omitted]

The revelation of a communication under the above circumstances is not a breach of trust or a violation of professional ethics; as stated in the Principles of Medical Ethics of the American Medical Association (1957), section 9: 'A physician may not reveal the confidence entrusted to him in the course of medical attendance... Unless he is required to do so by law or unless it becomes necessary in order to protect the welfare of the individual or of the community.' [footnote 15 omitted] (Emphasis added.) We conclude that the public policy favoring protection of the confidential character of patient-psychotherapist communications must yield to the extent to which disclosure is essential to avert danger to others. The protective privilege ends where the public peril begins. 17 Cal.3d at 441-2, 551 P.2d at 347

As is evident from the opinion, the court was concerned about the tension between patient confidentiality and the policy interest in protecting the public from "peril". In formulating a standard of legal responsibility, known as "duty", the court held that what is required of physicians is the exercise of reasonable "skill, knowledge, and care ordinarily possessed and exercised" by members of the physician's specialty. This means that what is reasonable and required of one type of practitioner may be different from what is required of a physician practicing another specialty. In other words, what would be considered reasonable conduct for a psychiatrist might not be required of an ophthalmologist.

Regardless of a physician's practice type, keep in mind that this rule of law does not mean that he will be held absolutely liable for any and all harm done to others by his patients. It means that under certain circumstances, he must take reasonable steps to protect any known intended victims of his patients. Whether conduct is reasonable under the circumstances of any given situation will be decided by a finder of fact, which is usually a jury.

In some cases it may be that making a phone call to warn a third person is sufficient. Leaving a message on an answering machine may or may not be adequate depending on the circumstances. Notifying the authorities may be reasonable and required in some cases, but not in others. Simply put, the determination of what is reasonable varies and is based on the facts of each situation.

Tarasoff –type Obligations

In many states there are cases in which the *Tarasoff rule* has been officially adopted. Those states in which it hasn't been officially adopted still may follow the reasoning of the *Tarasoff* case. Moreover, many state legislatures have enacted statutes that explicitly recognize a psychiatrist's legal duty to prevent harm to third persons under certain enumerated circumstances. Some statutes also delineate what conduct is necessary to discharge the duty.

Clearly, all psychiatrists should be intimately familiar with the *Tarasoff* law of the jurisdiction in which they practice medicine. In addition, *any* physician who has occasion to deal with potentially dangerous patients, such as inmates or mental health patients, should certainly be familiar with the law as well.

In the non-psychiatric setting, the issue of whether a physician can be held liable for causing injury to another has been variously considered. The types of cases in which this issue has come up often involve the administration or prescription of medications that affect a patient's judgment. Usually the courts analyze the cases by employing a balancing test to weigh the likelihood of harm, the reasonableness of the burden on a physician to guard against it, and the consequences of burdening a defendant doctor with a duty to protect against harm to others. As an example, consider a doctor who administers a narcotic pain medication or tranquilizer to a patient in the office. The patient then leaves the office, drives away, and causes injury to a pedestrian or other motorists. The doctor who administered the medication and knew or should have known that the patient was impaired, may be held liable for the injuries caused by her patient.

Any doctor who prescribes or administers medications that may affect a patient's judgement or perception should warn the patient *in advance* that he or she will not be able to drive a vehicle and must make arrangements for transportation from the office. It would be quite prudent to have patients sign a form acknowledging receipt of the warning and perhaps including a brief description of the arrangements that have been made for transportation home.

Case Illustration

In *Wilchinsky v. Medina*, 108 N.M. 511, 775 P.2d 713 (1989) the plaintiff filed suit against defendant Medina, who was the driver of the car that struck and killed plaintiff's daughter. Plaintiff also named Medina's physician as an additional defendant, alleging that he was negligent in giving Medina two medications that are known to cause drowsiness and impaired judgment.

On the morning of the accident Medina suffered from a debilitating headache and took Percodan as prescribed by the doctor. The medication did not provide relief so Medina went to the doctor's office and was given an injection of Meperidine, and shortly thereafter, Vistaril or Tigan for nausea.

Here is what the court decided, after reviewing the decisions of courts in other jurisdictions:

In *Joy v. Eastern Maine Medical Center*, 529 A.2d 1364 (Me.1987), the Supreme Court of Maine allowed a third-party cause of action against a doctor whose treatment included fitting his patient with an eyepatch. The court wrote "when a doctor knows, or reasonably should know that his patient's ability to drive has been affected, he has a duty to the driving public." Id. at 1366. In *Welke v. Kuzilla*, 144 Mich.App. 245, 375 N.W.2d 403 (1985), the Michigan Court of Appeals found that an injection given on the evening prior to the accident created a cause of action in malpractice for the third-party victim. The facts in these two cases are markedly different from the present case.

The facts of this certification present a stronger argument for finding a duty than any of the cases described above. Unlike Joy, facts here do not suggest that Medina should have known the extent of her risk in accepting medication. In Joy, the doctor argued the eyepatch created an obvious impairment for which no reasonable person required a warning. Here, one side effect of the drugs may have been impairment of the patient's ability to reason. In addition, it will require medical testimony to explain the probable diminishment of capacity when Demerol is administered, either by itself, or in combination with other drugs. Unlike Welke, facts here also suggest a stronger argument for proximate cause, as Dr. Straight injected Medina within seventy minutes of the accident. Finally, unlike the prescription cases, the administration of these drugs was within the doctor's presence, in the doctor's office under his direction and timing, making reasonable preventative measures of whatever type easier to implement, and, at the same time, creating a higher degree of patient reliance on the doctor's professional judgment. Having canvassed other jurisdictions, we return to the balance set forth from the Kirk opinion: the likelihood of injury, the reasonableness of the burden of guarding against it, and the consequences of burdening the defendant. The likelihood of a vehicular accident immediately following injection of a narcotic in combination with other drugs is high. When the narcotic is administered by a doctor in his office, the burden of guarding against that foreseeable danger is not unreasonable if the doctor is judged by standards of normal medical procedures, rather than subjected to after-the-fact speculative attack. Finally, if the scope of the doctor's duty is limited to the professional standards of acceptable medical practice, the additional burden on the doctor's treatment decision is neglible. 108 N.M. 511, 514-515, 775 P.2d 713, 716 – 717

Patient Confidentiality and Office Staff

Physicians in private practice need to be sure that staff members are educated about the legal requirements of patient confidentiality. It is a good idea to have written office guidelines for staff to follow on how to handle written and verbal requests for patient information, and on intra-office handling of charts. For instance, it is best to keep patient charts closed or covered whenever they could be in view of non-staff persons. The best rule of thumb is not to give out information to anyone, other than the patient (or patient's legal representative), unless the patient has signed your official office form permitting release of information.

Practice Pointers

Whether it relates to protecting patient confidentiality, reporting obligations, or warning and protecting third persons, two things are critically important. First, you must know the "law of the land" where you practice. You can't take steps to comply with the law if you don't what it is. Although general comments may be made about the law of confidentiality, as in this chapter, the requirements in each jurisdiction are different.

If you don't know the requirements of your state, there are several ways to find out what they are. Your malpractice carrier is certain to be able to provide help. The state licensing board is also likely to be a good resource. County and local medical societies can also help locate requirements that are most likely to be encountered in particular practice areas.

You, your group, or your local medical society should also consider inviting local attorneys to speak at seminars. In most areas there are a number of qualified lawyers nearby who will eagerly speak to small or large groups of doctors about various aspects of law that relate to medical practice. If this approach is of interest you, check around to be sure that you invite lawyers who are qualified to speak to your area of interest. It probably won't surprise you to know that there are lawyers around who are not at all reluctant to talk about matters on which they are unlearned!

Always keep in mind that if you have a specific situation for which you need advice and counsel, it is best to seek it one-on-one with a lawyer.

The second important aspect of complying with confidentiality and reporting requirements has to do with office procedures and record keeping. One of the best ways to ensure compliance is to set up procedures for yourself, your group, and your staff so that compliance is routine and automatic. To help standardize good practices and procedures, find, develop, and use forms that that apply to your practice and comply with state and federal laws.

The use of forms where applicable is a very good way to promote standardized documentation that can eliminate or reduce liability in certain areas. Forms can be as simple as rubber stamps or checklists, or more sophisticated such as complex HIV information releases.

When the use of forms is inadequate for the situation, it is always sound practice to document important positive or negative findings such as "patient is non-threatening", "patient advised and understands that he is not to drive while taking this medication", "have made arrangements for patient to leave office via cab", "patient threatened to '. . . x y z . . .' – police notified of specifics at 11:23 a.m."

These types of entries create a written record of your efforts to comply with the legal duties imposed upon you by virtue of the physician-patient relationship. An entry of this type becomes evidence of your thought process and good judgment. Even though the failure to document certain conduct or action doesn't indicate that things weren't done, a record that is silent about prudent conduct is certainly less than convincing, especially to jurors.

Liability for Violating Patient Confidentiality

A review of case law reveals a variety of lawsuits brought against physicians based on improper disclosures of confidential medical information. The legal bases for the claims often relate to breach of the fiduciary duty of confidentiality or breach of implied contractual term of confidentiality. Here are examples of some unusual cases.

> **Case Illustration**
>
> In *Home v. Patton*, 291 Ala. 701, 287 So.2d 824 (1973), a patient brought an action against his physician for damages because the physician revealed information about the patient to the patient's employer. The court held that there was a confidential relationship between the doctor and the patient that imposed a duty upon the doctor not to disclose information obtained in the course of treatment concerning his patient. By entering into the physician-patient relationship the physician impliedly contracted to keep confidential all personal information given him by the patient. The physician's release of information constituted an invasion of the patient's privacy. This case is of interest because it was decided in a state that did not have a doctor-patient testimonial privilege. After reviewing the law of other states, the court said: After a careful consideration of this issue, it appears that the sounder legal position recognizes at least a qualified duty on the part of a doctor not to reveal confidences obtained through the doctor-patient relationship. 291 Ala. at 706, 287 So.2d at 827

> **Case Illustration**
>
> In *Howes v. United States*, 887 F.2d 729 (1989) a military serviceman's wife brought suit against military and civilian doctors who disclosed information she told them about her husband's alleged alcohol and drug abuse. The court held that there was no patient/physician relationship between the wife and the psychologist and psychiatrist she consulted about her husband's alleged drug and alcohol abuse and, therefore, the psychiatrist and psychologist did not breach any Ohio law duty of confidentiality.

Next

In the next chapter the topic of informed consent is presented from the patient's perspective as well as the physician's. It is important to know when and how to make informed consent disclosures, as well as how to document the informed consent process in your records.

FAQ:

Q: *Can I give out patient information to insurance companies without patient consent?*

No, not without patient consent. You should have a standard intake form signed by the patient that authorizes your office to give pertinent information to insurance companies.

Q: *What do I do if I get a subpoena for a patient's records but do not have an authorization from the patient?*

Most states have statutes that direct a physician on how to respond to subpoenas if there is no patient authorization. It is a good idea to become familiar with the particular requirements where you practice. Also, see Chapter 8 - Releasing Medical Records.

Q: *Does it violate patient confidentiality to consult with other doctors about a patient's diagnosis or treatment?*

Usually not. It is recognized that doctors frequently get "curb side consults" and in those situations a patient's name often doesn't even come up. Discussions of that type tend to be rather generic and do not involve patient confidentiality. However, if you plan to actually review and show a patient's chart to another physician who is not currently connected with the patient's care (other than an existing consultant), technically speaking it could violate the patient's confidentiality. It is probably be a good idea in that situation to let the patient know in advance, and note in the chart that you have patient consent to talk with or meet another physician about his or her care. Certainly, where several physicians are involved in different aspects of a patient's care they are free to discuss the patient and her care without violating her confidentiality.

✦   ✦   ✦   ✦

6

INFORMED CONSENT

The root premise is the concept, fundamental in American jurisprudence, that every human being of adult years and sound mind has a right to determine what shall be done with his own body . . .

Canterbury v. Spence, 464 F.2d 772, 780, 150 U.S.App.D.C. 263, 271 (1972)

The concept of informed consent is grounded in the notion that each patient, or patient representative, has the right to make informed decisions regarding his healthcare treatment and all its attendant risks. In the simplest sense, informed consent involves the obligation of physicians to adequately inform their patients about treatments, treatment alternatives, risks and benefits associated with treatments, and in some cases, the risks of foregoing treatment.

The subject of informed consent comes up in many different contexts, and nearly all types of patient care. What we are really talking about when we look at informed consent from the physician's point of view, is the duty to disclose information to a patient. For it is based upon physician disclosures that patients then provide informed consent to the physician. The physician's duty to disclose, and the informed consent provided by the patient are two different sides of the same coin.

Informed Consent – A Legal Requirement

The laws in every state impose a legal obligation upon physicians to obtain *informed* consent from their patients. Looking at it more precisely, the law imposes a *duty to disclose* so that patients may then give informed consent.

Informed consent and *consent* are two different matters. If a patient does not understand a procedure, its risks, or alternatives, he cannot be said to have provided informed consent. What some physicians tend to overlook is that *un*informed consent is really no consent at all for legal purposes. The fact that a patient's signature appears on a form that briefly describes a procedure to be performed does not in and of itself show that the patient has given *informed* consent. It is often what does not appear on the form that determines whether proper disclosures were made to the patient. Obviously, a patient must be sufficiently educated about his treatment in order to make informed decisions about his care.

It is always in the physician's best interest to provide full disclosure to patients about recommended treatments, alternative treatments, risks associated with treatment options, and potential complications of options. If asked, a physician is even obligated to candidly disclose his particular experience and personal rate of success with any given procedure.

If it is ever revealed during the course of litigation that a physician has mislead a patient or withheld information regarding any aspect of a procedure or his personal experience, the consequences could be very serious. Not only could the conduct give rise to a claim for an intentional tort or a claim for punitive damages, the physician's license to practice could also be jeopardized. As with evidence of medical record alterations, jurors and judges are very harsh in their judgment of physicians who have mislead their patients.

> **Case Illustration**
> True consent to what happens to one's self is the informed exercise of a choice, and that entails an opportunity to evaluate knowledgeably the options available and the risks attendant upon each. [footnote omitted] The average patient has little or no understanding of the medical arts, and ordinarily has only his physician to whom he can look for enlightenment with which to reach an intelligent decision. [footnote omitted] From these almost axiomatic considerations springs the need, and in turn the requirement, of a reasonable divulgence by physician to patient to make such a decision possible. [footnote omitted] *Canterbury v. Spence*, 464 F.2d 772, 780, 150 U.S.App.D.C. 263, 271 (1972)

Informed Consent Disclosures – Physician Informs the Patient

In order to achieve the desired end result, which is obtaining a patient's informed consent for your treatment, your patient needs to become informed about any proposed treatment and its risks. It is your job as a physician to inform your patient. The most common way to inform patients is through face-to-face discussions with them. In some instances, such discussions might be supplemented with telephone discussions or reading materials.

When Does the Duty to Disclose Arise?

You do not need to have "informed consent" discussions with every patient each and every time treatment is provided. The physician's obligation to disclose information to a patient typically comes into play any time there is a *decision* of consequence to be made about treatment. The decision may involve a question of undergoing one of several treatments, or it may involve a question of treatment versus no treatment.

Patients are always entitled to know whether a recommended procedure is experimental or investigative, and if so, the success (or failure) rate associated with the procedure. Whenever there is a risk of failure or complication associated with a given treatment, test, or procedure, informed consent should be obtained before proceeding.

See Figure 6-1 for a checklist to help you decide whether you should disclose information to you patient to obtain informed consent.

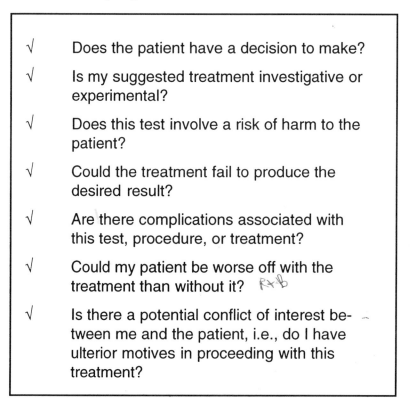

√	Does the patient have a decision to make?
√	Is my suggested treatment investigative or experimental?
√	Does this test involve a risk of harm to the patient?
√	Could the treatment fail to produce the desired result?
√	Are there complications associated with this test, procedure, or treatment?
√	Could my patient be worse off with the treatment than without it?
√	Is there a potential conflict of interest between me and the patient, i.e., do I have ulterior motives in proceeding with this treatment?

Figure 6-1: When to Obtain Informed Consent

What Disclosures are Needed to Obtain Informed Consent?

The specific requirements for obtaining informed consent are as varied as the medical treatments offered to patients. Generally speaking however, state statutes, case law, and various formulations of patient rights statements all recognize that the patient has the right to make decisions regarding his healthcare in collaboration with his physician. Because the decisions to be made by patients are often quite case specific, the requirements for making disclosures will depend on the circumstances of each case.

In general, the disclosure process should include discussion about all information necessary for the patient to fairly decide whether to undergo a particular treatment by a particular physician. Figure 6-2 lists the topics that should be covered in most informed consent situations.

Discuss With Your Patient:

1) the need for or reasons for considering a treatment option

2) the anticipated outcome if treatment is refused

3) the anticipated outcome if the treatment is successful

4) the risks associated with the treatment

5) alternative treatments and associated outcomes and risks

6) whether the recommended treatment is experimental

7) the extent of the physician's experience with each option

Figure 6-2:
What to Disclose to Obtain Informed Consent

In some situations an informed consent discussion may be relatively brief and fairly routine. In other situations disclosure discussions may involve a very detailed process that takes place over the course of several visits. Generally though, the basic requirements are the same. The variations will depend upon the seriousness of the decision to be made, and the nature and severity of risks and complications.

Disclose Information According to a Patient's Ability to Understand

A review of legal literature on the subject of informed consent reveals a difference of approach as to what is the proper area of focus in determining whether a physician has discharged his disclosure obligation. Some scholars emphasize the physician's perspective:

> In duty-to-disclose cases, the focus of attention is more properly upon the nature and content of the physician's divulgence than the patient's understanding or consent. Adequate disclosure and informed consent are, of course, two sides of the same coin - the former a sine qua non of the latter. But the vital inquiry on duty to disclose relates to the physician's performance of an obligation, while one of the difficulties with analysis in terms of "informed consent" is its tendency to imply that what is decisive is the degree of the patient's comprehension. As we later emphasize, the physician discharges the duty when he makes a reasonable effort to convey sufficient information although the patient, without fault of the physician, may not fully grasp it. (cite omitted).

> Even though the factfinder may have occasion to draw an inference on the state of the patient's enlightenment, the factfinding process on performance of the duty ultimately reaches back to what the physician actually said or failed to say. And while the factual conclusion on adequacy of the revelation will vary as between patients –

as, for example, between a lay patient and a physician-patient – the fluctuations are attributable to the kind of divulgence which may be reasonable under the circumstances.

Canterbury v. Spence, 464 F.2d 772, 780, 150 U.S.App.D.C. 263, 271 (1972)

In contrast, other scholars recognize that as a practical matter, jurors are likely to focus on the understanding of the patient when determining whether *informed* consent was given. Nearly all scholars recognize that a physician's disclosure needs to be "reasonable under the circumstances". This means that physicians should tailor their disclosure discussions according to their patients' ability to understand.

Because patients come in all shapes, sizes, and abilities, there is no "one-size fits all" script or formula for explaining a particular treatment and its risks to all patients. A standardized discussion may be too sophisticated for some patients, yet too simplistic for others. What this means is that you must convey information to your patients according to their various abilities to understand.

The words, terms, illustrations, and concepts you use to discuss a treatment option for one patient may be different from those you use to discuss the same treatment with a different patient. While you may talk with one patient about "the anticipated outcome if treatment is refused", you might talk with another about "what you expect to happen without treatment". The true test of whether informed consent has been obtained is not a matter of mouthing certain words; it is a matter of doing what is reasonable under the circumstances to ensure that the patient truly understands the proposed treatment and accepts the associated risks.

Case Illustration

In *Canterbury v. Spence,* 464 F.2d 772, 150 U.S.App.D.C. 263 (1972) the court passionately described the facts of the case and law of informed consent: The record we review tells a depressing tale. A youth troubled only by back pain submitted to an operation without being informed of a risk of paralysis incidental thereto. A day after the operation he fell from his hospital bed after having been left without assistance while voiding. A few hours after the fall, the lower half of his body was paralyzed, and he had to be operated on again. Despite extensive medical care, he has never been what he was before. Instead of the back pain, even years later, he hobbled about on crutches, a victim of paralysis of the bowels and urinary incontinence. 464 F.2d at 776

. . . Dr. Spence [the defendant] further testified that even without trauma paralysis can be anticipated "somewhere in the nature of one percent" of the laminectomies performed, a risk he termed "a very slight possibility." He felt that communication of that risk to the patient is not good medical practice because it might deter patients from undergoing needed surgery and might produce adverse psychological reactions which could preclude the success of the operation. 464 F.2d at 778

Patients ordinarily are persons unlearned in the medical sciences. Some few, of course, are schooled in branches of the medical profession or in related fields. But even within the latter group variations in degree of medical knowledge specifically referable to particular therapy may be broad, as for example, between a specialist and a general practitioner, or between a physician and a nurse. It may well be, then, that it is only in the unusual case that a court could safely assume that the patient's insights were on a parity with those of the treating physician. 464 F.2d at 780

The court disagreed with Dr. Spence's opinion that there was no need to disclose the risk of paralysis and held that the issue was for the jury to decide.

Just as the *content* of the informed consent process varies according to the test, procedure or treatment in question; the *form* of the informed consent discussion varies according to the patient you are dealing with.

Disclosure and Discussion of Specific Risks

One of the questions frequently asked by physicians about informed consent disclosure has to do with *risks*, and the extent to which a physician must discuss them. For many procedures, treatments, and tests there are lengthy lists of possible risks or complications that range from those that are quite benign to those that are fatal. Is it incumbent upon the physician to discuss each and every possible risk or complication? The answer will depend on a combination of qualitative and quantitative assessments of the risks and complications.

A risk that is very serious or deadly should be discussed even though its statistical likelihood is numerically low. On the other hand, there may be scores of risks that are more common, but not at all serious. In depth discussion about all of these risks is probably not necessary. Use of judgment is called for. If you are unsure about whether to discuss a particular risk, you should probably ask yourself the same question a juror would likely ask himself: "Is that something I would have wanted to know about this procedure before deciding to undergo this treatment?" If the answer is "yes", you should discuss the risk with your patient.

Timing of Informed Consent Disclosures

It is important to make sure that a patient is given enough time to thoughtfully and productively consider treatment options. Other than in emergency situations, the more serious the decision to be made, the more time the patient should be allowed to make a decision. For significant decisions it would not be reasonable to provide a patient with detailed information about treatments, risks and alternatives, and then immediately insist that a patient make a decision that same visit. It would also be inconsistent with the appearance of thoughtful decision-making to have a patient sign a consent form shortly before undergoing a surgical procedure.

Informed Consent Disclosures and the Patient's State of Mind

A patient's mental state may be a factor in determining when and how informed consent disclosures should take place. If you are dealing with a patient who is distraught, medicated, distracted, in pain, or otherwise temporarily mentally compromised, it would be best to schedule another time for a discussion about significant medical decisions and treatment options. If you go ahead and have a thorough informed consent discussion with a patient who isn't emotionally able to understand or process information, you may not have accomplished anything. Anytime it is apparent to you that the patient can't productively participate in a decision-making process, take the time to cover the information in a later discussion.

In some cases it is good practice to have informed consent discussions over the course of several visits. This gives the patient an opportunity to consider information and ask questions if they arise.

Informed Consent for Surgical Procedures

In some instances, obtaining informed consent for surgical procedures can become a complex affair. This is especially true at times when a recommended course of treatment will depend upon the findings revealed during surgery. When a patient is anesthetized, it is impossible to provide information about intraoperative findings that suggest a particular course of treatment. A patient simply cannot be given information at that time that is essential for making an informed decision about care.

A situation of this type is one that can frequently give rise to claims based on lack of informed consent, and therefore demands special attention by a surgeon.

Extra care should be taken by a surgeon to thoroughly discuss the recommendations associated with all the potential findings. The surgeon should give thought to both the anticipated and possible alternative findings, discuss them in detail with the patient, and map out with the patient the recommendations for *each* possible scenario. Make sure that you and the patient understand what is to be done in the event of particular findings.

Again, good rule of thumb is to be guided by common sense and the "Golden Rule". Ask yourself: knowing what you as a learned physician know about a recommended procedure, what information would you like to have about the procedure if you were the patient? The answer to this question will generally indicate the nature and extent of the informed consent disclosures and discussion.

Informed Consent and Emergency Situations

There are times in the practice of medicine when it is not always possible to make informed consent disclosures to a patient before proceeding with treatment. If you are presented with a true emergency situation of significance, rather than risk further harm to the patient, proceed with treatment.

From a legal perspective, consent will be implied in the case of an emergency. Here is a standard to follow: if a delay in treatment, which takes place because of efforts to obtain informed consent, increases the risk or harm to a patient's health or life, then an emergency consent situation is deemed to exist.

In those cases where treatment must be provided without actual informed consent, you should make a detailed entry in the chart setting forth the nature of the emergency. It is good practice to obtain consent after the fact if at all possible.

Implied Consent – A Legal Defense

The concept of implied consent is based on legal recognition that there are times when consent to a procedure is implied. For instance, if a patient has treated with a physician and previously consented to or submitted to a particular treatment, arguably it may be implied that the patient consents to the same procedure at a later date. Be aware that this is not always true. Aat times consent may also be implied when the risks associated with a treatment or procedure are so commonly known that a reasonable person of ordinary intelligence would be expected to know of the risks and consent to treatment anyway.

In effect, the concept of implied consent is a legal defense to a patient's claim of failure to obtain informed consent. However, you should recognize that although the facts of these types of circumstances may be argued as a defense in some cases, it is always best to obtain informed consent for each test, treatment, or procedure.

Informed Consent Waiver by a Patient

It is rare, but not unheard of to encounter a patient who wants to proceed with a certain treatment without knowing the associated risks or possible complications. If this situation presents, reasonable efforts should be made to persuade the patient that he should provide informed consent for treatment. If the patient insists on proceeding, and you intend to do so, be sure to have the patient sign the consent form as a waiver. However, if the suggested treatment is controversial, high risk, investigative, or one that no reasonable person would undertake without understanding the risks, it would be best for you to forego providing the treatment.

If a situation of this type presents, the most important thing to do is thoroughly document in the record either the waiver, or the fact that the patient refuses to provide informed consent. Referral of the patient to another physician may be advisable.

Legal Ability to Consent

Consent from one who is not competent to provide it is not valid consent. In legal terms this is referred to as "incapacity". The most common types of incapacity that physicians are likely to encounter are minority (under the age of eighteen) and mental impairment.

Minors

Generally, minor children are not legally capable of providing informed consent and therefore consent to proceed to treat must be provided by a parent or legal guardian. There are exceptions to this rule. For instance, parental consent may not be required for emergency situations. State statutes also specify situations in which minors can consent to treatment. Figure 6-3 lists examples of exceptions to the general rule from various states. This list is not exhaustive.

Minors Who May Consent

- married, homeless, and emancipated minors can consent to treatment

- minors over the age of twelve who are diagnosed to be under the influence of a dangerous drug or narcotic can consent to treatment

- a minor can petition the court to waive the requirement of parental consent for an abortion upon a showing that it is in her best interest

- a minor who has contracted a venereal disease can consent to undergo diagnosis and treatment

- when the parent of a sexual assault victim over the age of twelve cannot be easily contacted, the minor may give consent to treatment.

Figure 6-3:
Minors Who are Competent to Consent

Mental Incapacity

Whenever a patient is mentally incapable of understanding the nature of a recommended treatment or its consequences, the patient is not capable of giving informed consent to a particular treatment, test, or procedure. Mental impairment may be permanent or temporary.

If a patient is permanently mentally impaired he or she is likely to have a court appointed *guardian* who may give consent on the ward's (patient's) behalf. In most states, a court appointed *conservator* is not authorized to give consent for treatment. This is because there is a legal distinction between guardians and conservators. A conservator is only responsible for handling monetary affairs on behalf of a ward.

If a patient is unable to provide consent due to the temporary influence of mental illness, shock, trauma, physical injury, medication, drugs, or alcohol, a physician should not proceed with treatment. If treatment is necessary, a guardian or medical power of attorney should be appointed for the patient. The bottom line is that a physician should not seek to obtain nor honor the consent of a patient who is not competent to provide it.

Considerations for Specific Consent Situations

Medications

Whenever a physician prescribes a medication, drug, or therapy that is associated with significant side effects or risks, or is experimental in nature, informed consent should be obtained from the patient. If a pharmaceutical manufacturer has provided specific warnings about a particular drug, then the physician should use his judgment about passing on the specific warnings to the patient. Whether to warn a patient of a specific medication risk or complication will depend on how likely and serious the risk is.

Procedures and Surgeries

Many types of medical procedures are likely to involve risks or complications and therefore informed consent should be obtained from the patient. Any procedure that involves anesthesia should also include a discussion of anesthetic risks. Major surgical procedures will require thorough discussions about options, risks, and complications. As noted earlier, when the ultimate surgical course depends on intra-operative findings, the surgeon should make sure the patient understands the expected findings and other possible findings, and the recommendations associated with each. It is imperative that the physician and patient understand each other, and clearly outline together the desired approach. Far too often, informed consent claims arise in this context because the patient and physician had different conceptions of what the patient wanted.

At times, a surgeon will encounter an unexpected finding during surgery. The unexpected finding might suggest a course of action that has not been discussed with the patient. If this happens, in almost every case it is best to wait to talk with the patient before proceeding. This gives the patient an opportunity to decide how she would like to be treated. This is especially true when the recommended treatment involves permanent or irreversible changes. If an emergency situation is present, then the surgeon may proceed with reasonable medical treatment.

When a patient is already under anesthesia it may be tempting for the surgeon to "guess" at how the patient would like to proceed. However, he should realize that he might be held liable for the legal consequences if he guesses wrong.

It is also important to realize that unless there is a medical power of attorney or guardianship relationship, under the law of some states even a spouse or nearest of kin cannot authorize treatment on behalf of an anesthetized competent adult.

Case Illustration

In *Lounsbury v. Capel*, 836 P.2d 188 (Utah App. 1992), a patient brought suit against an orthopedic physician for operating without *any* consent, a battery. The doctor argued as a defense that the patient's wife signed a consent form on behalf of the patient. The court interpreted a Utah statute to mean that one can provide consent for his or her spouse *only* in emergency situations. Here are interesting excerpts of the facts of the case.

Prior to his being admitted to the hospital, the patient, his wife, the doctor, and the doctor's assistant were all present in the doctor's office. The patient told the doctor that he would not decide whether to have the surgery until after he had had an opportunity to see the new myelogram results and discuss them with the doctor. On the morning of May 14, the patient was admitted to the hospital. After the scheduled myelogram was performed, a nurse requested that the patient sign a consent form for the surgery. The patient refused, stating he had not yet decided about the surgery because he had not seen the results of the myelogram. The patient was returned to his room and given pain medication at approximately 1:00 p.m.

Sometime later that afternoon, a nurse anesthetist talked to the patient and his wife about the anesthesia for the scheduled surgery. The anesthetist had brought a consent form for the anesthesia services. The patient declined to sign the form, stating that he wanted an opportunity to talk with his doctor before he would agree to have the surgery. Between 5:00 and 6:00 p.m., the doctor and his assistant came to the door of the patient's hospital room and told the patient that they were going to get the results of the myelogram and would "be back later to talk." The doctor never returned to the patient's room. The patient's wife left the hospital that evening at approximately 9:30 p.m. The patient continued to receive pain medication and went to sleep that night.

The first thing the patient remembered upon awakening is that he received a shot—apparently of preoperative medication—around 6:20 the morning of May 15th. The patient has no recollection other than feeling the shot and apparently going back to sleep. Contrary to the proffer on behalf of the doctor, the patient has no recollection of telephoning his wife and asking her to come to the hospital to sign some paperwork. When the patient's wife arrived at the hospital the morning of May 15th, her husband was unconscious. She was given a "stack of papers" by "a couple of nurses" who said, "Here. You need to sign these." Under the circumstances, the wife felt "intimidated" and "pressured" and did not want to ask any questions. She assumed that her husband had talked to the doctor and had agreed to the surgery following review of the myelogram. Therefore, she went ahead and signed the papers. She had no opportunity to talk with the doctor or her husband. Immediately after she had signed the paperwork, the patient was wheeled out of his room and into surgery. Following the surgery, the patient did not recover and return to work as he expected he would. Rather he claims that he was, and still is, in "continual pain" and has been unable to work. Moreover, he has experienced "mental depression" and "psychological problems" associated with the surgery and his continuing pain.   836 P.2d at 190

Therefore, we construe section 78-14-5(4)(b) in a manner that avoids the potential for constitutional infirmity, by interpreting the authorization for spousal consent as a secondary option, to be relied on only in cases of emergency or other incapacity of the patient. [FN20] 836 P.2d at 198

Immunizations

Most states have enacted statutes making it improper to immunize a minor without the consent of a parent or guardian. If a particular immunization involves a series of several injections over a period of time, it is good practice to have the parent or guardian sign a consent form for each injection.

HIV Testing

With a few exceptions, no patient can be tested for HIV status without his consent. State statutes typically detail the form of the consent required for HIV testing. State statutes also recognize a private right of action against health care providers for unauthorized testing for HIV. The few exceptions relate to the testing of donated blood, organs or body fluids, subjects convicted of sexual crimes or other offenses that involve a risk of HIV infection, prisoners who pose a health threat to others, anonymous research, autopsy related testing, and emergencies.

Blood Transfusions

If a patient is expected to have, or may have the need for a blood transfusion, the risks associated with blood transfusions should be discussed and consent should be obtained in advance. There are some states that have enacted statutes requiring physicians to advise patients of the risks and benefits of autologous and homologous blood.

Case Illustration

In *Sargeant v. Beekman Downtown Hosp.*, Index No. 16068/91 (N.Y. Cty. Sup. Ct), March 2, 1994, a Jehovah's Witness was awarded $500,000 in a claim against the hospital and physician when he was given a blood transfusion even though he had orally and in writing indicated his refusal to have a transfusion.

Experimental Treatment

Federal regulations and state statutes govern persons involved as experimental subjects, whether as subjects or members of control groups. No person can be involved in drug or medical research without providing informed consent. Federal regulations require that experimental subjects be provided with the following information:

- a description of the experimental procedures associated with the research

- a description of any reasonably foreseeable pain or discomfort

- a description of the benefit expected from the research

- a description of other procedures that might be advantageous to the subject

- a description of the extent of the confidentiality of research records

- a description of what compensation and treatment are available in the event of injury

- a statement that participation is voluntary and that the subject is free to discontinue participation at any time

    21 C.F.R. § 50.25(a)

Documenting Informed Consent Discussions

Documentation of the informed consent process is very important for several reasons. First, it is evidence that a physician and patient actually had one or more discussions culminating in an informed patient giving consent to a particular procedure, test, or therapy knowing the risks and alternative. Second, it can often assist the physician by serving as an outline of what is required to be covered during informed consent discussions for a particular procedure, test, or therapy.

Documentation should not necessarily be limited to the patient's signature on a pre-printed form. You should document not only the end result of the informed consent process, which is the patient giving informed consent, but you should also document the disclosures made to the patient. Together, your record (office notes) and the patient consent form should reflect your disclosures and the patient's *informed* consent. If the issue of informed consent is ever raised as a claim, lawyers, judges, and jurors will look not only at the consent form, but also at your medical record to determine whether they believe the patient gave informed consent.

How and What to Document in the Chart

Physicians often wonder how far they should go to document informed consent disclosures. Although it may tempting for the sake of time to simply note, "informed consent discussion took place", it is not advisable to be quite so laconic. Your chart notes should reflect what was actually discussed. Figure 6-4 lists recommendations for documenting informed consent disclosures and discussions.

Even though it may seem tedious and time consuming to record informed consent documentation in the chart, keep in mind that enduring months or years of litigation can also be very tedious. Your notations are designed to be an indication of the quality of the informed consent discussions with patients. If you have, and document, a quality informed consent process, you drastically reduce the likelihood that a patient will bring a claim based on lack of informed consent.

- Note in the chart each particular procedure, test, or therapy you discuss with the patient.

- For each procedure, test, and therapy, note that common and serious risks and complications were discussed, and specify those that are significant or likely.

- If applicable, note any alternatives that were discussed with the patient.

- If the patient was provided with reference materials, make a note about what you provided.

- If you used any models, charts, diagrams or other visual aids during discussions with the patient, make note of that in the chart.

- If the informed consent discussions have taken place over several visits, make a note each time.

- If the patient asks questions that you consider to be significant, note them in the chart and include documentation of your responses.

Figure 6-4:
Documenting Informed Consent Discussions

PATIENT INFORMED CONSENT FORM

1. Identify the procedure, test, or therapy to be provided.

2. Specify the reason for, or purpose of, the procedure, test, or therapy.

3. State the fact that all procedures, tests, and therapies can be associated with risks and complications, then specify those that are most significant (most common and most serious) for the procedure chosen.

4. If anesthesia is necessary, state the significant risks associated with its administration.

5. For procedures that may depend on intra-operative findings, it may be prudent to specify the various options to be pursued. You may also want to include a general authorization statement such as, "I authorize my physician to perform such procedures as deemed medically necessary, except. . ." [This type of language can be very helpful to avoid confusion about what is and is not authorized.]

6. Include a statement that the patient has read and understands the form and has had an opportunity to ask questions, and that all questions have been answered.

_____   _____

Patient signature   Date/time

Physician Declaration: A statement that the document has been reviewed with the patient, questions have been answered, patient has been adequately informed and gives consent . . .

_____   _____

Physician signature   Date

Figure 6-5: Informed Consent Form

Informed Consent Forms

In addition to notes entered in the chart about informed consent discussions with a patient, it is absolutely necessary to have the patient sign a form that officially records the fact that he or she is providing informed consent. The precise language of an informed consent form will vary depending on the procedure, test, or therapy. In fact, it would probably be a mistake to try to use one form for all procedures. Even though consent forms vary according to their subject, there are some common features and provisions to include. Figure 6-5 shows typical consent form paragraphs.

Next

The last two chapters of this section deal with patient medical records—how maintain them and when to release them. Keeping medical records serves many purposes. These next chapters provide reasons and means to maximize the benefits of keeping good patient records.

FAQ:

1. Does a physician have to disclose to his patients that he is an alcoholic or HIV positive?

Although a patient is entitled to information about a physician's qualifications and experience with a particular procedure, there is no clear answer to this question. The American Medical Association published a statement in January 1991 recommending that HIV positive physicians either voluntarily disclose their HIV status to patients, or refrain from all professional activities that could result in transmission of infection to the patient. See 21 PROFESSIONAL LIABILITY NEWSLETTER, Feb. 1991.

In *Kaskie v. Wright,* 403 Pa. Super. 334, 589 A.2d 213 (1991), a Pennsylvania case, the court ruled that a patient could not bring a claim for lack of informed consent based on a physician's failure to disclose that he is an alcoholic. However, the general rule in Louisiana is that a physician must disclose known risks that a person standing in the patient's shoes would want to know about before deciding on a course of treatment. There, one court ruled that a physician's alcohol abuse was a material risk that a patient was entitled to know about. *Hondroulis v. Schuhmacher,* 553 So.2d 398 (La. 1988).

2. If my patient signs a hospital consent form, do I need to have another one signed for my office?

The hospital consent form may or may not suffice to serve as adequate evidence that an informed consent discussion took place with the patient. If you see a patient in your office before doing a hospital procedure, you should not rely on the hospital's consent form to take the place of your private practice consent form. It is important for you to have an office consent form because it reflects that informed consent disclosures and discussion took place in the office, rather than in the hospital shortly before a procedure. Because you will typically have obtained a signed consent form before the patient enters the hospital, your office consent form will indicate that the patient was not rushed or pressured to make a decision in the hospital.

3. Do I have to document each and every risk or complication that is discussed with a patient for a particular test, procedure, or therapy?

It is good practice to do so. If a risk or complication is worth mentioning to the patient, it is worth noting in the chart. This practice also develops the habit of being familiar with the risks and complications associated with a particular procedure. Some might be concerned that there is a downside to listing every risk and complication for a particular treatment because the absence of an entry could then be used to prove that an unlisted risk or complication was not discussed, leaving one vulnerable to a seemingly "automatic" claim. However, consider one's vulnerability for informed consent claims if vague, general descriptions of risks and complications are used. Then, a patient and her lawyer could easily argue that since a certain risk was not specifically listed, there is no certain proof of it being discussed. The patient will claim that it wasn't, and it will be her word against yours.

✦   ✦   ✦   ✦

7

Maintaining Medical Records

"Medical records" means all communications that are recorded in any form or medium and that are maintained for purposes of patient treatment, including reports, notes and orders, test results, diagnoses, treatments, photographs, videotapes, X-rays, billing records and the results of independent medical examinations that describe patient care. Medical records include psychological records and all medical records held by a health care provider, including medical records that are prepared by other providers.

Ariz.Rev.Stat. § 12-2291

Keeping and maintaining patient medical records is addressed in two ways in this chapter. The first part of the chapter looks at "why" and "how" records should be made and kept. The second part of the chapter relates to "what" should go in the patient record, looking particularly at the office chart.

Part I – General Considerations for Making and Keeping Records

Purpose and Uses of Medical Records

Medical records should be kept for a number of reasons. Obviously, one of the most important reasons for physicians to keep records is to help them provide good patient care and treatment. Here are other important reasons for keeping records:

- compliance with licensing, peer review, and research regulations

- compliance with requirements of funding or accrediting agencies

- compliance with governmental regulations (keeping vital statistics)

- compliance with insurance requirements

- for protection from legal action

The JOINT COMMISSION ON ACCREDITATION OF HEALTHCARE ORGANIZATIONS recommends that records be adequately detailed and organized to serve the purposes of keeping records. Records should be kept in such a way to permit:

- the responsible physician to provide effective continuing care to the patient, to determine later what the patient's condition was at a specific time, to review the diagnostic and therapeutic procedures performed, and to review the patient's response to the treatment

- a consultant to render an opinion after an examination of the patient and a review of the medical record

- another practitioner to assume care of the patient at any time

- retrieval of pertinent information required for utilization review and quality assessment activities

1 JOINT COMMISSION ON ACCREDITATION OF HEALTHCARE ORGANIZATIONS, 1992 Accreditation Manual FOR HOSPITALS 49 (1991).

Records and Patient Care

Good record keeping is presumed to be an integral part of good patient care, and the corollary which naturally follows is that the failure to keep good records is likely to be seen as a reflection of poor care. Whether or not this is actually true, you will have a difficult time trying to persuade regulators, judges, or jurors that good care can be provided without maintaining good records.

Many states seem take to heart the saying "if it's not in the records, it wasn't done". In most states, statutes define the failure to keep adequate records as "unprofessional conduct". Furthermore, legislatures and licensing boards often enact statutes and regulations that define "adequate records".

Here is a typical definition of the term "adequate records":

> . . . legible medical records containing, *at a minimum*, sufficient information to identify the patient, support the diagnosis, justify the treatment, accurately document the results, indicate advice and cautionary warnings provided to the patient and provide sufficient information for another practitioner to assume continuity of the patient's care at any point in the course of treatment. (A.R.S.§ 32-1401.2)

There are a few things to note about this type of definition. Importantly, most definitions represent only a *minimum standard* adequate for licensing purposes and should not be looked upon as setting the gold standard for record keeping. In fact, a conscientious physician would likely want to document certain aspects of a patient's care in greater detail.

Also, keep in mind that often there are additional record-keeping requirements set forth in other statutes and regulations. Such statutes and regulations relate to other types of information that are required to be noted in patient records under certain circumstances.

Some examples of other types of information that are usually required to be documented are mentioned elsewhere in this book. See Chapters 5 and 6 regarding experimental procedures, patient informed consent, highly confidential information, and prescriptions and administration of certain medications.

Legibility

Records must be legible to serve their purposes. Very important reasons for keeping medical records will be defeated if either you cannot read your own writing, or others cannot read it. If you are more comfortable making hand written entries in charts, make sure they are legible. If your handwriting isn't legible, type or dictate, and review the transcription. If you use abbreviations, make sure they are not simply personal shortcuts that would be unknown to others.

Entries need to be both legible and understandable by others. This is especially important to remember for hospital charting, where there are many different care providers of various backgrounds and levels of training who read records.

Any time you write orders, prescriptions, or referrals, be absolutely certain that what you have written is legible, understandable, and accurate. If your record is misread by others, you could be liable for the consequences.

Alterations

Although there may be legitimate reasons for making changes to records, whenever a record appears to be *altered*, it can create suspicion about the writer's credibility. A definition of *alter* is: "To make over or different; to make some change in; to modify; to vary to some degree; to vary in some degree, without an entire change." (*Lexicon Webster Dictionary*, 1981) Altering a record is different from *correcting* a record. See infra. Altering records involves a retrospective effort to *change* the record for purposes other than correcting an erroneous or mistaken entry, and often involves obliteration of the original entry.

Because the science of document examination has become so sophisticated, it is very unlikely that improper changes to records will be overlooked. Even though at times there may be a very strong temptation to just "fix" or "clarify" a patient's record once a medical malpractice claim or lawsuit has been brought, it is *very* unwise to do so.

It has been shown time and time again in court cases that juries do not look favorably on those who alter records. They are quick to draw the conclusion that alterations are made by those with a guilty conscience. Because of this fact, plaintiff's lawyers are quite sure to studiously inspect relevant records in the hope of finding any indication of tampering. In fact, many plaintiff medical malpractice law firms have in-house or part-time nurse paralegals to help them understand, organize, and summarize medical records. A savvy nurse who knows a great deal about patient record keeping is likely to spot inconsistencies, unusual entries, or other irregularities that are indicative of alterations.

Medical records are designed to provide a reliable indication of a patient's condition and care and are therefore accorded great weight by other medical providers, independent reviewers, and jurors. Any indication of an irregularity that suggests an attempt to hide an error will cast doubt on the credibility of the entire record. This means that even if an unimportant portion of a patient's record is altered, factfinders may be inclined to consider other critical portions of a record in a light that is to the disadvantage of the physician. Once your trustworthiness is called into question by jurors, the likelihood of a verdict in your favor becomes slim. In court, the impact of such a finding could mean a large verdict against you.

Case Illustration

In the case of *Henry v. Deen*, 310 N.C. 75, 310 S.E.2d 326 (1984) a treating physician and physician's assistant made false and misleading entries in a patient's chart. They also obliterated another entry in the record that dealt with the patient's true condition. Moreover, they conspired with a consulting physician by enlisting his agreement to destroy or conceal the patient's real record and create a false record. They all agreed that the consulting physician would provide the falsified record to anyone who asked about his participation in the patient's care. Upon these facts, the court recognized a cause of action for conspiracy to alter and destroy medical records.

Record Corrections

Having said that records should never be altered, it is important to note that inaccurate records should always be *corrected*. Whereas the term *alteration* connotes an improper change, concealment, or omission of portions of records that were appropriately written, the term *correction* implies the act of making something right. To *correct* means: "To set right; remove the errors or faults of; rectify; to point out or mark the errors in." (*Lexicon Webster Dictionary*, 1981)

Since one of the primary goals of good record keeping is to provide good medical care, all care providers should always strive for accuracy in record keeping. To knowingly leave inaccurate information in a patient's record would be just as wrong as after-the-fact re-writing a record to make it look better. The key to correcting errors is to use a reasonable and acceptable method of making corrections.

Here are recommendations for maintaining accurate records:

- All entries in records should be made in ink.
- The same pen should be used for each single entry.

- Inaccurate information should be corrected as soon as it is noted.

- The person making a correction should initial and date the correction in the margin of the record.

- A correction made *at the time* of one's current entry should be made concurrently by drawing a single line through the inaccurate part of a record. Be sure to leave the original entry otherwise intact.

- A correction made *after* the date of the original entry should be corrected by an addendum. Enter the current date, the word "addendum", the basis for the correction, and finally, the correction. Be sure to sign or initial the entry.

- Never obliterate an incorrect entry.

- Never tear out a page on which an incorrect entry is made.

- Never re-write a record and discard the original. If you re-write a record to make it more legible, be sure to keep the original record with it.

In some instances it may be important to bring a correction to the attention of other care providers. If so, verbal notification may be required if the correction relates to a matter of urgency. For non-urgent situations, it is usually adequate to reference the correction by making a note in the chart where it will be seen.

The point of making corrections is not just to have an accurate record, but to also correct potentially harmful mistakes or mis-impressions in the minds of other caregivers. Remember, all of these efforts are ordered toward providing good patient care.

If you have your own office, it is prudent practice to make sure that all staff members know how to keep and correct records. If they are your employees, you can be held legally responsible for their conduct. This concept, known as *respondeat superior* is discussed further in Chapter 9. If you work for a health care organization, make sure to be familiar with the policies and procedures regarding record keeping and record corrections.

Retention of Records

The length of time that patient records should be retained relates to the purpose for which a particular record is kept. Because records are kept not just for the purpose of providing care and treatment, they should be retained even when a patient is no longer being seen by a physician.

There are various state and federal statutes and regulations that apply to certain health care providers and direct the length of time records must be kept. For instance, hospitals that participate in Medicare must keep records for at least five years. 42 C.F.R. § 482.24(b)(1). State regulations often require as a condition of licensure that hospitals maintain patient records for at least three years.

Some states have regulations that require that patient records be kept seven years before they can be destroyed. For those who practice in a state that does not require retention of records for a specific time, some regard as reasonable a minimum retention period equal to the statute of limitations period for a medical malpractice action. Applying this standard would mean that those physicians who practice in states with a medical malpractice statute of limitations period of two years, should keep records for a minimum of two years.

Although reference to the statute of limitations is perhaps a convenient way to formulate a standard, it is most likely very inadequate for the vast majority of practitioners. It is inadequate because there are a number of things that can, and do, occur to affect the calculation of the statute of limitations period for a medical negligence action. For instance, the legal "infirmities" such as insanity, imprisonment, and minority all toll the statutory period from beginning to run. Many states also follow the *discovery rule*, which means that a cause of action does not accrue until the plaintiff discovers, or reasonably should have discovered, that he has been injured.

All of these legal principles can indefinitely extend the time within which a lawsuit may be brought well beyond the typical one, two, or three year statute of limitations period. The point, then, is that the statute of limitations period alone does not provide a reasonable guideline for determining how long records should be retained.

> **Case Illustration**
>
> *Kenyon v. Hammer,* 142 Ariz. 69, 688 P.2d 961 (1984) was a wrongful death case filed by a mother in connection with the stillbirth of her second child. The claim was based upon a physician's vicarious liability for alleged negligence of his nurse, who incorrectly recorded the mother's Rh factor during pregnancy her first child. The date of the nurse's negligence and the stillbirth of the second child were more than three years apart so the trial court ruled that the claim was barred by the then 3-year medical malpractice statute of limitations.
>
> The the Arizona Supreme Court said the claim was not barred because the statute of limitations period began to run not on the date of the negligent conduct (the nurse's error), but rather on the date on which second child suffered some injury. The action had been filed within two years from the date the second child was conceived.
>
> This ruling means that if a patient suffers injury due to the negligence of a physician, it is the date of the *injury* that determines when the cause of action "accrues", and it is that date which begins the running of the statute of limitations. In *Kenyon,* the negligent act was the error in recording the mother's Rh type. Injury from that error did not occur until the mother became pregnant a second time, with the resulting stillbirth. The rationale for the "discovery rule" is that was unfair, and in fact unconstitutional under Arizona law, to bar a cause of action before it could even be discovered. As a practical matter, the mother in this case had no reason to know of, or even suspect, the alleged negligence of the nurse until the outcome of her second pregnancy.

Many state hospital associations recommend keeping records for at least ten years after a patient has been discharged. This is also the recommen-

dation of the JOINT COMMISSION ON ACCREDITATION OF HEALTHCARE ORGANI-
ZATIONS.

If there are no regulations that apply to your practice, it is recommended that you consult the state licensing board, your malpractice insurance carrier, and others in your field of practice. If you treat minors (children under the age of eighteen), caution would suggest that you keep records for eighteen years plus the number of years in the statute of limitations. The reason for this is that a child's legal rights do not accrue until the age of majority (eighteen) and therefore the statute of limitations period does not begin to run until that time. Whether a child is injured in a car accident, by a dangerous product, or by a physician's malpractice, in most instances the child has two years from his eighteenth birthday within which to bring suit for his injuries.

> ### Case Illustration
> In *Barrio v. San Manuel Division Hospital for Magma Copper Co.,* 143 Ariz. 101, 692 P.2d 280 (1984), 19 year old Teresa Barrio brought an action against a hospital and two doctors for injuries allegedly caused by negligence at her birth. According to the opinion, "It is alleged that they allowed Teresa's mother to go through three days of difficult labor before delivering the child by cesarean section, even though a third physician had informed them that cesarean delivery was medically indicated for the patient. It is further alleged that these acts of negligence resulted in serious injuries, including partial paralysis, from which Teresa is still suffering." 143 Ariz. at 104, 692 P.2d at 283

For deceased adult patients, retaining records for 3 years from the date of death is probably adequate. However, anytime a physician receives notice of a claim or potential litigation, all records in question should be kept whether or not the recommended retention period has passed.

Remember, a good record is not only good for your patients, it can provide you with the best defense against unjust claims. Keep in mind that it may be difficult, or impossible, for a physician to defend against a claim without any records. For this reason, pay attention to what you put in, and how you and your staff write, your records.

Record Destruction

It is best not to destroy records. However, there are times when it becomes necessary to "do something" about records. When physicians move or retire, they need to address the issue of what to do with their patient records.

The most prudent practice for a physician who is moving is to transfer the records to the patient or another treating physician who will be assuming responsibility for care. If practicable, another alternative is to transfer records to a format that is more convenient to store, such as microfilm, computer scanning, or digital storage for computer retrieval.

A physician who is moving or retiring, should notify his patients and offer to transfer the records to another physician or to the patient. If his practice is being taken over by another physician, all patients should be notified and their written consent obtained before transferring their records to the new physician.

> **Case Illustration**
> In *In re Culbertson's Will*, 57 Misc. 2d 391, 292 N.Y.S.2d 806 (1968), a physician directed in his will that all his office records, including patient treatment records, be burned. Many records were those of current patients. Upon the death of the physician, upon reviewing the directions of the will, the court held that even though the physician owned the records, such a provision in the will was invalid because it was against public policy. The court found that the records could be extremely valuable to subsequent treating physicians and if the records were destroyed, it could have detrimental consequences for the patients.

In the event that records are destroyed, a record should be kept of the name of the organization or person doing the destruction, the date of the destruction, and a list of the names of the patients whose records are destroyed. It is best to follow a consistent policy for destruction of records. It might raise suspicion if any particular records were singled out for destruction.

> **Case Illustration**
>
> In *Carr v. St. Paul Fire & Marine Ins. Col,* 384 F.Supp. 821, 831 (W.D. Ark. 1974), the emergency room staff destroyed a patient's record right after the patient died. Not surprisingly, this conduct was inconsistent with hospital policy for destruction of records. The court found that the destruction was unreasonable and permitted the jury to infer that the record would have shown negligence on the part of the emergency care providers.

To summarize, options for retaining records, in order of preference are:

1. Transfer the records to the patient or physician who will assume the patient's care (with the patient's consent).

2. Store the records in their original format, or transfer them to a format that is more convenient for storage.

3. Only if allowed in your jurisdiction, destroy records as a last resort after the passage of a significant time period; and keep a record or log of the records destroyed.

Electronic Record Keeping

The reasons for keeping and maintaining complete, accurate, intact, and legible records apply to all means of record keeping, whether they are written by hand, transcribed from dictation, or entered onto an electronic medium using a computer. To accommodate these purposes when using electronic record keeping requires some special considerations.

To promote accuracy, either the care provider should make entries directly onto the system, or he should proof read notes that have been entered from his dictation or notes. It is advisable to set up a system so that the physician approves records before they become finalized as part of the permanent record. Legibility is not typically a concern with keyboard entries. However, it is still important to use accepted abbreviations and short hand notations.

Because alterations to electronic medical records might seem to be less detectable than alterations to handwritten records, the temptation to improperly change records is probably greater. Therefore, corresponding greater care must be taken to prevent alterations. If you have a large office with relatively little direct staff supervision, or are particularly concerned about alterations, the best way to prevent alterations is to set up your computer system in a way that physically prevents alterations. There are storage drives which can be built into a computer system that allow information to be entered, but once entered, the information can thereafter only be read. These drives are known as WORM-drives, meaning **W**rite **O**nce, **R**ead **M**any. Information stored on a WORM drive can be retrieved and read over and over by all those users on a system who need the information. However, those users cannot change, or in any way alter the information entered on the system. Access to the WORM drive itself should be limited to physicians and highly trustworthy staff persons. Use of this type of system is a good way to preserve authenticity and reliability of records.

As with non-electronic records, there are times when corrections to the electronic record are necessary and appropriate. It is important to develop and follow policies and procedures outlining the correction methods to be followed. Corrections should be made by separate entry, dated, and initialed. Never permit deletion of the incorrect information. Depending on the make-up of staff in a given office, it is likely that in most offices not every staff person needs or should have access to patient records for the purpose of making corrections. Designate those who do have access and establish a procedure for errors to be corrected if other staff members are involved. Passwords or codes should be used to restrict access to those with authority to make entries in or changes to records.

As with non-electronic records, confidentiality is critically important. When

using computerized records systems, maintaining security involves aware-
ness of an entirely new dimension. If your system uses modem connec-
tions to transmit patient charts or information, be aware that data can be
intercepted or read during transmission. It may also be technologically
possible for "outsiders" or "hackers" to access your system via your modem connection.

If your office relies heavily on computer technology as an integral part of
everyday practice, you would be well advised to consult with computer
system experts to address these types of issues. As long as you take reasonable precautions to maintain authentic, confidential records, it is unlikely
that use of computers in and of itself will give rise to liability.

In this next section, focus is shifted from the maintenance aspects of record-
keeping, to actual charting within patient records.

Part II – The Fine Art of Charting – What to Say and How to Say It

As with all patient records, there are both medical and legal reasons for
recording and keeping pertinent information in an office or hospital chart.
Common sense and consideration of the purpose of the chart should
dictate what information is important and how it should be noted. Essentially, the chart is the place where all relevant medical information about a
given patient is collected and kept. It should serve not only the current
treating physician, but also other concurrent and subsequent treating physicians. To meet the needs of the treating physician, and the potential needs
of other physicians, the chart should be contemporaneous, objective, thorough, accurate, up-to-date, and intact.

Chart Set-up

Physically, the chart should be designed to accomplish the objectives of
good care. In great part, this means seeing to it that the right information
gets to the right place and minimizing the chance of losing information.

A poorly organized or maintained chart cannot fully benefit the patient, the provider, or other providers.

The chart should contain places or sections for the various types and sources of patient information, including such categories as progress notes, telephone notes, referral and consultation notes, test requests and results, laboratory results, medications, and consents.

In the hospital setting the physical set up of the chart is directed by the hospital. Most hospitals also provide physicians with guidelines and mandates for charting. In private offices it is the physician who decides and directs how the chart will be set up. Consider the various parts of the chart and their purposes when you design the layout of your office chart. The idea of accessibility to important information should help determine what goes where, and in what form.

Progress Notes

The progress note portion of the chart is akin to a written ongoing eyewitness account of a patient's condition and care. It should reflect that the physician is undertaking a methodical thought process in making a diagnosis and providing treatment. It is best to use a standard type of format for each progress note, including information regarding the patient's complaints, the physician's findings, the physician's investigative thought process (assessment, differential diagnosis, etc.), and finally, the physician's plan. Some hospitals prescribe a format, such as "S.O.A.P.", which many physicians also use in their offices. See Weed, Larry, M.D., *Problem Oriented Medical Record* (1960)

The point of the progress note portion of the record is to provide a chronicle of the patient's care and all pertinent information should be included in this part of the chart. So, in addition to including information that fits within the standard progress note model, it is especially important to include notes regarding certain events or aspects of care.

As an example of the need for additional charting, consider a patient who refuses treatment. When this happens, a detailed entry should be made. You would want to in include in your notes the fact that a specific treatment was recommended, why it was recommended, the consequences of foregoing the treatment, and that the patient was fully informed as to these facts. A patient's reason for refusing treatment may dictate what more should be done by the physician. If the patient refuses treatment for economic reasons, the physician should make reasonable efforts to assist the patient, and document what he has done. This might mean making a referral to a public or private funding source. If the refusal is based on the patient's lack of understanding, or fear of the treatment, then the physician should further educate the patient, and, again, document his efforts. If the patient refuses for religious reasons, document this and detail that you have explained the consequences of refusing the recommended treatment.

In addition to documenting the details of a patient's refusal of treatment, it would be a good idea to also have the patient sign a form that outlines the discussion with the patient. This formality not only helps guide the physician's discussion, but it also serves to impress upon the patient the gravity of refusing recommendations or treatment. It may also prompt the patient to recognize and appreciate his own accountability for the decision.

Chart the Facts

There are several reasons to stick to the facts when charting. To do so helps you and other physicians to get an accurate picture of a patient's condition and treatment response. There are other less-than-medical reasons to chart objectively. One is the fact that patients are entitled to copies of their records. Another is that other health care providers may have occasion to read your records.

It is wise to avoid all unnecessary comments that do not pertain to patient diagnoses and treatment. It is human nature to make value judgments about others. It is asking for trouble to note in the chart the irrelevant judgments you make about your patients. Ideally, the record should be an objective account of the patient's care and treatment. Avoid the temptation to comment on perceived motives or attitudes of your patients.

If a patient ever had reason to get copies of his records and read uncharitable and unnecessary comments about himself in the records he might reasonably question your dedication to his well-being. If another physician read such comments about a patient, your professionalism might be called into question. Either outcome should suggest that you should avoid any comments in the records that are inappropriate to the patient's diagnosis and treatment.

If something is said by a patient that prompts a pertinent assessment by you about his or her attitude, quote the patient's language in the chart so that the basis for the assessment is memorialized. This will lend credibility to the assessment without making it appear that you are inappropriately judgmental.

Avoid Phrases with Double Meanings

It is best to avoid terms that have legal significance or double meanings. Lawyers or others may attach meanings to certain terms that are different from what is intended by an unsuspecting physician. Consider that even commonly used terms such as "probable", "standard of care", "duty", and "consent" have specific legal meanings. A physician who uses any of these terms is likely to have a non-legal meaning in mind, but may inadvertently convey other unintended meanings.

Avoid Summary Conclusion Phrases

Phrases that are conclusory in nature should be avoided. An example of this would be to state, "informed consent obtained", rather than setting forth the information given to the patient, and the patient's response. Not only does the phrase represent a legal conclusion, but its exclusive use also precludes an independent observer from determining whether appropriate information was disclosed to the patient. Another example of a phrase to avoid is, "patient understands". It would be much better to simply record what a patient was told.

When intending to communicate the status of a patient or situation, phrases such as "patient reassured", "patient better", or "patient improved" should be replaced with actual, objective descriptions.

Skip the "Legalese"

Don't write your notes as if you were defending yourself in court. You do not need to try to make your record "lawyer-proof". You are much better off focusing on good medical practice rather than subtly or otherwise rationalizing, justifying, or arguing your "position" in a record. Jurors expect your medical record to be an accurate reflection of a patient's condition and treatment, not an advocate's brief. If it appears to be the latter rather than the former, it will justifiably raise suspicions and cast doubt on a physician's priorities, intentions, and credibility.

Documenting Complications

If a complication in treatment occurs, document it. The fact that a complication occurs should never be concealed from a patient. Complications are a recognized part of treatment and should be noted in descriptive terms. It is not necessary to apologize or become defensive. Be factual and honest about the nature and magnitude of a complication. The straightforward approach is the best approach.

The way in which mistakes and errors are handled can greatly impact the reaction of the patient. Patients who have been dealt with candidly and fairly are much less likely to find fault with their physicians.

It is important to realize that not all mistakes are the result of carelessness or negligence. If a patient perceives that you are doing your best, that you care, and that you are trustworthy, he will be much less likely to bring a claim. On the other hand, in today's social-legal climate, patients who question their doctor's honesty or commitment to their well-being will readily look for any reason to bring a claim.

Remember, if you find that a mistake of significant consequence has been made, it is recommended that you contact your malpractice carrier for specific advice on how to proceed.

Telephone Notes

The set up of every office chart should include a method for recording the details of note-worthy phone calls. This would include telephone calls from patients in which important information is conveyed (change in condition, additional history, significant questions, requests for treatment), as well as telephone calls from the office to the patient by which important information is provided (test results, medication changes, interim advice or recommendations).

While the use of phone message forms is appropriate, it is also critical to make sure that all important information will be seen by those who need to see it. For this reason, either charts with important phone messages should be flagged in some fashion, or concurrent notes should be placed in the progress notes. The important thing here is to develop and consistently follow a system for making sure that the physician and pertinent others are made aware of significant information that is provided by patients via telephone conversations.

In certain specialties, such as pediatrics, where it is common for complaints and patient status to be reported over the telephone, a detailed form should be developed to help elicit, record, and convey information.

Lack of communication, poor communication, and miscommunication between patients and their physicians, or between staff and physicians, all provide very fertile ground upon which malpractice claims may germinate. Often claims arise because important information did not get from the patient to the physician, or vice versa. Recognizing this, every office should strive to devise and follow a flawless system of communicating about patients and their care.

Medication Records

Most practitioners find that keeping track of medications is easier if a separate medication record section is kept within each patient's chart. This is in addition to medication notes entered in the progress notes. The medication sheet should include information about each medication including the name, dosage, and date of each refill prescribed. There is a tendency to handle refills with less attention to details so it might be wise to include a reminder that Schedule II controlled substances are not to be refilled over the telephone and Schedule III and IV controlled substances are limited to five refills. 21 U.S.C.A. §§ 801 et. seq.

 The value of a medication sheet is that it provides any health care provider with convenient access to information about all of a patient's medications. Doctors, nurses, and others will not have to hunt through progress notes to see what and when medications have been prescribed.

In addition to indicating basic information about each medication, the medication sheet should provide space for information about allergies. This information should be elicited on the initial visit, placed in the progress notes, and noted on the medication sheet. Many offices use brightly colored stickers to alert and remind staff and physicians about patient allergies. Any new allergic reactions to medications should be noted on the medication sheet and detailed in the progress notes.

Other Chart Documentation

Other types of documents that make up the chart include laboratory reports, diagnostic reports, consultation reports, consent forms, correspondence, and perhaps legal documents. Different sections or dividers for each are recommended so that information is readily accessible.

Chart Integrity

Keeping and maintaining intact charts – meaning separate and distinct charts for each patient – is important for all practitioners. It is especially important, and challenging, for those whose practices involve either large volumes of patients or patients with voluminous charts. Good chart organization and structure are musts. Both will help to minimize misfilings and loss of documents.

As a practical matter chart integrity can be enhanced if you avoid placing documents loosely in folders where they are apt to fall out. Instead, all sheets of paper, whether they are progress notes, phone messages, lab reports or the like, should be physically attached to the chart in a secure fashion. Patient names should be clearly identified on each chart. Your chart coding system should be set up following a standard procedure that is known and followed by all staff who handle chart filings.

The whole point of chart organization is to keep and maintain information so that the information in it is accurate, complete, timely, and readily accessible to those who need it.

Patient Records of the Medical Malpractice Defendant

A physician who becomes involved in a medical malpractice claim or suit needs to see to it that all records of the involved patient are gathered and maintained in a secure place. It could be important to include records that are related to the patient but not necessarily part of the office chart. It is possible that telephone bills, telephone notes, scheduling records, billing records, or outside records could become relevant to the claim – either for the patient/plaintiff or the defendant physician. Although certain records may not directly relate to patient care, it is conceivable that such records will be pertinent to an issue raised by the claim. Either party may want to use them to support a claim or defense.

Charting Do's and Don'ts

Do:

- set up charts in an organized way
- establish office policies and procedures for charting
- train staff to follow charting policies and procedures
- chart all pertinent factual information, assessments, and plans
- make corrections of mistaken entries and information

Don't:

- destroy records
- make alterations
- chart irrelevant information and assessments
- use double meanings
- use legalese
- summary conclusions

Figure 7-1: Charting Checklist

Next

The next chapter outlines when, how, and to whom medical records should be released. A summary chart provides a quick reference guide for responding to medical record requests.

FAQs:

1. What should I do if I find that a staff member has altered a record to cover up a mistake?

This is a very serious situation. Your first priority should be to correct the error in the records, and any consequences stemming from it. If the mistake has produced a harm or potential harm to your patient, contact your malpractice carrier for advice on how to proceed. As for the staff member, you must admonish him or her, and decide whether you want such an employee to remain on your staff. Naturally, you would want to consider the gravity of the mistake, why it was made, and why it was covered up.

2. Am I responsible for charting mistakes made by my staff?

Yes. Under the legal doctrine of respondeat superior, an employer is legally responsible (liable) for the acts, including negligent acts, of his employees. This concept is discussed in more detail in Chapter 9. Because you are legally responsible for the acts of your employees, it is imperative that you provide training on how office records should be kept and maintained. It is especially important to set up and follow policies and procedures for entering and correcting information in patient charts.

3. How detailed should I be with respect to charting findings and treatments?

If you remember that there are several different reasons for keeping records, such as chronicling a patient's course so you or others can continue care, and documenting compliance with legal requirements, the amount of detail should be fairly clear. Chart enough information to meet those objectives. It is very helpful to develop a habit or routine way of charting "with the big picture" in mind. Certain situations will require that you be very detailed with respect to your charting, i.e., informed consent discussions, patient refusal of treatment, patient non-compliance, because you want to make it clear in your record that you have meet your legal obligations. A well-documented chart is often a key element of a successful defense to a medical malpractice charge. On the other hand, a poorly kept chart will either be of no help, or it will hurt your defense.

4. I hate to chart. Can I have a nurse do it for me?

It is not recommended that you delegate this task to someone else. Are you confident that the nurse knows what to put in, and what not to put in a chart? Are you willing to accept responsibility for inadequate charting? Does the nurse know your thought process? How will a jury react to the fact that you don't enter your findings and plan in the record? The answers to these questions indicate why it is ill-advised to have another do your charting. It is not necessary for you to do all the charting, but it is best for you to at least enter your findings, impressions, and recommendations in the chart.

5. Should I ever be concerned about charting too much?

The answer is "yes" if you are including irrelevant or unimportant information. The answer is "no" as long as you limit your entries to pertinent information and thought processes. Make sure that all those in your office who enter information into patient records know and follow charting Do's and Don'ts.

◆　　◆　　◆　　◆

8

RELEASING MEDICAL RECORDS

Confidentiality of medical records.
A. Unless otherwise provided by law, all medical records and the informa-
tion contained in medical records are privileged and confidential. A health
care provider may only disclose that part or all of a patient's medical record
that is authorized pursuant to law or the patient's written authorization.

Ariz.Rev.Stat. § 12-2291

The issues surrounding the "who", "what", "when", "how", and "why's" of releasing medical records can be confusing. This chapter is devoted to outlining who can have access to medical records, and under what circumstances. Hopefully, by chapter's end, responding to requests for records will be a routine task.

Ownership of Records

As a starting place for considering who has access to records, it may be helpful to understand who owns patient records. Who actually owns the records you maintain in your office – you or your patients? In most instances it is recognized that the physician who maintains records for his treatment of patients is the owner of the *records*. However, patients own and are almost always entitled to *information* about their conditions. Therefore, with few exceptions, patients are entitled to complete copies of their records.

A physician, as the owner and custodian of patients' records, has an obligation to ensure that records are not lost, destroyed, or "spoiled". There have been cases brought against physicians who lost or destroyed critical portions of a patient's record.

> **Case Illustration**
> In *Fox v. Cohen*, 84 Ill. App. 3d 744, 406 N.E.2d 1978 (1980) the defendant physician "lost or destroyed" his patient's EKG tracings and report. The surviving family of the decedent/patient alleged that the doctor's conduct precluded them from proving a wrongful death claim against the physician. The court held that if the doctor's loss or destruction of the records caused the plaintiff to lose the wrongful death claim, then the family had a claim against the physician for failure to maintain his patient's record.

Having said that the physician owns the records themselves, it is important to note that the patient, as owner of his or her medical *information*, has primary control over access to that information. The physician, as owner of the record he creates, has the right to use the information in the record for the purposes for which it was collected.

With the ease of copying records, it is possible for the physician to maintain ownership and possession of the materials making up a patient record, and at the same time allow patients to exercise their right of ownership to the information. See Hirsh, *Medicolegal Implications of Medical Records*, 1975 Legal Med. Ann. 171.

Patient Requests for Records

In most instances patients are entitled to copies of their records and they should be provided upon request. Written and verbal patient requests for records should be honored. In either case it is a good idea put a note in the chart showing that the patient asked for and was provided copies of the records. Some physicians have their patients sign a written release for copies of their files. This also serves to document that the patient has asked for, and been provided with, a copy of the records on a certain date.

Even when records requested are voluminous or not easily accessible because they have been stored, it is not customary to have the patient pay a retrieval or copy charge. Some states prohibit the physician from charging the patient a fee for copying records when the record is necessary for the patient's continued medical care. Other states set the amount that may be charged for providing copies.

Be aware that a physician is never justified in withholding records from a patient who threatens to bring or has brought a claim or suit against him.

Third Party Requests for Patient Records

When a request for copies of a patient's record comes from someone other than the patient, remember not to provide any copies of records unless the request is accompanied by a signed and dated authorization from the patient. It is imperative that staff be trained to never act in a way that violates a patient's confidentiality by giving out verbal or written information about any patient unless required by law or authorized by the patient. There are only a few exceptions to this rule and they should be recognized only by a responsible physician and not by staff members.

If you deal with highly confidential patient information such as that relating to drug or alcohol abuse, infectious disease or AIDS, be sure to follow state and federal statutes and regulations for disclosure of this type of information. These are discussed in more detail in Chapter 5, which discusses the confidential nature of the physician-patient relationship.

Records of Patients Involved in Claims

One of the most common situations in which physicians receive requests for records is when their patient is involved in a claim, not necessarily involving the physician, and the patient's medical condition is at issue. Although it may seem to certain physicians that they are endlessly and, seemingly needlessly barraged with requests for copies of records, keep in mind that in most instances the interested parties are engaged in a search for the truth, or at least, the facts. Whether it is an insurance company, an industrial or worker's compensation commission, or an attorney representing a plaintiff or defendant, all are usually trying to do their respective jobs. They are not trying to make your professional life difficult. See Figure 8-1 for a sample attorney letter requesting copies of his client's record.

Charges for Providing Copies of Records

Unlike with patient requests for records, it is appropriate to charge a reasonable fee for responding to third-party requests for records. As permitted by law, the charge for responding for a third-party record request can include clerical time and per page copying charges. If you are tempted to try to discourage requests for records by charging an exorbitant amount of money to third-party requestors, eventually you are likely to find yourself dealing with a judge. Sooner or later, a patient with an attorney who is familiar with the "going rate" will seek court intervention and ask a judge to set a reasonable fee.

In some states, the reasonableness of a copying fee is set by statute. Also, in many larger cities and counties, there are medical-legal committees that jointly establish and publish guidelines for various medical-legal charges, including copy charges and fees for preparing written reports. If you practice in such a community, these guidelines are likely to be the standards followed by a judge. Your time is better spent practicing medicine than arguing with patients and attorneys about how much you should charge for records. Set a reasonable fee for staff to charge, then go on doing what you do best – take care of patients.

Subpoenas To Produce Records

A subpoena duces tecum is a document that represents a process by which parties to lawsuits compel a person to produce documents or materials that are pertinent to some issue in the lawsuit. The word "subpoena" comes from Latin – "sub" meaning under, and "poena" meaning penalty. A subpoena compels one to appear under penalty of law. A subpoena duces tecum compels a person to appear as a witness and produce specified requested documents at a specified time and place.

As a matter of practice, it is rarely necessary to appear in person to produce the records. Rather, it is often acceptable to comply with a subpoena by mailing copies of the requested items to a specified place. If this is the case, the subpoena will be accompanied by a letter explaining your obligations for complying by mailing copies of the requested materials.

If you receive a subpoena to produce copies of your patient's records you may think that you should automatically comply with such an official looking document. However, the way in which you comply may depend on whether the subpoena is accompanied by a valid authorization from your patient.

Statutes in each jurisdiction will dictate the manner in which you are obligated to respond. In most cases, if you receive a subpoena for records that is not accompanied by a written authorization of the patient, you will probably have several options for responding to the subpoena.

Here are two common alternatives:

> 1. You can deliver a sealed copy of the records to the clerk of the court (whose identity and location should appear on the subpoena) along with an appropriate affidavit; or

> 2. You can object to producing the records on behalf of the patient whose records are protected by the physician-patient relationship.

Remember, the fact that records are requested pursuant to a subpoena doesn't automatically mean that you should respond by providing copies. Third parties seeking records must have a patient's permission to obtain patient records whether their requests are by letter or subpoenas.

Don't be surprised in some cases to receive several requests for records, followed later by a subpoena for the same records. Here is why this may happen at times. Initially, a patient's lawyer may request records to help evaluate whether the client/patient has a meritorious and worthwhile case. Once a lawsuit has been filed, the defense attorney may request a copy of the plaintiff/patient's records (with an authorization from the patient). If the case moves forward while the patient receives ongoing treatment it is likely that one or both attorneys will request record updates. If the case is headed for trial, either party may want to be sure of receiving an "official", complete set of the patient/plaintiff's current records, and request the records once again by subpoena.

Remember that each and every request must be accompanied by a valid authorization from the patient. A valid release is one that is both signed by the patient and dated. If not governed by a statute or regulation that sets a specific time interval between the date of patient's authorization and the record request, the date of the signature should be "relatively" current.

Be aware that subpoena statutes can be quite detailed and vary from state to state. Check with the local medical society, the board of medical examiners, or your malpractice carrier for assistance in complying with the subpoena statutes in your state.

Law Offices of Larry Lawyer

April 1, 1998

Phil Physician
987 Painless Place
St. Louis, Missouri 98765

Dear Dr. Physician:

Our firm has been retained to represent Patty Plaintiff for injuries she received in an automobile accident on February 29, 1999.

I understand that you have provided treatment for the injuries suffered by Ms. Plaintiff. In order to pursue a claim on Ms. Plaintiff's behalf, it is necessary to gather all pertinent medical information relating to her injuries. I would appreciate if you would send a complete copy of Ms. Plaintiff's pre and post accident records, including any diagnostic test studies and reports, such as x-ray films and reports. Enclosed is a signed authorization from Ms. Plaintiff.

Please submit an invoice for copying charges and payment will be remitted promptly. If you prefer to be paid in advance, please call and inform us of the charges.

Thank you for responding to this request. If you have any questions, please call.

For the firm,

Larry Lawyer

123 Easy Street • St. Louis, Missouri 12345
(123) 456-7890

Figure 8-1: Request for Records from Attorney

Request From	Requirements for Release	Limitations	Copying Charges?
Patient	Oral or written request	Usually none, except for minors and psychiatric patients	Usually no, but depends on state law
Personal Representative or Guardian of Patient	Official written proof of relationship	Usually none	Usually no, but depends on state law
Another Treating Physician	Patient's written authorization	HIV, drug, and alcohol treatment require specific authorization	Usually a professional courtesy
Third-party	Patient's written authorization	Records requested subject to proper authorization of patient for HIV, drug, and alcohol related treatment	A reasonable fee for copies and clerical time
Court Order	Signed Order	Whatever is ordered	Depends on Order
Subpoena	Refer to controlling state statutes, if any	Whatever is requested, subject to state law and patient authorization	A reasonable fee, or subject to state law, if any
Billing or claims management, medical data processors, utilization reviewers, accrediting bodies, or and other administrative service providers	Patient authorization is not required if you obtain a written statement from the requestor verifying the purpose of the request and committing that the records will not be used for any other purpose	Records requested	Usually no

Figure 8-2: Responses to Requests for Records

Next

The chapters of the next section each deal with potential perils commonly associated with three main categories of practice – private practice, hospital practice, and managed care practice.

F.A.Q.

1. If a patient asks for a complete copy of her records, what do I include?

The answer may depend on the purpose of the request. If the patient is consulting another physician for a second opinion, you would want to include all pertinent information. If the patient is transferring his care to another physician, include all treatment notes, lab notes, consultations, correspondence, phone notes – in short, everything. Technically speaking, a patient is entitled to everything, but may not really want everything. A phone call to the patient may help to clear up what is actually wanted.

2. If I get a request for records from an attorney requesting "all records, including progress notes, lab slips, phone notes, consultation reports, correspondence, insurance information, x-ray films, videotape films, and other diagnostic film", do I have to give up everything? Even the films?

Yes, as long as a written authorization has been included. Attorneys, or their nurse paralegals, who are familiar with medical charts will know if something has been withheld. You don't want it to appear that you have withheld information. If you give original films, be sure to document the name of the person accepting the films. If you need the originals for your treatment, copies can be made, with costs to be borne by the requesting party.

3. What is a "reasonable charge" for records?

Assuming no statutes or regulations apply, fees vary from community to community. Processing fees for private practitioners can range from $0 to $50 depending on the volume of records involved. It is probably not reasonable to charge a $50 processing fee and then produce two pages of records, unless they were stored offsite. If records are stored offsite and require a special effort to retrieve them, your "staff time" charges would reasonably be higher. If this is the case, it would be a good idea to explain this to the requestor. A reasonable per page charge for copying could be anywhere from 25¢ to $1 per page, again depending on the volume of records involved. Some states have statutes that define what charges are permissible. Check with your medical malpractice carrier for guidance.

Again, you are not in business to make money copying patient records. Make an honest effort to assess what it actually costs you to respond to record requests.

4. Can I ask for copying charges before I send the copies of records?

The answer depends on who makes the request. If a patient requests copies, they should be sent. Don't ever try to use the records as leverage against a patient who has an outstanding balance due. When records are requested or subpoened by a third party, it is usually acceptable to notify the requestor by phone or letter after calculating or closely estimating the cost of providing copies.

5. What if I get a request for a report in lieu of copies of the records?

Sometimes attorneys, on behalf of clients, want a summary statement of a patient's diagnosis, treatment, and prognosis rather than copies of the actual records. Providing such a report will require that the physician, rather than clerical staff, prepare the report. As such, a fee reflective of the time and thought spent on the report is appropriate. A good rule of thumb to follow is to charge based on what you would have earned if treating patients during the same amount of time spent on preparing the report. For instance, if you earn an average of $300 per hour treating patients, and spend one half hour preparing a report, a fee of $150 would be considered reasonable. It is not at all unreasonable to ask for payment in advance of providing the report. Make a reasonable estimate of the time it will take to prepare the report.

6. What if I can't answer the questions asked for in a report?

Your inability to respond to a question may be for one of several reasons. You may be unable to address a question because the question asked does not make sense. If so, call (or if appropriate, have a staff member call) to get a clarification from the attorney. It may be that the lawyer has inartfully phrased a question due to ignorance or carelessness. On the other hand, if the question makes sense, but you cannot answer it, explain in the report why that is so. Remember that it is not necessarily a reflection of your ability or competence as a physician to not be able to answer a question. There are some questions that no one can answer.

7. What constitutes a proper authorization?

The authorization must be **signed** by the person whose records are requested, and in the absence of applicable statutes and regulations requiring otherwise, should be **dated** within one year of the request.

If the patient is authorizing release of drug and alcohol related information, federal regulations require that the authorization include:

- the name of the person or program permitted to make the disclosure

- the name of the person to whom disclosure is to be made

- the patient's name

- the scope of the permitted disclosure

- a statement that consent may be revoked at any time

- the date the consent expires

- the patient's signature

- the date of the patient's signature

    See 42 U.S.C. §§290dd-3, 290ee-3, and 42 C.F.R. pt.2

8. Do parents have a right to the records of their minor children? Do minor children have a right to their records?

The answers depend on the state in which you practice. Generally, parents, as guardians of their children, have a right to obtain copies of their children's records. Stated conversely, minor children must provide the written consent of a parent or legal guardian before they should be given access to their records or the information in their records. However, married or emancipated children are entitled to their records without parental consent. Another exception arises when minors have been providing consent for their own treatment, such as that relating to HIV test results or reproductive treatment and test results. In such cases, minors may have access to their records without parental consent. When this type of situation arises, then parents are not entitled to the child's records without the consent of the minor. In any event, be sure to document in the chart the reason for granting or denying access to a minor or parent. The laws vary from state to state so refer to the law of your jurisdiction if you are confronted with this situation.

10. Can I respond to a request for records by facsimile transmission?

It is recommended that you obtain patient consent before responding by facsimile to a request for records. A concern arises because when sending records by fax there is no way for the physician to guarantee that confidentiality will be maintained on the receiving end. Assuming patient authorization has been provided, it is likely that faxing medical records will be viewed as reasonable and acceptable as long as steps are taken to minimize transmission errors.

Make sure that the user of the fax machine is familiar with the machine so as to minimize the chances of inadvertent or erroneous transmissions. If you are using a new or unfamiliar machine, "practice" using non-patient information and "friendly" recipients. If a wrong number is dialed make sure to follow up with a request that the information sent be destroyed. Your facsimile cover sheet should contain certain information about the nature of the transmission, the identity of the intended recipient, and standard information about the sender.

If you anticipate or find that you frequently send records by fax, you should include language in your standard records request authorization form (filled out by the patient) stating that the signer/patient authorizes you to transmit records by facsimile transmission.

If you receive patient documents, including authorizations, by facsimile and you have a facsimile machine that uses thermal paper rather than plain paper, remember that thermal paper quickly degrades. Any thermal paper documents that are to be put in a patient's chart should be copied onto plain paper first.

11. Do I have to do anything special when dealing with the records of a deceased person?

Generally, records of a deceased person can be released as long as there is a valid authorization signed by the personal representative of the estate. The personal representative will have an official court document that recognizes such an appointment. If no personal representative has been appointed, it is acceptable to honor a request from the decedent's surviving spouse or next closest living relative. Have the relative provide a signed statement that he or she is in fact the nearest living relative.

✦   ✦   ✦   ✦

SECTION
THREE

PRACTICE
PERILS AND
PITFALLS

9

THE PRIVATE PRACTITIONER

. . . it is well established that the right to pursue a profession is subject to the paramount right of the state under its police powers to regulate business and professions in order to protect the public health, morals and welfare.

Cohen v. State, 121 Ariz. 6, 10, 588 P.2d 299, 303 (1978)

The fact that the private practitioner not only practices medicine, but also runs a business enterprise (his office), requires that he be aware of and meet the legal responsibilities associated with his business. Apart from the business aspects of running an office (tax, OSHA, worker's compensation, and payroll issues) there are also relationships and responsibilities that give rise to particular malpractice risks for the private practice physician. It is these relationships, responsibilities, and risks that are discussed in this chapter.

Corporation, Partnership, or D/B/A?

There are many tax, business, personal, and legal consequences associated with the various forms of business practice for physicians. Corporations, partnerships, and sole practitioners all have distinct advantages and disadvantages, but it is not the aim here to discuss the legal consequences of forms of business practice. Which form of business practice is best for you will depend on a number of factors that are highly specific to each practitioner. It would be best to consult an appropriate expert if you have questions in this area.

The Private Practitioner and
Respondeat Superior Liability

Regardless of the form of business practice you choose to practice under, there is a legal precept that has great importance to you as a private practice physician. It is referred to as the doctrine of *respondeat superior*. Under this maxim, a physician whether practicing as an individual, partner, or corporate shareholder, who hires employees to work at his practice can be held legally responsible for the negligence of those employees.

Respondeat superior is a Latin phrase that translates to "let the master answer". It means that when a servant is acting within the scope of his employment with the master, generally, the master can be held liable for the wrongful acts of his servant. Another variation of this same theme is that a principal can be held liable for the acts of his agent when the agent is performing the work of the principal.

As a private practice physician it is important to keep in mind that you will bear ultimate legal responsibility for the overall operation of your medical practice. Even when you as a physician are completely free of any wrongdoing, if your office nurse is negligent in the care of one of your patients, it is more likely that you, and not she, will be named as a defendant in a lawsuit.

Note that *respondeat superior* liability only applies when employees are acting within the course and scope of their employment. You would not be responsible for an employee's off duty negligence. At times, however, the line between work and personal time is not so brightly drawn.

The ultimate legal responsibility you bear translates into *liability*, and ultimately *financial responsibility*, on your part for the negligent conduct of a staff member. This means that, just as with other types of business enterprises, you as the owner of your practice should carefully monitor how your employees conduct your business. If you appreciate the fact that "the buck" stops with you, the need to hire, train, and supervise your staff with the utmost attention to good and reasonable patient care should be clear. Moreover, you must impress upon your staff the fact that their conduct (or misconduct) could have significant legal consequences for you.

One of the best ways to instill good work habits and practice in your office is to use the "tried and true" team approach. Every staff member has an important job to do and contributes to the team effort, which is to provide optimal patient care. If your office team truly strives for excellence, chances are very good that you will rarely, if ever, fall short of the *reasonable care* standard.

The next sections of this chapter cover aspects of private practice that are of particular importance in view of respondeat superior liability.

Selecting, Training, and Supervising Staff

Considering that yours is the ultimate responsibility in your practice, you are well advised to take steps to ensure that *all* of your staff members are appropriately hired, trained, and supervised. Hire employees who are capable of performing the tasks they will be assigned. Make sure staff roles are well defined and that staff members perform within the parameters of their particular roles. Front office personnel, back office personnel, technicians, assistants, nurses, and insurance and billing clerks all have distinct functions. Don't expect or allow personnel to switch roles unless they are truly capable of performing other roles.

Policies

It is a very sound idea to develop and articulate for staff members what is expected of them in their various roles. Probably the best way to do this is to develop written statements, or policies, outlining what is expected of staff in certain situations.

Consider for instance which members of the staff are qualified to answer the telephone? It sounds simple enough, but what if a patient calls with an emergency situation and is given unreasonable instructions by an unqualified staff person? Which members of your staff are qualified to schedule appointments? Although it may seem that just about anyone could do either of these routine tasks, what happens when a patient calls to report on a condition that is worsening and should be seen right away? That type of call should be referred to someone (most likely a physician) with the judgment to determine when that patient should be seen. A medically un-trained staff person could not be expected to assess the nature of the patient's condition or make a decision about the urgency of being seen in the office. The office in which a non-medical staff person decides the urgency of seeing a patient for an office visit, is an odds on favorite to receive a claim brought by a patient who suffers deleterious effects of delay in treatment.

Policies and procedures should be developed for a very specific purpose. They should be practice oriented. Do not set as policy loftily worded goals that cannot be attained in every day practice. Policies and procedure statements should be developed (whether written or not) in a way that will help prevent errors, mistakes, and malpractice. They should not be adopted if they do not concretely further the goal of providing good patient care. For each office policy and practice developed, consider whether it is prudent, necessary and consistently achievable, or whether it creates an impossible or unwanted standard by which you may be measured. If you can't meet it, don't adopt it! Don't create unnecessary standards that may later be used against you by an unhappy patient and her lawyer.

The point in having policies or procedure statements is to clearly define roles and activities that are acceptable practice in your office. If you develop policies, make sure they·are followed. It may be just as bad to have policies and not follow them, as it is to have no policies at all.

Office Communication with Patients

It is very important that staff members be trained to properly screen patient telephone calls. Calls that deal strictly with scheduling of routine matters need not be passed on to someone with medical judgment. But staff should be trained, and policy should be developed, to help staff recognize the situations that do require medical judgment. When medical judgment is required, the matter should be passed on to the appropriate person in the office, usually the physician, to assess and decide the appropriate action. Once decided, staff members may then be able to communicate the recommended action to the patient.

Unfortunately, it is not unusual to see medical malpractice claims arise from patient contacts that were not handled appropriately. It may be that a patient who is scheduled for a return visit in several weeks develops a complication before that time, and calls in to report the difficulty. The office staff member taking the call should exercise the judgment to either have the patient seen immediately, or to have a physician talk to the patient to assess the situation.

Your staff should know that you or a partner must be made aware of each and every significant condition reported by a patient. A physician cannot successfully defend his non-feasance by asserting that his staff didn't tell him about a patient who clearly needed attention. Under the doctrine of respondeat superior, you will be held legally responsible for the failings of your staff. You can minimize your risk of claims in this area by ensuring that staff members know the limits of their authority and judgment.

Office Communication about Patients

Patient confidentiality must be maintained not only by a physician, but also by office staff. Your staff should be educated about physician-patient confidentiality and instructed not to give out patient information without written consent of a patient. Staff members who are responsible for dealing with requests for records or information about patients must be trained to know how to handle such requests without violating patient confidentiality. When in doubt, have staff check with you because you may be held responsible for any improprieties. At least one staff person should become familiar with the procedure to follow to respond to a subpoena of medical records. See Chapter 8 regarding medical records and subpoenas.

Keep in mind also that intra-office communication about patients should be handled with due care. It is not appropriate for patients to be able to overhear staff discussions about other patients. Not only does this violate the right to confidentiality of the patient being discussed, but it is also likely to cause the listening patient to question whether his confidentiality will likewise be disregarded. The overhearing patient would reasonably question the professionalism of a medical office with such practices.

Documentation and Records

Make sure that all staff members who handle records know the proper way to make entries in a patient's chart, and the proper way to correct errors in a patient's chart. This topic is detailed in Chapter 7. Alterations should absolutely not be permitted because such conduct could have very detrimental consequences for the physician as well as the staff member.

Written policies about making entries in patient charts should be provided to all staff members who deal with records. Also, the types of information that go into a chart, and the manner in which various types of information are handled, should be outlined for staff members. All staff members who have reason to make entries in charts should be thoroughly trained in charting and record keeping.

It is important to document all significant patient contacts whether they occur in person or by telephone. Each time a patient calls and reports information that is significant to her treatment, or non-treatment, a note should be placed in the chart detailing the information, the date, and the action taken, if any. Similarly, any time a call is placed to the patient to report test or consultation results, or to recommend further tests or treatment, a note should be placed in the chart to document the call, including the information or recommendation given, and the patient's response. Any time a patient refuses to follow a recommendation, it should be noted in the record that the recommendation was made, explained in detail (including the consequences of not following the recommendation), and that the patient refused to follow the recommendation. These types of entries, as all entries, should be dated and signed by the person making the entry. If these types of entries are made on message slips rather than on the actual chart, make sure the message slips are physically put into the chart.

One good way to standardize office procedure telephone calls to and from patients to develop and use specific forms for detailing telephone encounters.

Missed Appointments

Just as it is important to document most patient encounters, whether by phone or in person, it is sometimes equally important to document missed or canceled patient appointments. This is especially so if critical follow up treatment has been indicated. The private practice office must have a system in place to track and review the charts of each and every patient who misses a scheduled appointment. It would be prudent to have in place some sort of check system to indicate the action taken on each no-show patient. This means of course that ultimately a physician or skilled nurse should review the charts of no-show patients (probably daily) to evaluate whether, and what type of follow up is indicated.

A "no show" and follow up action can easily be tracked by using a check sheet placed in the chart, or by use of a rubber stamp that is placed in the chart and then appropriately marked. The check sheet or rubber stamp should allow you to indicate the fact that there was a no-show, including the reason for the no-show if known (i.e., "patient called and canceled", "patient re-scheduled"), and the action taken by the physician or office staff (i.e., "appointment re-scheduled", "letter sent to patient").

Follow-up on Diagnostic Results

Each office needs to have a systematic method of following up on the outcome of tests, studies, and consults that have been ordered for each patient. In most offices this should mean something more than simply filing test results in the file. The problem with such an approach is that it does not guarantee that positive or significant results will be seen and considered by the physician in a timely fashion, if at all. Because lab results, diagnostic test results, and consultation reports can reveal significant results, whether positive or negative, a physician or skilled nurse should review all reports *before* they are filed in the patient's chart. This way the physician is sure to read, assess, and act accordingly on each report.

Ideally, the progress notes should reflect that all tests ordered have come full circle. In other words, an order should be noted in the progress notes for each test. The test results should then be reviewed by a physician and initialed and dated at that time. Further, the progress notes should document the fact that the test results were seen, considered, and acted upon by the physician. Finally, patients often need to be notified of test results and a confirming note should be placed in the chart.

In many offices where high volumes of tests are ordered, it may make sense to use a log book to record in cursory fashion the fact that the appropriate action has been taken with respect to each test ordered. A color coding system can be used to flag items that need immediate action. This approach serves as an extra check to make sure that those items requiring immediate follow up receive the attention they deserve. Whatever approach is taken, the key is to ensure that test and consult results are not left unseen by the physician.

Far too many lawsuits arise from the fact that tests, lab work or consults have been ordered, but not followed through on. It is a situation that can easily create liability based on the reasonable perception that if it was important enough to order a test, it should be important enough to follow up on. This is often the factual basis for a failure to diagnose claim.

Along this same line, it is a good idea to have a system to track patient follow-ups and consultations. Liability can arise when a patient is referred to a consultant or specialist but never goes. Although a patient cannot be compelled to return for office visits, or to follow through with referrals to specialists, your record or log book should reflect that patients have not become lost in the system.

Again, liability can be predicated upon the argument that if an action is important enough to recommend, it is important enough to follow through on. The fact that patients should take responsibility for failures to follow up will not prevent the filing of claims. Such claims are often defended and won. But, whether or not a physician ultimately successfully defends a claim or suit, it is best to avoid going through the litigation process altogether. It is best to take action to prevent, or at least minimize, patient claims.

Office Computer Systems

In these times, it is almost unheard of for a medical office not to use a computer system for at least some parts of its operations. The extent to which computers are used in a particular office will depend on the type of practice, the interest and motivation of the physician, the interest and motivation of the staff, and financial resources. However, no matter what type of practice, amount of interest, and amount of resources, computers should be used for what they are best suited, and not to eliminate or replace critical functions of the physician.

Using computers can be an especially good way to record, store and retrieve large quantities of patient information or "data". The same concerns still obtain – confidentiality, accuracy, accountability, and follow-up.

It is very important to remember that no matter what the system used, patient confidentiality must still always be maintained. It is also essential that the "do's and don'ts" of charting be observed. All entries still need to be dated and signed (initialed) so that the author of the entry is clearly identifiable. Preventing alterations is more difficult because it is seemingly simple to delete and re-write entries.

Office policies and guidelines should strictly prohibit the alteration of computerized records. Not only is it wrong to alter any type of patient records, the consequences of "getting caught" could be very detrimental to the practitioner who is defending a claim. If possible, it is best to implement a system that precludes or minimizes the ability to alter records. Having such a system in place will lend credibility to any medical records that relate to a patient claim.

It is very important to include a back up system for all records that are maintained on a computer system. The inadvertent loss of medical information could have very significant consequences to the physician and his patients. In effect, your computer system should be designed and set up so that data can never be irretrievably lost. Even short term "down time" can be crippling, but it is the total loss of data that has the potential to produce disastrous consequences.

One of the most simple, yet effective ways to both minimize alterations and store patient records, is to transfer all entries to a permanent format at the end of each day. This may be accomplished by using tape storage, disk storage, or any of the emerging technologies developed for data storage.

If the use of computers in your office is significant, it is best to consult with knowledgeable persons about the hardware, software, and set ups best suited to your needs. A computer system should be viewed as a tool to enable your office to run efficiently and effectively. There is no doubt that the use of computers and technology can enhance the efficiency of your practice. Yet, a tool is only as good as the people who use it, and should never be used in a way that is counter to its best use.

Office Staff Meetings

One way of keeping track of your staff and how they are doing with office practices and procedures is to have occasional or regular staff meetings, depending on your practice. Recognizing that days are filled with patient care and regular duties, a lunch, evening, or weekend meeting at which a meal is provided (your treat!) is a simple, yet gracious way to provide a forum for you and your staff to communicate in a more relaxed environment.

Depending on your personal preference, meetings can be as formal or informal as you like. You may want to prepare a written agenda so that staff members can be prepared to discuss particular concerns you and they have. You can take the opportunity to inform staff of particular procedures you would like them to follow and your reasons for doing so. Handouts containing office policies might be provided and explained. Meetings also provide an opportunity for you to gauge to some extent how well your staff members are performing in their various roles, and whether additional guidance or supervision is indicated.

Essentially, office staff meetings should be looked upon as a means of providing open lines of communication for you and your staff. Indirectly, this is an excellent way to reduce the risk of claims arising from poor "handling" of patients, rather than those arising from actual physician malfeasance.

Overall Office Philosophy

It is important to realize that those who may be in a position to evaluate a patient's care, whether it be a judge, a juror, a claim handler, or professional reviewer, are likely look beyond the precise care provided to the patient. Whether it is actually pertinent, they are likely to be negatively impressed by such things as sloppy records, poor record keeping practices, lack of policies or guidelines, and the failure to follow policies. Would you prefer to take your car to a mechanic where the shop is neat, orderly and customer friendly? Or might you wonder about the quality of the workmanship at a shop that is messy, poorly organized, and poorly run? Most people would conclude that the work performed by the well-run facility was provided by competent, qualified mechanics.

For similar reasons, you want your office to appear to be (and actually be) a well-run professional office where things that need to be done are not only done, but are done carefully, properly, and efficiently.

You and your staff should develop a working attitude geared toward providing superior care and service in all aspects of the practice. This is true of portions of the practice that relate directly to patient care, such as patient visits, and those that do not, such as billing. Physicians and staff should keep in mind that it is best to err on the side of caution. The adage that *an ounce of prevention is worth a pound of cure* applies not only to patients, but to running physician offices as well.

Staff should be taught to check with the physician when in doubt. With this approach, nonfeasance will rarely be the basis for a claim against the physician. It is much easier to prevent *non*feasance (a failure to act) than it is to prevent *mal*feasance (a negligent act).

As a private practitioner, whether as an individual, partner, or corporate shareholder, you should have a hands-on approach to your practice. Because you are legally responsible for your enterprise, including your employees, you should administer your practice as closely as practicable. Remember that it is no defense to a respondeat superior claim that you didn't know what was going on in your office.

Next

Physicians who practice medicine partially or totally in a hospital setting should be aware of the legal significance of their relationship with the hospital and the patients seen there. Chapter 10 focuses on these relationships and outlines their legal and practical significance.

FAQ:

1. May I and my staff discuss patients when scheduling lab work, diagnostic studies, or seeking consults?

Yes. If the purpose of the disclosure of information about a patient is directly related to providing treatment, such disclosures cannot be avoided. However, it would be improper to formally discuss a patient's condition with a consultant without first advising the patient. Generally speaking, a physician and his staff may disclose and discuss a patient's medical information and records with other physicians or health care providers who are currently treating the patient. It is also permissible to disclose related information to other physicians who have treated the patient in the past.

2. If I send my nurse on an "office errand" during lunch and she drives recklessly could I be held responsible for damage she may cause?

If your employee is conducting your business, you may be held responsible. However, in the case of a car accident the nurse is more likely to be named as a defendant as well. Your malpractice carrier may not provide coverage for you in this instance. See No. 3.

3. Will my malpractice carrier defend me if I am sued based on the negligence of an employee?

Yes. Almost all policies provide coverage for acts and omissions of employees that are within the course and scope of their employment "while assisting in the rendering of health care services". You may not be covered for all activities of your employees. A carrier may argue that an employee who is running an office errand on the lunch hour is not assisting in the rendering of health care services. If your policy does not cover you for acts and omissions of your employees, you should be sure to get a policy that does provide coverage.

4. I employ nurse practitioners to work in my office. Am I responsible for their negligent acts and omissions?

Probably yes. However, in most instances, your insurance policy is not likely to cover you for the malpractice of employees who practice in an "extended role". They should have their own malpractice coverage or be named as additional insureds on your policy.

✦   ✦   ✦   ✦

10

THE HOSPITAL PRACTITIONER

. . . basic principles of due process of law require that criteria established for granting or denying privileges not be vague and ambiguous, and that as established, they be applied objectively.

Keister v. Humana, 843 P.2d 1219, 1225 (1992)

For those whose medical practice is conducted primarily or exclusively within a hospital setting, it should be appreciated that there are certain aspects of providing medical care that are unique to that setting. Some legal principles have particular application to hospital based practitioners that private practitioners rarely encounter. Conversely, it also generally true that hospital based practitioners will not have to be concerned about many legal considerations that affect private practice physicians on a daily basis. It would not be reasonable to suggest that either type of practitioner fares better or worse in terms of potential involvement with the legal system; the practices simply raise different concerns.

In general, those who practice in the hospital setting will be subject to hospital rules and regulations. Many of the medical-legal aspects of providing patient care will be subject to those rules and regulations. Thus, by following the hospital's protocols, the hospital practitioner will have automatically addressed many legally related concerns that the private practitioner should know and address. However, hospital based practitioners have to deal with another dimension of potential medical-legal issues that arise from the relationship with the hospital. It is these somewhat unique issues that are presented and discussed in this chapter.

Relationship with the Hospital

There are several types of relationships that practitioners may have with a hospital, and each gives rise to its own set of potential medical-legal issues. Some physicians practice exclusively within the hospital setting. Other types of practitioners have a private practice office but spend a significant amount of time seeing patients in the hospital. Yet others have an active private practice and rarely see patients in the hospital. In any event, the physician should take care to learn and follow all hospital regulations that pertain to his practice. Most of the pertinent practice specific rules and regulations will be learned as part of the credentialing process required for obtaining privileges. It is also a good idea to check with the hospital's risk management department for additional recommendations.

Vicarious Liability Issues

One of the most commonly encountered issues that can have significant legal consequences is whether an individual practitioner is an independent contractor or an employee of a hospital. The distinction may seem to be of little consequence, but just the opposite is true. The status of one's relationship with the hospital can have very significant legal consequences because it will determine whether vicarious liability applies. In the previous chapter, respondeat superior liability was discussed from the perspective of the physician's liability. Now, it is considered from the hospital's.

Vicarious liability is a legal construct that occurs in several forms – respondeat superior, master-servant, and principal-agent. In all types of vicarious liability the conduct of one gives rise to legal liability on the part of another based on the relationship between the two entities. In each form of vicarious liability, certain characteristics of the relationship involve some aspect of control by the employer, master, or principal over his employee, servant, or agent.

The types of work relationships that can often give rise to vicarious liability frequently occur in the hospital setting, but are also discussed in Chapter 9 in connection with private practitioners. In the private practice setting application of vicarious liability means that the physician is responsible for the negligent conduct of his employees. In the hospital setting, vicarious liability typically involves the question of whether a hospital will be held liable for the negligent conduct of physicians who work there.

Hospital Employee or Independent Contractor?

It is generally recognized that employers are responsible for the acts of their employees, but they are not responsible for the acts of independent contractors. You might expect that two parties could contractually determine which type of relationship they would like to have. Although this is sometimes true, contracts alone do not always control. Contract language notwithstanding, if two parties work and act as though they have an employer-employee relationship, the law of most states will subject an employer to vicarious liability for the negligent acts of a so called independent contractor.

Consider for instance, the commonly occurring case of an emergency room physician or group of physicians that has a contract to work exclusively at a hospital emergency room. The contract may explicitly state that the physician or group is an independent contractor and not an employee of the hospital. Yet, under the agreement the physician's hours are set by the hospital; patient scheduling and billing services are performed by the hospital's staff; the physician is paid by the hospital based on the fees collected from patients (after a deduction for hospital administrative fees); and the physician is subject to hospital policies and procedures governing nearly all aspects of providing care and treatment to emergency room patients.

Under this set of facts, is the physician truly an independent contractor or should he be considered to be an employee of the hospital? In many cases with facts such as these, a judge or fact finder has found that the hospital should be subject to liability for the misconduct of the physician.

As a practical matter, the issue of vicarious liability can be very significant in medical malpractice litigation. If an individual physician or physician group, such as the emergency medicine physician in the situation described above, is sued by a patient for medical negligence it is likely that the issue of vicarious liability will be a significant battle in the litigation war. Here is why.

You will recall that under the vicarious liability doctrines the employer/ master/principal is liable for the conduct of the employee/servant/agent. In order for vicarious liability to apply, there must be evidence that an actual master-servant relationship exists. If there is sufficient evidence of a master-servant relationship, a hospital could be subjected to legal responsibility for the negligent conduct of its contracted emergency room physicians, despite contract language to the contrary. Absent indications of a master-servant relationship, the hospital would have no legal responsibility for the negligent conduct of independent contractors.

In many cases where the issue of vicarious liability becomes important, a physician may find himself in the middle of a heated legal battle between an injured plaintiff and a defendant hospital. In those cases involving significant damages it may be critical for the plaintiff (the party claiming damages) to establish that the hospital is, or should be, liable for the conduct of the emergency room physician, radiologist, or pathologist. It may be that the individual defendant physician is uninsured or underinsured for the damages claimed in the case.

Assume for instance that a hospital-based physician negligently caused an injury or loss to a patient worth $2,000,000. The physician may have medical malpractice insurance with a limit of $1,000,000. If supportable by the facts, in order to recover the full amount of his damages, the plaintiff will advance the position that the hospital controlled critical aspects of the conduct of the defendant physician and should bear some responsibility for the patient's damages.

In other cases, regardless of the amount of damages claimed, there may be instances where a hospital is brought into the case because it (through its employees) truly was a contributing factor in causing a patient's injury. In most instances, even though there may be contract language that defines the physician–hospital relationship as that of independent contractor, it is a legal fact finder who will ultimately decide the nature of the relationship. The decision of the fact finder will be for purposes of that specific case only.

The factors and evidence typically weighed by judges in making a determination about the physician-hospital relationship are those that relate to the issue of control over the hospital over the physician, and/or whether the hospital held the physician out as its agent.

In almost every situation similar to those described here, whether it involves radiologists, pathologists, or emergency room physicians, the hospital will likely automatically include or insist on including contract language in the professional services agreement whereby the physician or physician group is described as an independent contractor. Furthermore, it might specifically state in the contract that it (the hospital) assumes no liability for the actions of the physicians or group hired to provide care to its (the hospital's) patients. The obvious reason for this is that the hospital wants to avoid legal responsibility for the physician's conduct. Being relieved of legal responsibility equates to being relieved of monetary responsibility for negligent conduct. Notwithstanding such language, the facts of a particular case may lead a plaintiff's attorney to take the position that the hospital should bear responsibility for the conduct of its contract physicians.

For a physician to enter into an independent contractor relationship is fine, as long as the contracting parties understand the consequences of the contract. Most importantly, a so-called independent contractor physician must understand that although his medical practice may be highly regulated by the hospital, the hospital seeks to avoid responsibility for his conduct.

Whether or not terms defining the legal relationship between a hospital and physician are negotiable varies from institution to institution. However, in nearly every case, efforts to eliminate such clauses from standard contracts are likely to be met with resistance. A contracting physician or group has very little bargaining power over a hospital institution. Even so, it is still helpful to understand the meaning, purpose, and consequence of being an independent contractor versus an employee.

Captain of the Ship Doctrine

The *captain of the ship* doctrine is another variation of vicarious liability that applies most often to surgeons. For the most part, this doctrine has become outdated as a result of development of the law relating to hospital liability. The theory arose in the 1930's at a time when hospitals were almost universally protected from liability for malpractice claims by what was known as the charitable immunity doctrine. This meant that according to public policy at the time, even if hospital employees, such as nurses, were clearly negligent, the hospital could not be sued for malpractice because it was seen as performing a strictly charitable function.

In order to find a source of recovery for malpractice claimants, the "captain of the ship" doctrine evolved and was most successfully applied to surgeons and nurses working in operating rooms. When applied in that context, liability could be imposed on a surgeon for negligent acts of hospital nurses assisting during a surgical procedure. The underlying theory was that the surgeon was like the "captain of a ship", and as such he had the responsibility to control and direct everyone and everything that went on during a surgery.

As the nature, perception, and reality of providing health care services changed, the charitable immunity doctrine was gradually eroded, and ultimately abandoned altogether. Since then, the captain of the ship doctrine has been similarly eroded or expressly rejected in many states, although vestiges of the doctrine can still be found in some jurisdictions known as the "borrowed servant doctrine" or "non-delegable duty doctrine".

Staff Privileges

Although most physicians who practice within the hospital setting are not employees of the hospital, they share some responsibility with the hospital for delivering good medical care. Because hospitals are required by law to provide quality health care to patients they enact rules and regulations to be followed by those who provide care within their facilities.

Recognizing that not all physicians practice to the same extent within the hospital setting, traditional categories of hospital staff have been developed that define the responsibilities and limitations of various staff types. These categories are taken from the *GUIDELINES FOR THE FORMULATION OF MEDICAL STAFF BYLAWS: DEPARTMENTALIZED HOSPITALS (1971)*, prepared by the Joint Commission on Accreditation of Hospitals (JCAH), renamed as the Joint Commission on Accreditation of Healthcare Organizations (JCAHO) in 1987):

> **Active Staff** – includes physicians who regularly admit patients to the hospital and are close enough to the hospital to assume all the functions required of active staff. Appointments are made to specific departments. Active staff can vote and hold office and must attend staff meetings.

> **Associate Staff** – typically includes new physicians who are at the entry point, awaiting advancement to active staff membership. They can sit on committees, must attend staff meetings, but cannot hold office in the general medical staff.

Courtesy Staff - includes physicians whose primary practice is elsewhere and who therefore only occasionally admit patients or act as consultants. Usually there are no committee or meeting attendance requirements, and there is no right to hold office.

Honorary Staff – includes physicians who have been recognized for their status in or contributions to the profession. Often they are retired active members. They have no medical staff responsibilities or duties.

Hospital Staff Privilege Requirements

Each hospital sets its own requirements for granting staff privileges. Examples of requirements that have been held by the courts to be reasonable include the following:

- experience and training from American Medical Association accredited programs

- allopathic residency training (in contrast to osteopathic training)

- current medical malpractice insurance

- obedience to a hospital's rules and regulations

- right to make unilateral temporary suspensions of privileges in cases of emergency involving danger or health to patients

- hygienic precautions

- cooperation and coverage for another physician who requests professional assistance (*Findlay v. Board of Supervisors* 72 Ariz. 58, 230 P.2d 526 (1951); *Pick v. Santa Ana-Tustin Community Hospital*, 130 CalApp 3d 970 (1982); *Ross v. William Beaumont Hosp.*, 678 F.Supp. 655; *Miller v. Eisenhower Med. Center*, 27 Cal. 3d 614 (1980)

- geographic proximity (Kennedy v. St. Joseph Me. Hosp. 482 N.E.2d 268)

- economic credentialing - the ability to bring in a minimum number of patients or referrals to the hospital (*Desai v. St. Barnabas Med. Center*, 103 N.J. 79, 510 A.2d 662; *Berman v. Valley Hosp.*, 103 N.J. 100, 510 A.2d 673 (1986)

- absence of criminal convictions (*Miller v. National Medical Hosp.*, 124 Cal.App. 3d 81(1981)

- sufficiency or insufficiency of present staff *(Oliver v. Board of Trustees of Eisenhower Med. Center,* 181 Cal. App. 3d 824 (1986)

- absence of AIDS / HIV infection (*Estate of Behringer v. Medical Center*, 249 N.J. Super 597, 592 A.2d 1251 (1991)

The issue of economic credentialing promises to be controversial. The term refers to the practice of applying economic data and efficiency criteria to decisions regarding medical staff appointments and reappointments. The American Medical Association, which is strongly opposed to the concept of economic credentialing, defines it as the use of economic criteria unrelated to quality of care of professional competency to determine physician qualifications for staff membership or privileges.

Hospitals that use economic credentialing in their physician privileging decisions typically consider the following types of criteria:

- lengths of stay by diagnosis-related group
- charges by diagnosis-related group
- charges adjusted for severity of illness
- length of stay for severity of illness
- utilization review denials
- bad debt expenses
- timeliness of medical record completion
- incident reports

Economic credentialing, an outgrowth of managed care, is likely to continue to generate debate about whether it is an appropriate tool to measure a physician's entitlement to participation in an HMO or on a hospital staff. Opponents argue that physicians should be measured according to the quality of patient care they provide. Proponents see cost-effectiveness as a valid statistical component of an overall measurement of quality of care. It is likely that physicians, hospitals, HMOs, and court decisions will continue to refine the limits of economic credentialing.

Court Review of Privilege Determinations

Deciding the question of whether or not a hospital has been reasonable in denying or suspending staff privileges to a physician involves looking at a number of factors. Historically, courts were not quick to become involved in reviewing the decisions of hospitals with respect to staffing. Public hospitals were more likely to be scrutinized by the court because they were considered to be instrumentalities of the state, founded and owned in the public interest, and funded by public funds. Private hospitals, those not subject to direct control of a governmental agency, were more reluctantly scrutinized with respect to staffing decisions.

Essentially two standards of court review have developed. For private hospitals, courts in most states only consider the issues of whether the hospital has followed its own constitution, charter, by-laws, rules, regulations, and policies, and whether a fair hearing was provided. For hospitals that are determined to be "state actors", courts will look to see that a party's constitutional rights are protected and will review whether hospital standards are arbitrary or capricious.

When courts review credentialing decisions they are inclined to give great deference to medical staff and hospitals with respect to substantive requirements for privilege determinations. As for review of procedural issues, courts are more exacting in their scrutiny. Broadly speaking, courts look to ensure that the process by which a hospital denies or suspends privileges to a physician is a fair one. Precise requirements vary from state to state but minimum procedural requirements for a fair hearing tend to include such elements as:

- adequate notice of the hearing date and place

- adequate notice of the deficiencies or charges

- access to evidence by the aggrieved physician

- a hearing (which can be handled a variety of ways, including personal appearance at a formal hearing or the opportunity to respond in writing)

- requiring the hospital to carry the burden of proving the charges it raises against a physician

- requiring the reviewing panel to be impartial

- requiring that factual findings be supported by substantial evidence

Although privilege hearings must be conducted so as to be "fair", it is not necessary that they include all the accoutrements of a formal court trial. For instance, there is no right to be represented by an attorney. Hearsay evidence is often competent evidence as long as other reliable evidence supports it. Witnesses need not be sworn before they testify in the absence of a statute or regulation requiring that testimony be given under oath.

If you are confronted with an adverse staff privilege determination that you believe to be unfair, it is best to consult with an attorney who is experienced in representing physicians in such matters. Although there are procedural guidelines for fair procedure established by JCAH and JCAHO, they are guidelines only and the law of each state will control.

Next

The legal landscape of practice in a managed care setting is for the most part still in the process of being developed. The next chapter outlines the premises of the managed care model of medical care. Physicians whose practices involve contact with managed care entities, as most will, should have a basic understanding of physicians' roles in managed care health care models.

FAQ:

1. I am a resident at a hospital. Am I an employee of the hospital or an independent contractor?

In almost all instances, you would be considered an employee of the hospital. Thus, the hospital could be held liable if you are sued for malpractice.

2. I work for a group of emergency room physicians. The group has a contract with the hospital to provide emergency medicine services. What is my status for legal purposes?

It depends. There are several issues that may arise. First, is the question of your relationship with the group — whether you are an employee of the E.R. group or an independent contractor will depend on how you function. If you work for the group part time and have your own separate practice, you are likely to be considered an independent contractor. If you work solely for the group and you are treated as an employee, you will probably be considered by the court to be an employee (only for purposes of a particular lawsuit, should the issue arise). The relationship between the group and the hospital raises yet another issue as to status, and again, will depend on how members of the group function at the hospital. In essence, courts regard physicians as independent contractors if they are truly acting independently. Likewise, physicians who are treated as employees will be considered employees, sometimes regardless of what the parties say in their contract about their relationship.

Keep in mind that the question of one's status in these types of situations usually only becomes an issue when a lawsuit is brought against the physician and hospital. Determining one's status relates to the question of whether the hospital can be held vicariously liable for the misconduct of the physician. If the physician is its employee, the hospital is liable. If the physician is treated as an independent contractor, the hospital is not responsible for his misconduct. The hospital will want to avoid responsibility for the physician's conduct and will therefore take the position (through its lawyer) that an independent contractor relationship exists. If the physician has adequate insurance coverage, the determination as to his status will not be critical. However, if the physician is underinsured for the damages claimed, it would be to his advantage for the court to determine that he was acting as a hospital employee.

✦　✦　✦　✦

11

THE MANAGED CARE
PRACTITIONER

An HMO, regardless of its organizational format, may be liable in bad faith when it has denied a request for out-of-network care or coverage without a reasonable basis. Such a bad faith cause of action may arise when an HMO refuses to consider a patient or physician request for care or coverage, if the HMO makes no reasonable investigation of a request for care or referral put to it, if the HMO conducts its evaluation of a care or coverage request in such a way as to prevent it from learning the true facts upon which the plaintiff's claims are based, or if, as the plaintiffs allege in this case, the HMO conducts its evaluation of a request and bases its decision primarily on internal cost-containment mechanisms, despite a demonstrated medical need and a contractual obligation.

McEvoy v. Group Health Corporation of Eau Claire, 570 N.W.2d 397, 405 (1997)

Medical practice within the managed care setting presents the practitioner with a number of unique considerations and concerns that are not typically encountered in the traditional model of medical care. From a legal perspective, many of the nuances of the law of medical malpractice in the managed care setting are still in the process of being carved out. For the most part, this is happening on a state by state, case by case, basis and by means of regulatory and statutory enactments. The purpose of this chapter is to provide the practitioner with some background on the basic development of the managed care model of medical practice, and to identify the unique practice considerations for any physician who practices within a managed care model.

Traditional Medical Care Model — A Point of Reference

To appreciate the features of a managed care model of providing medical care and treatment it may be helpful to first look at the traditional medical care model as a starting point. In the traditional model, a patient selected a physician of his choice for medical care. Payment for the physician's services was made directly by the patient, or by the patient's medical insurance carrier. Importantly, the physician and the insurance company had no relationship to each other and they performed their respective responsibilities independently.

It was the physician's job to manage and treat the patient; it was the insurance company's job to pay covered claims on behalf of its insureds. An insurance company had no direct control over what a physician charged for medical care, nor over the quantity of services provided for any given patient condition.

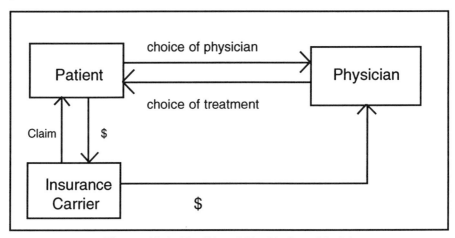

Figure 11-1: Traditional Health Care Model

Under the traditional model, control over delivery of health care was largely in the hands of the physician. That meant control over costs, access to care, and quality of medical care. As concerns about rising medical care costs grew in past decades, economic, social, and political pressures converged to invite a shift from the traditional medical care model to one in which costs could be better "managed". With that shift, came a loss of physician control over patient care.

Basics of the Managed Care Model

It is not our purpose here to enter the debate (and debate there is) about whether the managed care model of providing medical care is a "good" model, or whether it is better than the traditional model. The aim here is to provide physicians with a basic understanding of the managed care model, and to highlight areas of potential concern for the practitioner who practices within that model. Because of the rapid growth of managed care in this country, the likelihood that you will encounter or practice within some form of managed care is extremely high.

The American Medical Association defines *managed care* as "a system or techniques that affect access to and control payments for, health care services." One of the distinguishing features of the managed care model is cost containment. At the heart of the managed care model is the managed care contract. The contract can be one of several varieties, but all are basically the same in that the goal, or purpose, of the contract is to achieve cost control or "containment".

In the managed care model it is the terms of a contract that direct who is entitled to receive care, when and where care can be received, from whom care can be received, and last but not least, the monetary charges for care provided. Thus, the control that in the traditional model was largely held by the physician has been shifted in the managed care model to the managed care entity. Physicians practicing medicine in the managed care model have less control over how, and how much, care is provided to patients. Moreover, they often have no control over who they see as patients, nor how much they charge for their services. All of these aspects of the physician's practice are *managed* by a managed care organization whose goal is to control access to, and cost of providing medical services.

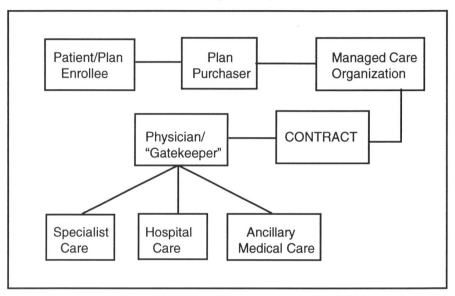

Figure 11-2: Managed Healthcare Model

In essence, the design, purpose, and structure of managed care organizations are all geared toward the containment of health care costs.

One aspect of cost containment in managed care organizations is administratively based and does not directly involve physicians and the provision of health care services. Factors such as underwriting, the selection of physician providers, design of enrollee benefits packages, and determination of patient eligibility are examples.

Another aspect of cost containment involves measures that more directly impact patient care, such as: (1) reducing the frequency of medical services and claims; (2) reducing the cost for services rendered; and (3) changing the points of service to less costly locations or procedures. See Wrightson,

Jr., Charles William, *HMO Rate Setting and Financial Strategy*, Health Admin. Press, Perspectives, Ann Arbor, Michigan, 1990.

Managed care organizations employ a variety of mechanisms to actually achieve the cost reductions. It is these mechanisms that tend to have a direct impact on physicians, and the way they practice medicine. Among these are:

- Risk Sharing Plans – these are physician reimbursement plans designed to reward the "efficient" use of medical services. If the managed care organization as a whole, or as a particular "pool", has a quarterly or annual surplus, profits are distributed or shared with the physicians. Conversely, if overall earnings for the organization, or a particular pool are down, physicians receive no "bonus" or may be financially penalized.

- Setting Goals to Minimize Utilization – a managed care organization may set concrete goals to limit the number of hospital admissions, limit lengths of stay for hospitalizations, and increase the use of out-patient procedures or lower cost treatments as alternatives.

- Medical Review/Pre-Approval Requirements – the form of this tool can range from pre-certification requests handled by managed care "certifiers", to use of third party medical review organizations whose physicians or nurses review requests for treatment and hospitalization and then make specific recommendations as to what types and amounts of treatment should or should not be given.

- Quality Review Evaluations – these may include retrospective reviews of a physician's pattern of using medical care resources or services. Indicia of such usage include such things as numbers of specialist referrals, laboratory referrals, physical therapy referrals, and pharmacy utilization. If it is determined that a physician has an unacceptable pattern of usage, steps may be taken to encourage more acceptable usage.

- Direct Financial Incentives – managed care organizations may use a variety of formulations to financially reward/penalize physicians who meet/don't meet pre-set goals or practice "cost efficient" medicine. Some organizations withhold a percentage of a physician's fees until the end of a period (quarter, semi-annual, or annual), and release the fees to the physician only if certain utilization goals are met. Some organizations have arranged it so that primary care physicians keep all unused funds allotted by the managed care entity to the physician's budget.

It is not too difficult to see that many of the cost containment tools used by managed care organizations have the potential to perhaps unduly or improperly motivate physicians to make medical care decisions based on their own financial interest rather than on the best interests of the patient. Managed care patients who have been denied treatment, and then successfully show that the denial was related to a physician's personal financial interest, have been awarded large litigation awards. Large damage amounts have also been awarded against managed care organizations based on the improper denial of or delay in providing patient treatment.

Types of Managed Care Organizations

Although no two managed care organizations are exactly alike, most can be identified as fitting into one of several broad categories of managed care entities. These managed care sub-groups are distinguished primarily by the degree of structure provided and control exercised by the managed care entity:

Preferred Provider Organization ("PPOs")

PPOs are typically used by employer group health plans who contract with physicians or physician groups to provide discounted health care services. Physicians enter into an agreement with a group health plan, directly or indirectly, to be a "preferred provider" for employees who enroll in their employer's group health plan. In exchange for having patients directed to the physician for care, the physician agrees to provide medical care to enrollees for set discounted fees.

Independent Practice Associations ("IPAs")

IPAs are individual physicians or practice groups that form a legal entity for the purpose of contracting with insurance plans to provide health care services to the plan members. Physicians in the IPAs maintain their own offices and medical practices. They are not limited to seeing plan member patients. The contractual agreement between the IPA and the insurance plan will often dictate such things as: limitations on the services IPA physicians are authorized to provide, to whom specialist referrals may be made, the number of referrals authorized, when prior approval for treatment is required, the circumstances under which patients may be hospitalized, and where patients may be sent for hospitalizations and ancillary medical services.

Health Maintenance Organizations ("HMO"s)

As the name suggests, HMOs are entities which provide all health care services to enrollees in the HMO plan. Enrollment in an HMO most often comes about through the employment setting. An employer purchases health care insurance for employees from a managed care entity that offers a group HMO plan. Employees who wish to receive their medical care through the HMO enroll in the Plan and typically agree to receive all their medical care through the HMO. The HMO may provide care to enrollees using both physicians who are actual employees of the HMO and physicians or physician groups who contract with the HMO to provide care to its enrollees. For the physician and the patient, medical practice within an HMO setting is highly structured. Both physician and patient must follow extensive plan directives that control or regulate nearly all aspects of medical care services including control over: which physicians patients have access to; which consultants or specialists are "approved"; when, where, to whom, and how often patients can be referred for consultations; when, where, and how long patients can be hospitalized; what treatments or procedures are "medically necessary"; and the number of patients a physician must "accept".

These are brief overviews of the major categories of managed care entities. It is possible to further distinguish sub-categories, but not necessary for our purposes here. The goal here is to provide an abbreviated summary of the most common types of managed care entities the practitioner is likely to encounter.

Physicians Practicing in A Managed Care Setting

There are a number of reasons that physicians who practice in the managed care setting are exposed to unique risks of legal liability. Those reasons, and suggestions for minimizing your risk, are discussed in these next sections.

Physician Responsibilities Are Determined by Contract

As a physician who practices wholly or partially within a managed care setting, you will need to consider and understand your working relationship with the managed care entity. Although it may seem like a nuisance to pore over IPA, PPO, or HMO contracts, it should be done. Whenever contract language impacts the way you manage your practice, or the manner in which you treat patients, it should wave a red flag in your mind. What you want to minimize or avoid are contractual constraints on the exercise of your medical judgment and independence.

Figure 11-3 contains a list of questions to keep in mind as you read through a managed care contract. These questions highlight the areas which may give rise to tensions between you, your patients, and the managed care entity. You should give some definite thought to the aspects of your practice that will be controlled or impacted by a managed care contract.

AGREEMENT

1. Who has authority to approve medical services?

2. What can you do under the Plan if you disagree with a denial of medical services for your patient?

3. Are there limitations on referrals to specialists?

4. What are the exceptions to limitations on "outside" referrals?

5. Who is responsible for making referrals to specialists outside the Plan - you or the managed care entity?

6. Who is responsible for obtaining second opinions for surgical procedures - the primary care physician or the specialist?

7. Who has the authority to approve or deny a specialist's recommendations - you or the managed care entity?

8. Are there limitations on your ability to admit patients to particular hospitals?

9. What are the qualifications of other providers with whom you will be treating patients?

10. What non-patient obligations does the contract impose? (Credentialing, peer review, or quality review responsibilities?) Does the Plan indemnify you for claims arising out of those activities?

Figure 11-3: Contract Questions

Upon review of a particular contract, if there is a clause or term that you are uncomfortable with, it may behoove you to actively negotiate for more acceptable language. This can be accomplished by striking though the terms that are disagreeable. You may even want to suggest substitute language as a compromise. Although it may seem that you as an individual physician have little bargaining power to negotiate with managed care organizations, they are likely to become sensitive to physicians' concerns and demands the more frequently they are expressed.

Patient's Rights Are Determined by Contract

Patients/enrollees in a managed care plan have a contractual right to receive needed medical care according to the terms of the plan. If they do not receive the benefits (diagnosis, care, and treatment) they are entitled to under the managed care contract, the managed care entity and its provider-physicians could be subject to claims for breach of contract. In some cases, patients bring actions against the managed care entity alone on the basis that the managed care entity's system did not work properly for them.

Patients may also bring suit against individual managed care physicians and may or may not include the managed care entity as a defendant. Usually the decision about whether to pursue an individual managed care physician as party is made by the plaintiff's attorney. The decision will be based in great part on whether the facts and the law of that particular jurisdiction will support a claim that the physician was an employee or agent of the managed care entity. Refer to Chapters 9 and 10 for discussions about respondeat superior liability.

Physicians Are Part of a "System"

Those physicians who practice in an HMO setting and are actual employees of the HMO find that they are part of a medical care provider *system*, and that as part of the system, they have to operate (so to speak) according to their place within the system. The system is set up to deliver medical care to its enrollees by means of established procedures and policies. As long as patient/enrollees receive appropriate care and treatment within the system, all is well. However, as with many *systems*, there are occasions when the system does not meet the needs of a particular situation, either because it is uniquely challenging or requires handling different from that provided by the system.

In the same way, sometimes patients' presentations or conditions can be unusually complex or difficult to diagnose, treat, or manage. A particular HMO system may work efficiently and well 99% of the time for its patients/enrollees. However, 1% of the time patients may "fall through the cracks", or somehow fail to receive the diagnosis, treatment, or management needed from the system. The point here for the HMO practitioner is that he must be able to recognize, respond, and adjust to, those patients whose legitimate medical needs are not adequately met by "routine" handling within the system.

Physician-Patient Relationship in the Managed Care Setting

One consequence of the way many managed care organizations are set up to provide health care to enrollees is that "continuity of care" is often harder to maintain. Managed care patients and physicians may be less likely to develop solid physician-patient relationships because different providers are often seen on different visits, lists of approved providers and specialists change frequently, and providers and facilities are determined by the plan rather than the patient and physician. From the patient's perspective, it is naturally more difficult to invest in a relationship with a physician knowing that the particular physician may or may not be seen again. Physicians too are probably less likely to commit professional and emotional resources to patients whom they will not likely see on a consistent basis. Not too surprisingly, an expected outcome of this is that patients and physicians in managed care settings don't often have the opportunity to develop trusting, caring, physician-patient relationships that naturally develop with long-term relationships. As a result, patients may be quicker to blame managed care physicians for any real or perceived problems with their medical care or the system.

With this in mind, it is especially important for the managed care physician to convey to the patient sincere concern for his or her well-being. See to it that the patient does not feel lost between visits or referrals. Make sure that you and your staff are familiar with the plan you work under so that you can properly direct patients through the plan requirements. It is very important that patients be directed through the system appropriately. Both you and your staff should know and follow the procedures for making referrals, arranging ancillary care, and arranging hospital admissions.

Imagine how frustrating it can be for the patient who is told to do one thing, and then finds out that proper channels were not followed, resulting in a delay of treatment. Even if you are not really to blame, to the patient, you may be seen as the most visible and tangible ambassador of the managed care system. Therefore, feelings of frustration or ill-will may be directed to you if a patient has a bad experience with the managed care system.

In many instances it may be appropriate and helpful for the patient to understand your role within their medical plan. If there are limitations that impact your ability to treat the patient, explain that to the patient. When there are procedures within the plan for exceptions that may apply to your patient, advise the patient that you are attempting to get approval for treatment in accordance with plan requirements.

If there are limitations on your ability to provide care or treatment, it may be important for a patient to understand the source of those limitations. In some instances where there are limitations placed on you by a patient's plan, it might be appropriate to make clear to a disgruntled patient that her plan places restrictions upon you, but that your best medical judgment will always be followed. Explain to the patient that you are exercising your best medical judgment within the constraints of the patient's plan. As long as a patient rests assured that she is receiving care as a result of your best efforts, the likelihood of complaints, or worse, is low. This means that when necessary, you must be candid, yet tactful, in explaining plan limitations that impact the treatment options you can provide to a particular patient.

Plan Restraints versus Physician-Recommended Treatment

Because various plans often place limits on what and how treatment can be provided to its enrollees, physicians sometimes find that the treatment they recommend for a patient is not authorized (and therefore not paid for) by the patient's plan. As a practical matter, the patient may then go without recommended treatment and suffer harmful consequences. To minimize your exposure in this circumstance it is important to act with the patient's best interest in mind, and show that you have done so. It is recommended that you take the steps listed in Figure 11-4.

PLAN DENIAL OF RECOMMENDED TREATMENT

1. Discuss the recommended treatment with the patient. Advise why it is needed and the consequences of not receiving it. Document it in the record.

2. Follow the Plan's procedures to appeal a benefit denial. Advise the patient of the steps you have taken and note them in the record.

3. Prepare and submit a letter to the Plan's medical director outlining your findings, the need for the recommended treatment, and the consequences of not receiving the treatment. Keep a copy for the record.

4. Make sure you have and document a detailed discussion with the patient outlining your efforts on his behalf, your advice, the risks of not following the recommendation, and the patient's decision. Consider having the patient sign a "refusal of treatment" statement if the patient decides to forego the treatment.

5. If you believe it advisable or necessary to end your relationship with the patient, refer to the Plan and follow its requirements.

Figure 11-4: Approach for Unauthorized Treatment

Managed Care and Financial Incentives
for Physicians

Managed care physicians must always be mindful of the fact that cost containment mechanisms of managed care entities can affect their vulnerability to legal claims. If managed care physicians are paid based on profits of the managed care entity or a capitation agreement, a litigious patient (through her lawyer) will be sure to investigate whether there is any basis for claiming that the physician put his pocket book ahead of his patient's well-being.

A capitation agreement is one in which a physician or group of physicians is paid by a managed care entity a set fee (often monthly) for each patient enrollee. The capitation fee is paid to the physician without regard to the actual cost of providing medical care to the patient during that month. Under this system of compensation there is certainly a financial motive for the physician to avoid over-treating patients. But it is the motivation to under-treat that must be spurned. In fact, capitation agreements are the subject of much scrutiny and criticism because there is a financial incentive for physicians to under-treat patients. The following example illustrates the criticism:

> Freelance Physician's Group contracts with Tip Top Managed Care Company to provide primary care physician services to Tip Top's enrollee/patients. Tip Top pays a capitation fee to Freelance of $100 per patient per month. Tip Top sends a panel of 50 patients to Freelance, and therefore pays $5000 per month to Freelance ($100 per patient x 50 patients). If Freelance Group provides more than $5000 worth of medical care to Tip Top's panel of patients in one month, it loses money because it has spent more than it was paid. If Freelance Group provides approximately $5000 worth of medical care to Tip Top's patients, it has been reasonably compensated for the care provided. However, if Freelance Group provides $3500 worth of medical care in a given month, it has in effect received a bonus of $1500.

Of course this example oversimplifies the situation and ignores the fact that there are likely to be legitimate monthly fluctuations on the medical care demands of a given population of patients. However, from a risk management/litigation perspective, it is fair to say that if a physician or group consistently "comes out ahead" month after month, the claim that the physician or group put "profit before patients" is likely to surface in a medical malpractice case.

As a practical matter, whenever managed care contracts include financial incentives for you to control or minimize patient care costs, you must make sure that you do not pursue financial incentives at the expense of good medical care for your patients. Jurors will not look with favor upon any physician who even appears to put his own financial interest before reasonably necessary medical care for a patient. Juror dissatisfaction or anger will likely be shown with a significant damage award against the HMO and physician.

Gag Clauses

Some managed care contracts with medical providers contain clauses that preclude the provider-physicians from saying certain things to patients that negatively impact the HMO. For instance, physicians may be prevented from informing patients about treatment options that are not provided by the HMO. From the HMO's perspective, there are several reasons it wants to discourage patients from seeking treatment not provided by the HMO. First, the HMO has a financial incentive to provide treatment through its contract providers, with whom it has negotiated a discount rate, or with its employee providers with whom costs are highly regulated. Second, the HMO does not want patients to "dis-enroll" with the HMO and seek treatment with another HMO or plan that does cover the desired treatment.

This situation can have serious consequences for the HMO physician because it may directly impact his ability to obtain informed consent. An HMO physician may find himself in the uncomfortable position of being "caught in the middle" with respect to complying with the contract and meeting his professional obligation. On one hand, the HMO contract may require that the physician not discuss non-covered treatments; on the other hand, the physician is obligated by standards of reasonable medical care to fully inform his patient of all pertinent treatment options. The difficulty lies in the fact that the physician who honors his contractual obligation may find himself as a defendant in a malpractice claim brought by a patient who claims that all treatment options were not disclosed and therefore informed consent was not provided.

Other types of "gag" clauses that have been sometimes found in managed care contracts preclude physicians from advising patients to obtain second opinions, or to seek care from certain facilities or providers that do not have contractual arrangements with the managed care entity. As a result of these types of restrictions, physicians sometimes feel hampered in their ability to provide good medical care to their patients. If a physician is contractually constrained from providing what he deems to be standard medical care, he may in fact be held responsible by the patient for the failure to provide such standard care.

Other types of gag clauses that managed care entities have included in provider contracts are those that prevent the physician from saying anything unfavorable about the managed care entity. This could impact the physician whose managed care patient blames him for substandard care. Based on the provider contract language the physician may find that he is precluded from defending himself by pointing to the managed care entity and its mandatory policies and procedures to explain his conduct.

In some states legislation has been introduced that would ban gag clauses in managed care provider contracts. If you practice in a state where such clauses are not banned, you should review all contract language and carefully note any clauses that appear to restrict either the way you manage your practice or your ability to treat patients. If the limitations are unacceptable you have the option of rejecting the contract or trying to negotiate for more favorable contract language.

As a practical matter, individual physicians may have little bargaining power compared to managed care entities. Groups of physicians – practice groups, partnerships, or associations – are more likely to have success in eliminating contract clauses that unfairly limit the physicians' ability to practice in accordance with accepted medical standards.

Terminating Managed Care Contracts

Managed care contracts usually contain language that sets forth the requirements for terminating a contract. Regardless of who it is that terminates the contract, beware of contract language that restricts your ability to discuss termination with patients. There may be some patients you are treating with whom discussion about arrangements and recommendations for further care is critically important.

You do not want to be subjected to claims that you have abandoned patients, so it is important to document in each and every patient chart that the relationship has been terminated, that transfers to other physicians have been made, or that other arrangements or recommendations have been made. If language in the contract makes it difficult for you to take steps to protect yourself against abandonment claims, negotiate for acceptable language. To the extent possible, never agree to contract language that leaves you especially vulnerable to legal claims.

In the event that continuity of care concerns make it preferable for you to continue to see a particular patient, make arrangements with the managed care entity for you to continue to see the patient. The arrangement should include a provision for reimbursement for your services.

Physicians in the Role of Utilization Reviewers

One method used by managed care entities to control costs is the use of a utilization review process. Most managed care plans contract with enrollees to provide and/or pay for care and treatment that is *medically necessary*. Many plans include a schedule of treatments that are automatically deemed to be medically necessary, and further provide that other categories of treatments, such as certain surgical procedures, will be reviewed on a case by case basis to determine whether a particular treatment is medically necessary for a particular patient.

In order to carry out the screening process managed care entities use *reviewers,* usually physicians, whose job it is to review cases and assess whether particular treatments are "medically necessary", as defined in the plan. If a reviewer determines that a certain treatment is not medically necessary, the managed care entity will neither provide the treatment nor pay for it to be provided elsewhere.

Physicians who work for managed care entities and perform the task of determining whether certain treatments are medically necessary should be aware that they could be subject to review and discipline by state licensing boards for their decisions. There are instances of patient and physician complaints filed with licensing boards against reviewers who have determined treatment to be unnecessary.

Case Illustration

In *Murphy v. Board of Medical Examiners of the State of Arizona,* 190 Ariz. 441, 247 Ariz.Adv.Rep. 35 (1998) it was recommended to a patient that she undergo gall bladder surgery. Dr. M, the medical director for the patient's managed care plan, determined that the gall bladder removal was not "medically necessary". Based on Dr. M's determination, payment for the surgery was not authorized. Both the patient and her doctor believed that surgery was needed, and the patient went ahead with the surgery without her plan's authorization. Interestingly, it was the patient's surgeon who subsequently sent a letter to the state licensing board complaining about Dr. M's "unprofessional conduct and/or medical competence". The surgeon complained to the board that Dr. M: (1) decided that the surgeon had offered his patient a treatment that was not medically necessary; (2) caused the patient to question the surgeon's professional judgment about surgery; (3) caused the patient to take on the financial responsibility of the recommended treatment; and (4) compromised the relationship between the surgeon and his patient. Ultimately, the licensing board issued an advisory letter of concern to Dr. M, finding that he made an inappropriate medical decision that could have caused harm to the patient.

For the physician who practices in the managed care setting, which can include a variety of forms, it may be helpful to always keep a couple of concepts in mind. First, remember that for the patient, physician, and managed care entity, their relationships, rights, responsibilities, and limitations are all defined by contract. Take the time to carefully read contracts before you sign, and once you sign, see to it that both you and your staff know and follow the plan's procedures. Strike or negotiate terms that leave you unfairly vulnerable to malpractice claims. Second, try to always keep the patient's best interest in mind and advocate for the patient if necessary. Don't let managed care plan cost controls and savings unduly interfere with your best medical judgment. Third, as in all areas of medical practice, document the records so that they faithfully reflect your best efforts to provide quality medical care.

Although managed care physicians face unique risk management challenges, by keeping these concepts in mind it is possible to reduce the likelihood of unfounded claims by disgruntled patients.

Next

The final section of this book will be of interest to physicians who find themselves directly involved in some aspect of litigation, either as a witness or party. If you want to know why some patients sue, and what happens when they do, these next chapters will tell you. For those who find themselves facing their first deposition and those who are seasoned "pros", see how lawyers prepare for deposition examinations.

FAQ:

1. I work for an HMO and feel very secure about my role? Am I too naive?

Not necessarily. There are many physicians who enjoy working for HMOs. If your bliss is from ignorance, that's not good. If you understand the system and your role within the system, your sense of security is justified.

2. My group has a contract with an HMO, but we're not happy with the constraints imposed on us. What should we do?

It would depend on the specific situation. Generally speaking, you could attempt to negotiate to eliminate the constraints you are uncomfortable with. If you cannot do that to your satisfaction, your group will have to decide whether to keep the contract. It may help to review your specific situation with a knowledgeable attorney.

3. If I work for an HMO and follow its rules and procedures could my patients sue me and charge that I am motivated by financial incentives?

If the HMO you work for does in fact compensate physicians based on financial incentives you could be vulnerable to such charges. Whether the charge is ulitmately successful against you will depend on the specifics of the claim.

4. I work for an HMO that rewards me in small part based on how much my patients utilize HMO resources. Is there anything I can do to protect myself from claims by patients that I put my financial interest above their best interest?

The best way to protect against such claims is to treat patients without regard to impact on the HMO's resources. Treat patients according to their needs and your best professional judgment. In general, satisfied patients don't bring claims.

5. I work for an HMO. If I am sued by a patient, who pays for my legal defense and any liability award?

In most instances, if you are named as an individual defendant and have your own professional malpractice insurance, your carrier is likely to provide a defense and indemnification. If the claim for malpractice is against the HMO and you are not named as a defendant in the case, the HMO's malpractice carrier will assume the defense and pay if an award is made to the plaintiff. There are exceptions to these general rules. If you have any doubt about whether you or the HMO provides malpractice coverage for you, be sure to inquire about your responsibilities.

6. Are there certain lawyers who specialize in representing the interests of HMO-employed physicians?

Yes. The trick is to find those that are truly qualified as specialists. Because HMOs are relatively new, the laws (statutory and common) regarding HMO are still developing. There are relatively few attorneys who truly specialize in this area.

✦   ✦   ✦   ✦

SECTION
FOUR

PHYSICIANS AND
LITIGATION

12

PHYSICIANS AS EXPERTS

If scientific, technical, or other specialized knowledge will assist the trier of fact to understand the evidence or to determine a fact in issue, a witness qualified as an expert by knowledge, skill, experience, training, or education may testify thereto in the form of an opinion or otherwise.

Rule 702, Federal Rules of Evidence

In the context of litigation, an expert is anyone who, by reason of special education, experience, or training, has knowledge about a particular area, field, or discipline not familiar to the average layperson or juror. Usually, the ultimate function of an expert in the context of litigation is to educate the triers of fact (judges and jurors) so that they can make reasonable and fair efforts to decide issues presented in cases they must decide.

Why Are Experts Used?

Under our legal system, whenever the legal search for truth involves matters that are beyond the understanding of the average lay person, it is recognized that the average juror may need assistance to help understand and fairly decide the issues presented to him. One way of assisting the fact finder in his search for the truth is to permit, and in some instances, require, those with specialized training (experts) to give opinions about matters at issue. Courts permit "experts" to testify about relevant issues because it aids jurors in understanding and deciding certain aspects of a case.

Consider how difficult it would be for the average person (or even the average physician) to sit as a juror on a hypothetical case involving the question of whether a rocket scientist properly designed and built a rocket engine component. Most likely, the average juror would be totally unequipped to consider and decide whether the conduct of the rocket scientist was unreasonable, or whether the conduct conformed to accepted practices within the field of rocket science. To fairly evaluate the conduct of the hypothetical rocket scientist, jurors would need to be educated, at least to some extent, about designing and building rocket science components. Experts are the witnesses who perform that function.

In addition to using experts to testify at trial, there are some other reasons a party may consult an expert. One reason is to evaluate the conduct of either, or both, parties. Because lawyers are not experts in non-legal areas they often need the assistance of experts to determine whether a potential case has merit. A defense lawyer may consult an expert to help find weaknesses in the plaintiff's case and to help find the best way to defend a case. Either side may want the help of an expert to recognize and prepare to handle the strengths and weaknesses of the opposing side.

At trial, the primary purpose of calling an expert to testify is to educate the jurors on what each side thinks is needed to know, and to persuade the jurors to decide the case one way or the other. Trial experts may be employed by parties to accomplish this in a variety of ways.

In our hypothetical rocket scientist case, it would be expected that each side (plaintiff and defendant) would have expert witnesses (qualified rocket scientists) to testify at trial. The plaintiff would likely have an expert to explain what a reasonable rocket scientist should have done under the circumstances, and then to describe how the defendant rocket scientist failed to act accordingly. The defendant rocket scientist would want to retain and call his own rocket scientist expert to rebut the opinions of the plaintiff's expert, and to explain to the jury why the defendant's conduct was reasonable under the circumstances. It would then be up to the jury, once educated by the experts, to ultimately decide whether the defendant rocket scientist acted reasonably.

Are Experts Used in Every Case?

Not all cases require the assistance or testimony of experts. In those cases that involve issues within the common knowledge of the average layperson, experts are not needed. Fault issues in personal injury cases arising out of automobile collisions don't usually involve experts because the typical juror drives a motor vehicle. Those who drive motor vehicles are presumed to have knowledge and experience sufficient to evaluate the reasonableness of the conduct of other motorists. However, in complex motor vehicle collision cases where questions about such things as calculations of vehicle speeds or angles of impact are important, accident reconstruction experts could be used to analyze and "reconstruct" an accident.

Separate and apart from the issue of deciding *fault*, in just about every personal injury case there is also a question of the extent of *damage* or injury to the plaintiff. One of the issues frequently decided by jurors in such cases is the nature, extent, and duration of injury or harm to the plaintiff. Physicians are often sought by lawyers, and the parties they represent, to help analyze and explain these damage issues.

Before cases are even filed, lawyers often call upon physicians to educate them about a party's injuries. When cases proceed to trial, physicians may then be called to testify as expert witnesses to educate the jury about a particular aspect of injury, or lack thereof.

Physicians as Experts

In the eyes of the law, the fact that physicians possess knowledge and training in the field of medicine, which are not commonly possessed by the average person, renders them "experts". While physicians are experts solely by virtue of the fact that they are medically trained, within the broad field of medicine there are also physicians who are experts in their particular specialties and sub-specialties.

The basis for recognizing physicians as experts, that is, the fact that physicians possess skills and training in a specialized body of knowledge, is the same reason for recognizing other types of experts. The rationale applies as much to physicians as it does to mechanics, architects, accountants, psychologists, and the like.

In medical malpractice cases, the general rule is that expert testimony is *required* in order for a medical malpractice plaintiff to present his case to the jury. In other words, the only way he can "prove" that the defendant physician committed malpractice is by having another physician (expert) opine that the defendant fell below the standard of care.

Without a qualified medical expert supporting his case, a medical malpractice plaintiff will not be able to pursue a case unless it falls within a narrow class of exceptions. If the medical malpractice case does not fall within an exception, and the plaintiff does not have an expert, the case will be dismissed.

The medical malpractice plaintiff cannot use just *any* physician to establish his claim. He must do so with the support of a qualified expert witness who is familiar with the medical setting in which the defendant physician practices. Usually this means that the plaintiff needs to consult and retain a physician from the same specialty area as that of each defendant physician.

Generally, if the defendant physician is a cardiologist, the plaintiff will need to consult and retain a cardiologist who is of the opinion that the defendant's care was substandard in order to proceed with a case.

One class of exceptions to the expert witness requirement in medical malpractice cases relates to those cases where the substandard care or resulting injury is apparent and obvious even to a layperson. Exceptions of this type are consistent with the rationale for requiring experts: if the alleged substandard care is obvious even to a layperson, no expert is needed to educate the jurors. Cases that fit into this type of exception are rare and usually involve glaring (truly obvious) malpractice.

> **Case Illustration**
>
> In *State v. Orsini*, 155 Conn. 367, 232 A.2d 907(1967) the court said: Although it is true that expert medical testimony is generally required in proving the condition from which a person claims to be suffering, this is not the case in obvious or simple matters of everyday life, especially where one is testifying about his own physical condition. No one would claim that one whose arm had been amputated could not testify to the fact of the amputation, although he might not be allowed to testify as to a particular diseased condition which had made the amputation necessary. The state of pregnancy is such a common condition that a woman may give her opinion that she herself is pregnant. [cites omitted] 155 at 372, 232 A.2d at 910.

Another related exception to the expert witness requirement in medical malpractice cases is based on a legal principle known as *res ipsa loquitur*. This Latin phrase translates as "the thing speaks for itself" and is ordinarily used to describe a situation in which the occurrence of an accident itself is an indication (but not absolute proof) of negligence. If under normal circumstances, a certain accident, injury, or outcome would not ordinarily happen in the absence of negligence, then the res ipsa loquitur doctrine could apply and give rise to the legal presumption that a defendant was negligent. There are specific conditions that must be established in order for the doctrine to be applied.

In order for the doctrine to apply, the instrumentality that causes injury must have been within the exclusive control of the defendant. Application of the doctrine in personal injury cases is rare, and rarer still in medical negligence cases. If applied in a medical malpractice case, it may eliminate the need for expert witness testimony on the standard of care, thereby giving rise to a rebuttable presumption of negligence.

Case Illustration

"It is the law in Arizona, as expressed by our Supreme Court in *Capps v. American Airlines,* 81 Ariz. 232, 234, 303 P.2d 717, 718 (1956), that the conditions necessary for the application of the doctrine are:

'(1) the accident must be of a kind which ordinarily does not occur in the absence of some one's negligence;

'(2) it must be caused by an agency or instrumentality within the exclusive control of defendant;

'(3) it must not have been due to any voluntary action on the part of the plaintiff;

'(4) plaintiff must not be in a position to show the particular circumstances which caused the offending agency or instrumentality to operate to his injury."

Tucson General Hospital v. Russell, 7 Ariz.App. 193, 195, 437 P.2d 677, 679 (1968)

In this case the plaintiff was injured when an x-ray machine fell on her in the surgical suite. The court held that plaintiff was entitled to proceed on the theory of res ipas loquitur because x-ray machines don't ordinarily fall on patients in the absence of negligence.

In personal injury cases other than those for medical malpractice, physicians are often consulted about a variety of issues that relate to medical aspects of patient's damage claims. The physician/expert's role depends on the reason the expertise is needed. A physician may be asked to provide expertise about a plaintiff's pre or post injury status, the impact of an injury, the causes of a plaintiff's condition, the type and amount of treatment needed by a plaintiff, or the likely course and extent of a plaintiff's recovery from injury.

Why Lawyers Consult Physicians

Regarding Their Patients

One of the most common reasons you may be consulted as an expert by a lawyer is about one of your own patients. Whether a client is pursuing a worker's compensation claim, an insurance claim, a disability claim, a social security claim, or a personal injury claim, his lawyer may want to speak or meet with you to get a better understanding of his client's medical condition.

You may also be consulted in your role as what is known as a "subsequent treating physician". This happens when the care or treatment provided to your patient by a previous treating physician is at issue or under investigation. In this situation you should be careful about offering gratuitous comments about the care and treatment provided by the previous treating physician.

If you are asked to comment about the treatment provided by another physician, you do not have to provide an opinion if you do not want to do so. You can respond by saying that you are willing to discuss the patient's present condition and your treatment, but that you do not know the details of the treatment previously provided and have not formed, or do not want to give, an opinion about that. This is a perfectly acceptable response. On the other hand, if you feel qualified to comment on the care and treatment provided by another physician, and *want* to give your opinion, you may do so. The fact that you offer an opinion does not necessarily commit you to testify in court about your opinion. However, if you provide an opinion favorable to the lawyer's client, you could be subpoened to testify. Though, as a practical matter most lawyers will respect your desire to "stay out" of the case if you express it with earnest.

Most commonly, your patient's lawyer (on behalf of his client/your patient) may want you to provide "expert" opinions to support the patient's claim for benefits or damages. In this type of situation it is important for you to realize the potential impact of your "opinion". It may be that your opinion alone will determine whether, or the extent to which, your patient is entitled to benefits. Therefore, be sure to be thorough and fair in formulating and reporting your medical opinions.

Regarding Another Physician's Patient

There are times when a lawyer needs to consult with a physician about a particular aspect of his client's medical status. Although the client may be under the care of another physician, it may be beneficial for the lawyer to have an independent assessment of the patient. You might be asked to review a case or see the client for an evaluation or assessment with a particular issue in mind.

A lawyer may need to know such things as the status of his client's injury, the client's prognosis for full recovery, or the amount and cost of further treatment. Understanding the purpose of the patient's consultation with you will help you to focus your examination and opinions.

In any evaluation of a case or patient's status you should be sure to steer clear of offering any comments on or criticisms of other physicians unless you have a good understanding of the facts and feel strongly about wanting to offer your comments or criticisms. Keep in mind that what you may intend to be a harmless comment about another physician, the patient may take to be a serious criticism. In general, it is best to refrain from offering gratuitous comments about the care and treatment provided by former or concurrent treating physicians. If you offer a criticism of another doctor, the chances are very good that the patient or his lawyer will follow up on it with you. It may simply be best to avoid getting into an awkward situation.

Regarding Another Physician's Care and Conduct

Every lawyer who considers whether to pursue a potential medical mal-practice case knows that eventually he or she will need to consult with a physician-expert to determine whether the case has merit. This is because statutes and case law in nearly every jurisdiction require that most medical negligence cases be supported by the opinions of qualified medical experts.

Attorneys often approach the medical expert requirement in two steps. The first step may be to consult with a qualified physician for the purpose of determining whether malpractice occurred, but not necessarily for the purpose of having the physician agree to testify at trial. It may be that the lawyer wants an informal opinion about the case and does not yet want to worry about securing an expert to testify. If the physician/expert informally renders a favorable opinion, the lawyer will then take the second step and ask the reviewing physician, or another physician who is qualified and willing to testify on behalf of the patient.

Some doctors are comfortable reviewing potential malpractice cases and giving informal opinions about the quality of care and treatment provided by other physicians, but feel constrained from actually serving as the testifying expert against another physician in a medical negligence case. Other physicians see it as part of their professional obligation or moral duty to support patients who have been harmed as the result of substandard medical care. Yet other physicians want nothing to do with evaluating medical malpractice cases either because they are too busy treating patients, they have no particular interest in reviewing cases, or because they want as little involvement in the legal system as possible. No one approach is right or wrong. For the most part, it is simply a matter of personal preference.

Some physicians find it thrilling to venture into the medical-legal arena. They enjoy the professional challenge of reviewing cases to determine what went wrong, if anything; and in finding no negligence they then enjoy the challenge of trying to find out how else a patient's outcome can be explained. For other physicians the idea of "sleuthing" through medical records for pieces of a medical-legal puzzle is one of the most dreadful tasks imaginable. Fortunately, both types of physicians, and those in between these extremes, can for the most part, be involved in medico-legal matters according to their level of interest.

One important caveat to note is that it would never be right to conceal the misdeeds of another physician knowing that a patient was likely to suffer serious harm. As an example, an assistant surgeon who knew that a foreign object or instrument was improperly left in the body of a patient could not mutely stand by while the patient suffered from consequences of the misdeed.

Regarding A Specific Medical Condition

If a case involves a particular medical condition whose cause, treatment, or prognosis is so complex, rare, or critical to the case, a medical expert may be consulted for the sole purpose of educating a lawyer, and ultimately a jury, about that one condition. Such a case may or may not be a medical malpractice case. In some cases it is possible to have several such experts consulted – one for each aspect of a condition, disease process, or treatment.

Independent Medical Exams

When a plaintiff brings a personal injury claim in which her medical status or injuries are disputed, as they often are, a defendant may want to either verify that the plaintiff and her physicians are accurately reporting her condition, or he may want to disprove the claim outright. To accomplish either purpose, the rules of procedure permit the defendant to have the plaintiff seen for an [I]ndependent [M]edical [E]xamination, or "IME" for short.

Under the authority of court rules, a defendant may request that a plaintiff submit to a medical examination for purposes of expert evaluation of any and all medical conditions at issue in the litigation instituted by the plaintiff. If a plaintiff were to claim both psychiatric and bodily injuries, separate IMEs by separate physicians could be done at the request of the defendant's attorney.

The IME physician may be designated by the court or by the agreement of the attorneys. Many lawyers and law firms have relationships with certain physicians who are agreeable to doing IME examinations. Note that the existence of any such relationships are usually not lost on plaintiff's attorneys and will likely be brought out to the jury if a case proceeds to trial.

IME physicians are often asked by defense lawyers to review pertinent medical records in addition to conducting an examination of the plaintiff. Once the review and actual evaluation are done, the IME physician may verbally report his findings to the defendant's attorney. The physician is also required by court rules to prepare a written report of his findings and opinions. This report then made available to lawyers for both sides.

A physician who thinks he would like to perform IMEs should be aware that he may subsequently be asked to provide deposition testimony and/or trial testimony in any case in which he performs an IME. If you prefer not to do either, you probably should not become involved in doing IMEs on a regular basis.

Regarding the Cause of Injury or Harm

The legal element of *causation* is one that must be established in every case. What is meant by *causation* is a showing, or proof, that the alleged negligence of the defendant *caused or contributed to* the harm or damages alleged by the plaintiff. In order to proceed with any personal injury claim, including medical malpractice claims, the plaintiff must establish:

   (1) that the defendant's conduct was unreasonable

   (2) that the plaintiff was injured or suffered harm

   (3) that it was the defendant's conduct that *caused* the injury or harm.

If one of these elements cannot be proven, the plaintiff's claim will fail.

The following two hypothetical examples help illustrate the concept of causation more clearly.

HYPOTHETICAL NO. 1

Pam Patient presented to Dr. Careless with a lump in her right breast. Dr. Careless noted the lump on palpation but did nothing further. He told Pam to return in six months. Pam returned in six months, by which time the lump had doubled in size. A biopsy was done and showed malignant metastatic cancer. Pam died within six months. *Do Pam's husband and three young children have a claim against Dr. Careless for Pam's wrongful death?*

(1) Was it below the standard of care for Dr. Careless to wait six months before doing anything? YES.

(2) Did Pam suffer harm? YES.

(3) Was the negligence of Dr. Careless a proximate cause of Pam's death? IT DEPENDS.

This causation issue requires "expert" analysis. It may be that Pam could not have been cured of this particular type of cancer even if it had been diagnosed and treated six months earlier. However, a qualified expert may be of the opinion that a six month delay in receiving treatment precluded Pam from receiving life-saving treatment. If Pam's family finds a qualified expert who is of the opinion that earlier treatment would have made a difference, a claim could proceed. The defendant may look for and retain an expert with a differing opinion. It will be up to a jury to decide which expert's opinion is more plausible and persuasive.

Hypothetical No. 2

Larry Leadfoot, Wanda Wheeler, and Valerie Victim live and drive in Pothole City, USA. One day, Larry Leadfoot fails to pay attention to traffic and his truck strikes the back end of Wanda Wheeler's car. Moments before the collision, Wanda Wheeler's car hits a pothole in the road, which causes a hub-cap on her car to fly off into the direction of oncoming traffic. It hits Valerie Victim's front windshield, which shatters. Valerie loses control of her car and ultimately comes to rest in a bush by the side of the road. As a result of the accident, Valerie has injuries to her face and neck. *Does she have a case against Larry?*

(1) Was Larry's conduct unreasonable? YES

(2) Was Valerie injured? YES

(3) Was Larry's unreasonable conduct the cause of Valerie's injury? NO

Because Valerie was injured as a result of Wanda's flying hub-cap, and not due to Larry's negligence, Wanda does not have a valid claim against Larry.

Expert Consultations with Lawyers

As one might imagine from the previous headings, there are a number of different reasons why lawyers call upon physicians as experts. Regardless of the purpose for which a physician-expert is consulted, it is not unusual to have several telephone or face-to-face conferences with a lawyer.

Initial contact may be made by a lawyer or his office staff to ask simply that a consultation take place. If the doctor is agreeable, in all likelihood the lawyer will provide specific information relevant to the purpose of the consultation. In some cases the physician will only be asked to review records; in other cases he may asked to see a patient and give an opinion; in yet other cases he may simply be asked questions about a particular patient, treatment, or condition.

At times, lawyers will ask physician experts to prepare reports or letters that address specific areas of inquiry. If you are asked by a lawyer to serve as an expert medical consultant and prepare a report don't hesitate to "orient" yourself to the case by asking questions. Sometimes lawyers take it for granted that physicians are familiar with the legal landscape in a given case when in fact the physician would have no reason to be. Other lawyers routinely provide background and a list of categories or questions to cover in the report.

Whenever you are asked to be an expert it is important to understand what function you are being asked to perform in the case so that you can prepare and respond appropriately. If it is not clear to you, ask whether the lawyer represents the plaintiff or the defendant. It is usually permissible to ask about the main allegations and defenses in the case that might be pertinent to your role. You may want to know whether any other physicians have been retained as experts by either side. If so, you may want to know their positions on the medical issues. If for some reason it is not appropriate for you to be provided with information of this type, the lawyer can let you know. More often than not, there is no reason for you not to be generally familiar with the case if you want to be.

Some physicians want to know nothing more about a case than what they absolutely need to. (The trick is to determine what that is.) It's a matter of personal preference. The point here is that if you are the type of person who likes to have background information, don't hesitate to ask for it.

Affidavits

In the physician's role as an expert there may be times when he is called upon to prepare or sign an affidavit. This differs from a formal report in that it is a notarized document, in which the physician "swears" or "affirms" the truth of what is asserted in the document. In most instances, a patient or lawyer will ask a physician to sign an affidavit to support a specific factual or legal assertion that the party is required or wishes to make.

Usually, the lawyer will prepare the affidavit for your signature. You should be given the opportunity to review it and make changes before signing it. It is perfectly proper for you to make corrections or changes to a proposed affidavit if you are uncomfortable with the version you have been asked to sign. Keep in mind that an affidavit is regarded as being an "official" statement by or position of the person who signs it. If you are asked to sign an affidavit, but disagree with its contents, or are unsure about your role or the purpose of the affidavit, don't hesitate to ask the requesting lawyer for clarification or changes.

Expert Fees

Many physicians who are frequently involved in medical-legal matters develop a fee schedule for various "expert" services. The lower end of the fee schedule might be for matters that are regarded as somewhat perfunctory. This would include such tasks as filling out simple reports or question forms submitted by a lawyer on behalf of a patient. The higher end of the fee scale is often for those matters that require more "work" on the part of the expert physician.

Physicians who review and analyze potential medical malpractice claims often spend hours reading through records, researching literature, and meeting with attorneys to discuss their conclusions. This type of expert work may be more demanding and therefore worth more to the physician.

It may surprise you to know that there are some physicians who charge nothing or very little for medical-legal work. They may have a particular interest in developing medical-legal expertise, or they may find that medical-legal work is professionally stimulating or novel. For those who think otherwise, see Figure 12-1 – a sample fee schedule for illustrative purposes only. The actual "going rate" will vary from community to community and specialty to specialty.

MEDICAL-LEGAL SCHEDULE
FOR DR. LEX

Simple reports/questionaires	$100
Complex medical reports	$250
Attorney consultations (per half-hour)	$150
Medical record review (per hour)	$150
Deposition preparation (per hour)	$250
Deposition testimony (per hour with 1 hour minimum)	$350
Trial preparation (per hour)	$250
Trial testimony (half day minimum)	$1000
Trial testimony (full day)	$2000

Figure 12-1: Sample Fee Schedule

There are several ways to determine what fees are reasonable for the legal work you may be asked to perform. To some physicians, time is time no matter how it is spent, and they have a set fee for all work that is based on the fees they would have generated if patients had been seen during the same period spent on the legal work. A physician who typically generates $200 - $300 per hour seeing patients may be inclined to charge for all legal work at that same rate.

Another way to consider what is reasonable for your medical-legal fee is to see what fees are being charged by other physicians in the same specialty. This gives you the opportunity to see what the "market will bear". Although you are not bound to charge what others charge, it will serve to provide a point of reference to consider when setting your own fee or fee schedule.

You may want to consider discussing your fees with the attorney who has asked you for your medical-legal services. Some physicians may think that the effect of this is to reveal a lack of experience or a sign of uncertainty about one's professional worth. In fact, it may reflect an earnest effort to charge a reasonable fee and many attorneys will respond sincerely. Attorneys are likely to know what charges are customary and should be willing to share this with you. If you are not agreeable to a suggested fee, you are free to negotiate or stand firm on a "bottom line".

Whether this latter approach is appealing may depend on the attorney you are dealing with. There may be times when the above approach is definitely not the preferred one. This is especially true if you find that you do not have a pleasant relationship with the attorney who is calling upon your expertise. On the other hand, if you find that the lawyer you are working with is sincere, reasonable, and perhaps even likeable, you may want to talk over the issue of fees in advance of your work.

If you are asked to perform a medical-legal service the issue of fees may not come up until after the work or service has been performed. However, it is more and more common for lawyers and insurance companies who pay for expert services on behalf of their clients to ask about fees in advance. Even if you are not asked in advance about your fee for a particular service, it is probably good business practice to set your fee and inform the lawyer in advance of performing the service. Many physicians have found that it is best to request payment of fees in advance of performing the work requested. Whether you do this is most likely to be a reflection of your general business practice. If you develop or have a good working relationship with a particular attorney or law firm and know that payment of your fees will not be questioned, you may want to forego requesting advance payment as a sign of good will. However, if you have never worked with or for a particular attorney or insurance company, or you have reason to think that payment of your fee could become a "sticky" issue, then it would be best to resolve any payment issues in advance of your work.

For the most part, the physician is in the driver's seat when it comes to setting expert witness fees. That does not mean that fees will never be scrutinized. In some jurisdictions there are limits and restrictions on fees for certain medical-legal services. In Chapter 8, reasonableness of medical record copying charges is discussed. The same considerations apply to fees.

With respect to fees for expert services, keep them within the local "going rate" to avoid scrutiny by a judge. Judicial oversight of expert fees is rare, but can occur when the adverse party (the one other than the side who has consulted you and agrees to your fees) wants to take deposition but believes your deposition fees are too high.

Experts and Professional Responsibility

Physicians who testify as experts should be aware of growing concern within the profession regarding "rogue" experts - those who testify beyond their areas of expertise or who go beyond the bounds of reasoned and supportable expert opinions.

All jurisdictions have laws of civil procedure and evidence that are to be applied by judges to prevent experts from offering unreliable opinions and from testifying beyond their capabilities. Even so, there are rare occasions when unsupportable opinions are in fact presented to juries. The reason for this is severalfold. First, judges are sometimes unable to discern whether an expert's opinions are based on valid medical science or upon "junk science". In the interest of erring on the side of allowing the jury to decide the case, a judge may believe it is best to allow an expert to testify if it at least appears that his opinions are reliable. Second, through the adversary process, a skilled and prepared lawyer should be able to debunk through cross-examination the credibility of an expert who offers unsupported opinions. Unfortunately, not all lawyers are skilled and well-prepared. In a perfect world, an expert who offered opinions that were ill-founded or flat out unfounded, would be so "beat up" after cross examination that the jurors would not give any credence to his unreliable opinions. In our real world, it is sad but true that crafty parties, doctors, and lawyers can sometimes find a way to beat the system.

Recognizing that ours is not a perfect world, and due to concern about the honor of the profession, there have been several approaches considered to stem the incidence of "hired gun" experts. The American Medical Association has studied this issue and is formulating an approach to discourage physicians from giving falsified or fraudulent testimony. An approach that appears to be gaining support is one in which doctors who testify as experts (presumably on standard of care and causation) would be viewed as practicing medicine by virtue of offering their opinions, and therefore subject to peer review.

It is reasoned that all physicians have vowed to uphold the standards of their profession, and that if a physician were to actually treat a patient in a way that was inconsistent with standards of reasonable practice, the physician could be subject to disciplinary scrutiny. A physician should not then be able to testify in court offering opinions that are not in accord with standards of good medical practice without any accountability.

The AMA concept, based on a model program begun by a Florida county medical association, involves peer review of complaints brought against physician experts by patients, or plaintiff or defendant physicians. A committee (known as an Expert Witness Committee) comprised of board-certified physicians reviews the complaint and pertinent materials to determine whether there is evidence of deceit or fraud in the expert's testimonial statements regarding the standard of care. The committee may then either dismiss the complaint or take further action. Ultimately, the committee may recommend that action be taken against the expert by the state board of medicine.

Such an approach is not without its critics. Some argue that such a system could unfairly penalize physician experts who testify as to honestly held beliefs that are not necessarily mainstream or widely accepted. What about physicians whose opinions are shared by only a minority of their peers? Are only majority held practices and opinions valid? What about opinions regarding controversial medical issues?

Others believe that the practice of disciplining doctors for opinions they give in court may be unlawful. First Amendment free speech protections and restraint of trade issues are raised and likely to be litigated if the AMA's model is applied by state medical boards and public hospitals. Legal scholars fear that witness scrutiny will have an overall chilling effect on the willingness of physicians to testify. As a result, it is argued litigants' will suffer, and the system will suffer.

Whether or not this model or any other is adopted in the community where you practice, it shouldn't impact you if you testify and offer opinions in good faith. As in all things, honesty is the best policy. This approach would not prevent an expert from offering a minority opinion, or even an unpopular opinion as long as it was acknowledged to be so. It is fraud, deceit, and dishonesty that are sought to be sifted out of the courtroom.

Next

Testifying in a deposition, hearing, or in court can be an intimidating experience. Rookie and first-time testifiers will benefit from the next chapter, in which the how's, why's, when's and where's of being a medical witness are dissected and outlined.

FAQ:

1. What if my patient specifically asks me whether I think another physician committed malpractice, and I think he did – do I have to tell the patient what I think?

No, you do not have to give an opinion if you don't want to. If that is the case, it is best to tell the patient that you routinely do not comment on the care of other care providers. This is better than denying that you have an opinion and leading the patient to believe that you are approve of another's conduct.

2. Can a nurse serve as an expert witness "against" a physician?

It is difficult to conceive of an instance in which a nurse would be qualified to testify on the standard of care for a physician. In order to render an expert opinion on what conduct is reasonable for a physician, an expert is generally required to be someone with the same education, training, and experience. This usually means that an expert physician must be of the same specialty as the defendant physician. It is possible to have experts from different specialties as long as the care and treatment at issue, are commonly treated by either specialist. For instance, a pediatrician would be qualified to testify regarding a family practitioner's care and treatment of a child.

3. If the doctrine of res ipsa loquitur applies, does that mean that the plaintiff automically wins the case?

No. Application of the doctrine only creates a rebuttal presumption of negligence. A defendant physician could introduce evidence to persuade a factfinder that he should not be held liable for the plaintiff's injury.

4. Can I be subject to peer review if I am summoned to a deposition or court to testify about treatment I provided to my patient?

Testifying in and of itself should not subject you to peer review. If the treatment you provided is questionable, whether or not you testify, peer review is likely to be triggered by some other event, such as a complaint from your patient or another physician. However, if you testify about your treatment, you are creating a sworn statement that could be "used against you" in a peer review proceeding. Remember to always testify truthfully.

✦   ✦   ✦   ✦

13

Testifying in Depositions, Hearings, or Court

Do you swear to tell the truth, the whole truth, and nothing but the truth, so help you God?

Oath of sworn witness.

A physician may be called upon to testify in a case for a number of different reasons. Whether testifying as an expert is something you relish or loathe, chances are that sooner or later in your career you will find yourself saying "I do" in response to the witness's oath to tell the truth. The primary purpose of this chapter is to explain the deposition process, explain the mechanics of testifying in court, and suggest how to prepare to testify in either type of proceeding. This chapter relates to depositions of non-party deponents, those who are not directly involved in a case as a plaintiff or defendant. Because there are different considerations to bear in mind when being deposed as a party-defendant, that situation is covered in the next chapter.

Reasons to Testify

Physicians are often called upon by patients, insurance companies, lawyers, and other physicians to provide formal testimony on their behalf in court cases and administrative hearings. The purpose of testifying will depend on the physician's role as an expert. These various roles have been outlined in more detail in Chapter 12.

A physician's testimony may be desired because he has treated a particular patient and knows her medical history. A research physician who has expertise in the treatment of or prognosis for a particular condition may be called to testify because that issue is critical to the evaluation of a case. In medical malpractice cases, physicians are called to testify as experts about the applicable standard of care for the defendant physician. A physician who evaluates a patient-litigant (an IME) at the request of an insurance company may be called to testify about his findings.

Considering that there are many different reasons for physicians to testify as experts, it will be very important to understand the purpose of your testimony in the event that you are requested or subpoened to provide testimony. If you are unexpectedly asked (or subpoened) to provide testimony in an administrative hearing or court case, and do not have a clear understanding of why you have been asked, there a couple of things you might consider doing.

You can try to guess the reason your testimony is needed, prepare accordingly, and hope you are right. This is a bit risky in the event that you guess wrong. Another approach is to contact the lawyer of the party who has requested your testimony and ask why you have been called to testify. As long as you are not a party to the lawsuit, it is not improper for you to contact the requesting lawyer. If the request comes from a lawyer on behalf of one of your patients, you may consider contacting your patient to find out why your testimony has been sought. Keep in mind that the whole point of making such an inquiry is not to be unduly meddlesome, but to allow you to properly prepare to testify.

Preparation

Understanding the reason for your testimony is vital if you are to prepare properly and efficiently. The nature and extent of your preparation will depend in great part upon the object of your testimony. If you are testifying as a treating physician, in all likelihood, it will be sufficient for you to prepare by reviewing the patient's record. If you are testifying as an expert on a particular condition, disease, or treatment, your preparation is more apt to involve research, review of literature, and study on the topic in question. If you are testifying as a medical malpractice defendant, you will need to understand each claim brought against you, the specific allegations of medical malpractice, and then thoroughly review all details of the patient's medical care and treatment.

Preparation to provide testimony is very important because it impacts your credibility as a witness. If your testimony relates to a patient's record, be familiar with the organization of the record before the deposition. If the chart is disorganized or difficult for you to refer to, be sure to organize it so that you can easily find and refer to information that relates to your testimony. In the event that you have read and relied on studies, articles, or materials that are not in a patient chart, you might consider bringing them with you when you testify.

When witnesses, including physicians, are asked to testify, they are evaluated not only based on *what* they say, but also on *how* they say it. Lawyers, judges, and jurors are more favorably impressed by witnesses who answer questions directly, than they are by those who fumble, mumble, or hesitate while testifying. It is usually fairly apparent when a witness is ill-prepared, or worse, unprepared. Testifying in deposition or court is a stressful event for most physicians (and most every other type of witness). Although it is unlikely that due preparation will obviate all tension, it will surely help to eliminate the pressure that can be avoided.

In the next section, the particularities of preparing for testifying in the deposition setting are explained.

Depositions

Nature of a Deposition

A deposition is one of several methods by which parties to a lawsuit *discover* facts and opinions known by witnesses. In most instances, depositions are taken once a lawsuit has been filed, as each party tries to find out what is known by witnesses identified by the opposing party. It is the practice in most jurisdictions that parties are required by statute or court rules to list all persons who are known to have information about the events in question. The statutes and rules often further require that the subject matter known to witnesses be disclosed as well. For expert witnesses, including physicians, a detailed summary of anticipated trial testimony or opinions is usually required. This means that if your deposition is requested, it is because you are thought to be a potential witness with evidence that is relevant, or even critical, to the case.

Attorneys typically approach a deposition with one or more goals in mind. One reason for taking a deposition is to find out, or "discover", what is known by a witness. It may be that neither party knows what a potential witness has to say about any issue in the case. Both sides may want to find out what information the witness has — either to see if it is helpful, or to prepare to rebut or counter the evidence if it is unfavorable.

Once the lawyers learn what a witness knows, or that a witness is likely to have pertinent information, they then decide whether the information relates to or helps decide an issue in the case. If the witness has relevant information, it is likely to be more helpful to one party than the other. In that case, the party helped will probably list and call that person as his witness at trial.

Another reason a lawyer might want to take the deposition of a witness is to preserve his testimony for trial. This may be done when the witness is unavailable at the time of trial, yet the lawyer would like to present the witness's testimony to the jury. These types of deposition proceedings may be videotaped weeks or months in advance of the trial. Then at the time of trial, rather than having the witness testify in person, the video-taped proceeding can be shown to the jury. Even if a deposition proceeding is not videotaped, the deposition questions and answers can usually be read to the jury at trial. Whether or not a deposition is videotaped, the proceeding will always be stenographically recorded by a court reporter.

Lawyers sometimes have a fairly good understanding of what a particular witness knows regarding an issue in the case, but will decide to take the deposition of a witness to "pin down" his testimony and avoid surprises at trial. If this is the objective of the lawyer in taking a deposition, then his questions are likely to be geared to having the witness commit to knowing certain things, but not others. In effect, the lawyer will attempt to carefully proscribe the limits of the witness' knowledge. In this way, the lawyer hopes to prevent the witness from changing or adding to his testimony at the time of trial.

Scheduling Deposition Date, Time, and Location

Once witnesses and potential witnesses are identified, each party decides whether to take the deposition of a particular witness. A deposition is a legal proceeding attended by all parties, or in most instances, their lawyers, in which a witness is subject to oral examination.

The witness, all other parties, and a court reporter, are notified of the intent of one party to take a deposition by a formal document known as a *Notice of Deposition*. The Notice will show the names of the parties, the name of the witness to be deposed, the date, time and location of the deposition, and the name of the party requesting the deposition. Figure 13-1 depicts common contents of a typical Notice of Deposition.

Out of courtesy and recognition of the fact that physician's days are tightly scheduled, the date, time, and location of the deposition are usually set weeks in advance based on agreement of the parties and physician-witness. Usually when a lawyer decides that the deposition of a physician needs to be scheduled, either his office staff or the office of the opposing attorney will contact the physician's office and ask for the physician's availability. When scheduling a deposition, lawyers are often able to estimate the length of time required so that an appropriate amount of time is blocked out on the physician's schedule. It is not uncommon for physicians and lawyers to schedule depositions at the end of the workday.

Able Attorney
Able Law Firm
123 Central Avenue
Yourtown, Anystate

SUPERIOR COURT of
Central County

Pamela Patient,
      Plaintiff,
vs.

David Doctor, M.D.
      Defendant.

No. 99-123456

Notice of Deposition

The State of Anystate to: Your Name and address

You are commanded to appear and give testimony at the time and place specified below:

Date: Wednesday, April 1, 1999
Time: 4:30 p.m.
Place   Your Office
      Your address

Signed and sealed this date: _____

Clerk of the Superior Court

Figure 13-1: Deposition Notice

As a practical matter, the location of a deposition is usually determined according to the physician. This is because lawyers don't want to pay for a physician's time to travel to a site away from his office. For convenience, most physician depositions are taken at the physician's office. They can be held in a conference room, lunch-room, or office, depending on the number of lawyers attending. Since each party is likely to be represented at the deposition by a lawyer, in multi-party lawsuits (more than one plaintiff and/or defendant) larger rooms will be needed to accommodate the witness, court reporter, and attorneys.

If for some reason you prefer not to have a deposition taken at your office, you can ask to have it taken at the lawyer's office. As a practical matter, it may be necessary to do so if the number of attendees at the deposition cannot physically fit into your office. Some physicians find that it is disruptive to their or their partners' practice to schedule a deposition while patients are being seen in the office. Others simply prefer to avoid a parade of brief case toting legal types through the office.

Assuming the deposition is scheduled for the physician's office, as they most commonly are, the date, time, and physician's office address will appear on the *Deposition Notice*. Otherwise, the *Notice* will reflect the location as any other agreed upon place, which could be a lawyer's office, a hospital conference room, a hotel meeting room, a court reporter's suite, a business meeting room, or even a private residence.

There are times when lawyers attempt to schedule depositions without first checking on the availability of the witness or opposing counsel. In some jurisdictions this is more common; in others it is considered to be quite uncivil. The legal culture varies from community to community and so does the level of attorney courtesy. In most communities, it is an aggressive attorney who presumes to schedule a physician's deposition without extending the courtesy of first checking on his availability.

If you receive a *Notice of Deposition* commanding you to appear at a place or time that is inconvenient, or when you are unavailable, call the office of the attorney who has requested your deposition and explain your conflict. In most cases, a convenient date, time, or place will be substituted and an *Amended Notice* will be issued. If the lawyer gives you a difficult time about making a change, send a letter to the attorneys for both sides in the case explaining why you cannot attend as requested. That is likely to produce the desired result. A lawyer who refuses to re-schedule a deposition when presented with a legitimate reason runs the risk of angering the judge assigned to the case.

Although it is extremely rare for a lawyer to insist that you appear when you cannot, if the *Notice of Deposition* is accompanied by a *subpoena*, you will have no choice but to either attend or obtain a protective order. If this situation arises, contact your insurance carrier and ask for recommendations on how to proceed. If the services of a lawyer are needed, you can get a reliable referral from your carrier.

Deposition Procedure

Seating

The mechanics of a deposition follow a fairly standard procedure. One of the first items of business is to decide on a seating arrangement. There is no set arrangement, but several concerns usually dictate the placement of attendees. The court reporter needs to be able to clearly hear the testimony of the deponent (physician-witness) and will therefore want to sit in close proximity to the witness. The lawyer who is taking the lead on questioning the deponent will then sit close by as well. Other lawyers are likely to sit according to their anticipated participation. Lawyers representing other parties also have an opportunity to question the witness, although it is not unusual for other lawyers to ask few or no questions once the lead questioner has concluded.

Figures 13-2 and 13-3 show typical seating arrangements for physician depositions - one is in a lawyer's office; the other is in a physician's office. Variations are often dependent on the number attending and available room.

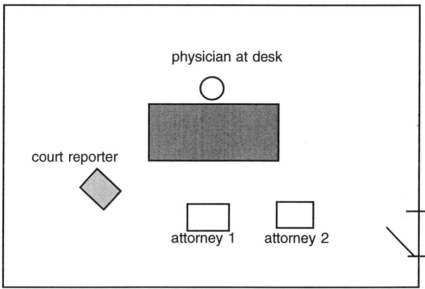

Figure 13-2: Deposition in Physician's Office

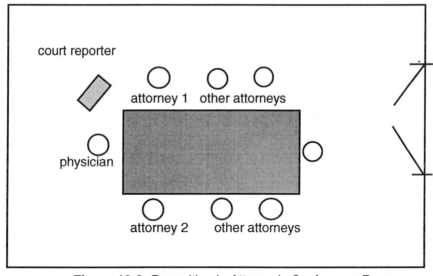

Figure 13-3: Deposition in Attorney's Conference Room

Swearing-In

Once everyone attending the deposition is situated and introductions have been made, the deposition begins with the oath of the witness to tell the truth. The oath is administered by the court reporter, who begins by asking the deponent to raise his right hand. The deponent is then asked whether he swears or affirms to tell the truth, to which he responds, "I do" or "Yes".

Order of Questioning

The party who requested the deposition will typically begin the questioning and ask questions about most of the material to be covered during the deposition. Once the initial lawyer-questioner has finished, he will "pass" to the next lawyer as lawyers for each party are given the opportunity to ask questions of the witness. If a party is represented at the deposition by more than one lawyer, only one of those lawyers is permitted to ask questions of the deponent.

Questioning of a witness is always done by one lawyer at a time, although each lawyer may take more than one turn at questioning. The turns at questioning the witness will continue until lawyers for each of the parties indicate that they have no further questions.

In general, the term *direct examination* refers to testimony given by a witness in response to the party who calls the witness to testify. *Cross-examination* refers to questioning by an adverse party. There are rules that govern the manner in which lawyers can question witnesses at trial depending on whether the questioning is done on *direct* examination or *cross*-examination. In most instances, questions on direct examination tend to be more "friendly", whereas cross-examination is often more "grueling".

Objections

During the course of a deposition it is likely that one of the attorneys in attendance will have objections to questions asked of the witness by another attorney. Lawyers make objections when it appears that the question asked is or might be considered improper, confusing, misleading, or unanswerable. The purpose in making the objection at the time of the deposition is to preserve the right to have a judge rule on the propriety of the question at a later time if the need arises.

The practice for stating objections varies from state to state. In some jurisdictions, both the manner of making and the content of objections are dictated by court rules. In other jurisdictions, there is little regulation and objections tend to be lengthier and more frequently made. From the perspective of the deponent, it shouldn't make much difference what the practice is.

Once an objection is stated, the deponent will usually be instructed to go ahead and answer the question if he is able to. However, because objections can at times be lengthy and distracting, it is sometimes hard to remember the offending question. A request to repeat the question is perfectly acceptable.

Deposition Transcripts

In addition to the person who is testifying, known as the deponent, and the lawyers, a deposition is always attended by a certified court reporter. It is the court reporter's official responsibility to swear in the witness and stenographically record every question, answer, objection, and discussion during the deposition proceeding. The court reporter creates the official record of the proceeding, which consists of stenographic notes that are transcribed into a written, readable transcript. An original transcript of the proceeding is filed with the court prior to trial. Copies are made available to each party in the case who wants one.

Because a reporter's transcript becomes an official record in the case, each deponent is given the opportunity to review, correct if necessary, and sign the transcript before it is filed with the court. It is not required that a deponent "read and sign" his transcript, but usually it is a good idea to do so. If the deponent chooses not to read and sign the transcript, it is said that he has "waived signature".

Reasons you might have for *not* reading and signing the transcript include the following:

- the deposition proceeding was straightforward and brief;

- your testimony did not involve a significant issue in the case;

- you are unlikely to be called as a witness at trial;

- you believe you understood the questions and answered appropriately.

Reasons to read and sign the transcript include:

- you have not had your deposition taken before (or rarely have) and would like to review the transcript to see if you might learn from the experience, or improve your ability to testify (it is always interesting to see how questions and answers appear in print);

- the deposition proceeding was long and the questions were difficult;

- you are likely to be called to testify at trial and therefore will want to make sure your answers are clear and consistent;

- you believe that some of your answers were not clear, or that upon reflection or review, were incorrect or misleading;

- there were uncommon, technical, or key words, terms, or phrases used in your testimony that might have been misunderstood by the court reporter;

- it is recommended by the lawyer who asked you to testify.

If you decide to read and sign the transcript, you will be given a copy of the transcript, a correction page, and a signature page. The correction page is to enter changes in your testimony by referring to page and line numbers in the transcript. After making changes, the correction and signature pages are signed and returned to the court reporter.

It is important to remember that the correction page should not be used to re-state or edit your testimony. It is best to limit corrections to testimony that was given, taken, or transcribed in error. If you make a number of corrections it will have a negative impact on your credibility as a witness. This is because even though witnesses are permitted to make corrections, it is permissible for those changes to be shown to the jury. So, if it is shown that you repeatedly change (rather than truly correct) your deposition testimony, it casts doubt on your reliability as a witness.

Charges

It is expected that physicians will charge a reasonable fee for the time spent giving testimony in a deposition. Often, physicians charge on a per hour basis, with a minimum one hour fee. That means that if the deposition actually lasts forty-five minutes, the lawyer who requested the deposition still pays for the full hour. In order for a fee to be considered reasonable, it should bear some relation to what would normally be earned by the physician as if seeing patients during the same amount of time. In some jurisdictions there are constraints on the maximum amount that can be charged depending on the specialty training of the physician. See Chapter 12 for additional discussion of expert fees.

In order to be assured of payment for time spent in deposition some physicians ask that their charges be paid in advance based on an estimate of the expected duration of the deposition. An advantage to this approach is that you will know in advance of the deposition whether the attorney is going to take issue with your fee. If there is a problem or dispute about your charge, it can be addressed before the deposition. You may have bargaining power with a party who really wants your deposition.

Whether you can expect to be paid for the time spent preparing for the deposition depends on the type of witness you are. If you have been retained by a party to serve as an expert witness to testify on issues of standard of care, causation, damages, or an independent medical examination, it is likely that the party who has retained you will pay for the time spent preparing for the deposition. However, if your role in the case is as a treating physician and you have not been specially retained by one of the parties, usually the time you spend preparing cannot be charged to a party.

Sample Deposition Questions

Although the specific questions asked in each deposition will vary according to the facts of the case, there are some fairly standard approaches to questioning physician-deponents who are treating physician experts, independent medical exam (IME) physician experts, standard of care experts, or causation experts. The samples that follow are designed to provide a basic familiarity with routine questions. They are presented as an outline of questions and notes that a lawyer might follow.

One of the most common situations in which physicians are deposed is as the treating physician of a patient who has brought an injury claim against another arising out of an accident. The lawyer for the defendant will want to find out what the physician has to say about the patient-claimant's injuries and treatment.

Nearly all attorneys prepare notes from which they question a witness. Some attorneys script out lengthy, detailed questions; others jot down cryptic notes of topics to cover; most use an approach in between.

On the pages that follow are outlines of questions that might be followed by attorneys preparing to question medical witnesses in two different cases. First, is a defense attorney's examination of a plaintiff's treating physician in an automobile accident case (Figure 13-4). Second, is an outline of questions asked of a defendant's medical malpractice expert by a plaintiff's attorney (Figure 13-5).

```
DP of Dr. Allright
Polly Patient v. Fender Bender
3/3/03

1. State your name and professional address.

2. Introductions (explain who each lawyer represents).

3. Go through deposition ground rules (role of court
reporter, need verbal responses, answer clearly, no ges-
tures, talk one at a time, okay to take breaks, ask for
clarification if question is confusing, wait for objections,
answer unless told not to).

4.  Purpose of deposition is to ask questions about Polly
Patient who has brought a claim for injuries from acci-
dent with defendant Fender Bender. Establish that
witness has treated Polly Patient.

5. Please go through your professional education and
training, including medical school, residency, licensure,
and board certification.

6. Please summarize your professional activities, includ-
ing professional memberships, committees, publications,
etc.

7. Have you ever been deposed before - if so, how many
times; what types of cases?

8. How long have you know Polly Patient as a patient?

9. For what types of conditions have you treated her?

10. Did you know that she was involved in an automobile
accident on x/x/x? - how and when did you become
aware of that?

11. Did you provide treatment to Polly Patient for inju-
ries allegedly received in the accident?
```

Figure 13-4: Deposition of Treating Physician

12. What history did Polly provide about the accident and her alleged injuries?

13. What were your findings on x/x/x?

14. Go through each date of treatment post accident.

15. Did you ever treat Polly for any of these symptoms before the accident? If so, when?

16. For how long did you treat Polly for these symptoms?

17. In your opinion, was the accident of x/x/x the cause of the condition(s) you treated on x/x/x?

18. Has she completely recovered from those injuries? If not, when do you expect a full recovery?

19. If there is a permanent impairment, can you quantify the nature and extent of the impairment?

20. Do you expect that she will need further treatment in the future? If so, what?

21. What is the cost of the accident related treatment you have provided to date?

22. What is the estimated cost of future treatment, if any?

23. Ask to look at doctor's complete medical record. Get copy of chart.

24. What have you done to prepare for the deposition today?

25. Have you spoken to the patient or the patient's lawyer about this deposition? If so, when? What was discussed?

26. What are your charges for giving deposition testimony?

27. What are your charges for providing trial testimony?

Figure 13-4: continued from previous page

If you agree to be an expert to testify in a medical malpractice case regarding standard of care, causation, or damages, expect to be put through a very thorough deposition examination. If you are testifying for the plaintiff, the defense attorney will likely schedule your deposition once preliminary depositions of fact witnesses have been concluded. This is to give you an opportunity to review their deposition transcripts, which may contain facts or information upon which you will rely to render your opinions.

If you have been retained to testify on behalf of the defendant, the plaintiff's lawyer will want to take your deposition. In either situation, it is likely that the attorney who questions you is one who specializes in medical malpractice litigation. He or she is likely to have specialized training and experience and will be very well prepared.

In anticipation of taking the deposition of an opposing party's expert, the thoroughly prepared lawyer will have taken the time to understand the medicine involved. He will have read up on the anatomy, physiology, and pharmacology involved and it is likely that his expert witness will have given him a crash course as well. If you have written expert articles or books, he will have read them and may have copies at the deposition. He may have checked the state licensing board to see whether you have been subject to any disciplinary action. If you have testified in other depositions, he may have access to transcripts in advance of the deposition from networks of other lawyers.

Not all lawyers are skilled and well-prepared to take the depositions of medical malpractice expert witnesses. However, it is generally true that lawyers who specialize in medical malpractice litigation tend to be well-trained, experienced lawyers who excel at taking depositions. At times you may be surprised to see how well a malpractice specialist handles seemingly complex medical issues during questioning.

If you anticipate that you would like the professional challenge of serving as a medical malpractice expert, be ready to match wits and skills with lawyers who will try to test the limits of your medical knowledge and verbal jousting skills.

DP of Dr. Yardly
Paul Paine v. Dr. Dolittle
4/4/04

1. State your name and professional address; introductions; go through standard DP rules.

2. Dr., please give a summary of your professional education, training, and work experience.

3. You have been identified by Dr. Dolittle's attorney as an expert on the standard of care in this case – when were you first contacted about this case?; by whom?; what information were you given?; when did you agree to be an expert on his behalf?

4. Do you know the defendant, Dr. Dolittle? If so, what is your relationship? Do you ever socialize outside of a professional setting?

5. Have you served as expert witness in other cases? If so, give details about each time including names of parties, attorneys, whether you were deposed, whether case went to trial, and the subject of your opinions in the case.

6. Have you ever been sued for medical malpractice? If so, how many times? Provide details of each case including claims brought against you, name of plaintiff, names of attorneys, whether you were deposed, outcome of case, and names of experts who testified on your behalf.

7. Go through licensing file and ask about any complaints.

8. Are you board certified? When did you first obtain certification?

9. Have you written or published any articles? If so, when, where, what topics? (Ask for curriculum vitae.)

Figure 13-5: Deposition of Defense Standard of Care Expert

10. Describe in detail all materials you have been provided with in connection with this case, including, but not limited to, records, diagnostic studies, reports, articles, pleadings, deposition transcripts.

11. Who have you spoken to about this case? (defendant, defense counsel, colleagues, treating physicians?) For each conversation, provide the date it took place and details about what was discussed.

12. Have you conducted any research regarding issues in this case? If so, what, when, your findings?

13. Please provide a factual summary of the case as you understand it.

14. Please enumerate each and every expert opinion that you have formed regarding this case. (Go over each opinion in detail, including factual basis.)

15. What does the term "standard of care" mean to you?

16. Under the circumstances of this case, in your opinion what did the standard of care require a physician to do?

17. Is it your opinion that Dr. Dolittle complied with the standard of care in every respect in this case?

18. What have you charged for your work as an expert in this case? How many hours have you spent working on this case? Do you expect to do any additional work? If so, what?

19. Have you ever worked with Dr. Dolittle's attorney before? If so, how many times? What cases?

20. What do you charge to testify at trial?

Figure 13-5: continued

Testifying in Court

General Considerations

As when testifying in a deposition, the reasons a physician might be called to testify in a court or administrative hearing are many and varied. Physicians who work in specialties where patients are seen for the treatment of injuries are more likely than others to be called to testify in legal proceedings.

If you are asked or subpoened to testify in court, review the section on deposition testimony because the basics are the same. One of the most significant differences is that your court testimony is likely to be given in front of a judge and jury. These finders of fact will be evaluating not only *what* you say from the witness stand, but also *how* you say it. Your overall appearance, dress, demeanor, and manner of testifying will make an impression on jurors so it is best to see that it is a positive one.

The best way to prepare to testify in court is to review your deposition in the case if you gave one. If you did not, it is very likely that the attorney for the party who has asked you to appear in court will meet with you ahead of time to prepare for your testimony. The attorney should have a good idea of what to expect in the way of cross-examination and should spend the time to go over anticipated questions that may be tricky or challenging.

It is very important that you have a complete understanding of your role in the case because otherwise you may be blindsided at trial, which could leave you in a compromised position professionally. This is especially true if you are testifying as an expert in a medical malpractice case. If you are apprehensive because you do not think you have a good understanding of the case (or your role) ask the attorney who has requested your appearance to explain more about the case. Also, read Chapter 12 regarding experts.

There are occasions when you will not be able to, or perhaps will not want to, talk to the lawyer demanding your appearance. This situation may also arise when a physician is subpoened to appear and testify at trial by a party who does not want to or can't meet to prepare beforehand. Here are examples of why these situations arise:

> When a plaintiff brings a case against a hospital or HMO, under the law in most jurisdictions, his attorney is not permitted to speak to employees of the defendant hospital or HMO without the consent of the attorneys who represent the hospital or HMO. In the event that a physician-employee of the hospital or HMO is a witness who is favorable to the plaintiff, the plaintiff will want to have the physician testify at trial on his behalf. The plaintiff will likely subpoena the physician to testify at trial, but will not be able to meet or speak to the physician beforehand.

Keep in mind that in this type of case it is probable that the attorney for the hospital or HMO will meet with and prepare the physician-employee for his testimony, including a review of likely questions from the opposing attorney. Here is another possible situation:

> When a person brings a personal injury case against another person, as in an automobile accident case, the injured plaintiff may have received treatment from several different physicians either before or after the accident. If the defense attorney believes that a physician will testify in his client's favor (i.e., that the plaintiff's injuries were minimal), he will want to have that physician appear at trial. However, neither the defendant nor his attorney can talk to the physician about the plaintiff because to do so would violate the physician-patient privilege of the plaintiff.

In the latter case, the defendant will have to make arrangements for the physician to appear at trial without speaking him – either by subpoena or through the plaintiff. If the anticipated testimony of the doctor-witness will not be in favor of the plaintiff, his attorney may not meet and prepare the physician to testify at trial. The best the physician can do to prepare is to review his deposition, if one was given, and if not, to prepare by thoroughly reviewing the records.

Pretrial Preparation

For those who have never been in a courtroom, it can be a bit intimidating to walk in to one for the first time on one's way to the witness stand. To lessen the anxiety of testifying for the first time in an unfamiliar setting, you may want to consider a field trip to the courthouse in advance of your testimony. As an alternative, arrive early and allow some time to watch the proceedings if allowed. In most cases, you won't be permitted to watch in the courtroom of the case in which you are to testify. (This is based on a court rule that is designed to keep witnesses from being unduly influenced by hearing the testimony of other witnesses in the trial.)

Courtroom Personnel and Set Up

Not all courtrooms are exactly alike, but there are some standard conventions and roles that permit general instruction. The typical cadre of court personnel and their jobs include the following:

Judge – is the official presider over a trial whose job it is to control the proceedings and decide questions of law;

Clerk – is the official independent record keeper of the court who swears witnesses, marks and secures exhibits, and records the start and end of proceedings, including the appearances of witnesses, introduction of exhibits, and recesses;

Bailiff – is the court person who is entrusted with the care of the jurors during a trial; he assembles the jury members at the beginning of each session and conducts them to and from the jury deliberation room; he is the person to whom jurors communicate when they have a question and when they have concluded their deliberations;

Court reporter – is the stenographer who takes a verbatim record of the trial proceedings, including lawyer questions, witness answers, objections, and court rulings;

Jurors – are the triers of fact who decide each case based on the evidence presented during the trial proceedings.

Although the arrangement of courtrooms varies to some extent, the components shown in Figure 13-6 are nearly always present in some fashion. There are several aspects of courtroom arrangement that do not vary. Notice that the plaintiff's table is closest to the jury box. This is standard in every courtroom. Also, the defense counsel table is always on the other side of the plaintiff's table, farther away from the jury box. The number of jurors placed in the jury box can vary depending on the nature of the case being tried, but the jury box will always be on the side closest to the witness chair.

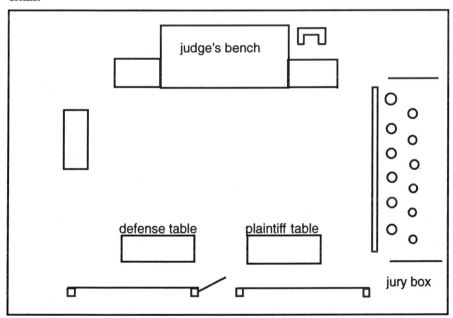

Figure 13-6: Courtroom Layout

Scheduling Trial Testimony

One of the most frustrating administrative tasks a trial lawyer has to deal with is scheduling trial witnesses. This is because it is very difficult to predict with real accuracy just how long direct, cross, and re-direct examinations will take for each witness. A lawyer may plan to call five witnesses on a particular day, allotting anticipated time for direct, cross, and re-direct examination of each witness. In actuality, he may only complete the testimony of three witnesses due to unexpected evidentiary problems, long cross examinations, or shortened court scheduling.

Often it is crucial to have testimony presented in a certain sequence so rather than bumping the two extra witnesses for later in the case, it will be tactically preferable to begin the next day with the unfinished witnesses. Of course, this creates a scheduling nightmare because all the remaining witnesses will need to be rescheduled (bumped). Even so, in the interest of presenting evidence in sequence, it is likely to be the more desirable course in most instances.

For trials that last more than a few weeks, preliminary witness schedule estimates can easily be off by days after the first week of trial. Sometimes, witnesses need to be re-scheduled more than once.

The point of this explanation here is that once the trial is underway you shouldn't be surprised to receive a very apologetic phone call from the lawyer's office advising you that your testimony time or date need to be rescheduled. Although it may be hard to adjust your patient schedule, sometimes it can't be helped.

To avoid or minimize the chances of rescheduling physicians' trial testimony, very often lawyers will try to schedule medical witnesses at the beginning of a morning or afternoon court session, or at the beginning of a trial week. If your work schedule is very tight and you have little or no scheduling flexibility, be sure to inform the lawyer who has scheduled your testimony. That way the lawyer can plan to make adjustments that don't involve re-scheduling your trial appearance.

Courtroom Procedure

When you arrive at the courthouse to testify as a trial witness you will probably have to wait outside the courtroom until you are actually called to testify. Once you are called to the witness stand you will first be directed to the courtroom clerk to be sworn as a trial witness. Then you will be directed to the witness chair. Take a moment to get comfortable. If you will be referring to notes, records, diagrams or charts, it is all right to set them out where they can be referenced as needed.

Normally, the attorney who has called you to testify will question you first on direct examination. Next, the opposing attorney will conduct a cross-examination. In most courts, the judge will then permit re-direct, but no further re-cross. In contrast to the procedure regarding deposition objections, trial objections will be ruled upon right away by the judge. If an attorney raises an objection to a question, wait for the judge to rule on the objection. Go ahead and answer questions when the objection is *overruled*; do not answer if an objection is *sustained*.

Impeachment

When used in relation to trial witnesses, the term *impeachment* generally refers to the process of adducing proof that any given witness is not worthy of the jury's trust. In other words, it is an effort on the part of a trial lawyer to discredit a witness so that the jury will not be persuaded by his testimony. A trial witness may be impeached on a critical aspect of his testimony, or on ancillary matters. Impeachment on ancillary matters can still be effective because it can cast a cloud of doubt in the mind of the fact finder about a witness's overall reliability.

One of the most common and effective means of impeaching a trial witness is to show inconsistencies or conflicts between his trial testimony and deposition testimony, entries in the records, statements, articles, or testimony given in another matter. Any physician who testifies frequently should be aware that testimony given in another case could be obtained by a resourceful lawyer and introduced in another case for purposes of impeachment. Physicians who have published papers, articles, chapters, or text-books, should remember that lawyers can impeach them if their testimony differs from what they have written in such documents.

The most often-used source of trial impeachment is one's deposition testimony given earlier in the same case. For this reason, one of the most important and effective ways to prepare to give trial testimony is to review the transcript of your deposition if you gave one. Be assured that the lawyer who is going to cross-examine you will prepare by summarizing your deposition testimony page by page. He is apt to ask you some of the same or similar questions that were asked of you in your deposition. Any time you give a different answer, he will probably point it out to the jury by referring and comparing to page and line numbers of your deposition testimony.

The best way to avoid being impeached is to be honest and well prepared each time you testify. As long as your answers are reasonably consistent, you will not have to worry about being impeached.

Next

If you have ever wondered what motivates some patients to sue their doctors, the next chapter will provide you with some insights. Although patients often have valid reasons for "suing" doctors, sometimes, patients are just plain mad.

FA**Q**:

1. My patient was injured in a car accident and has brought suit against the other driver. If I am subpoened to testify at a deposition or trial, can I testify about my patient without the patient's consent?

Generally, speaking, yes. The patient/plaintiff is presumed to have waived the privilege by putting his or her condition at issue in the case.

2. I like being an expert witness and I testify frequently. If I testify in a case differently from what I said in another case, can I be impeached?

If your testimony is drastically different without good reason, it is likely that you will lose credibility. However, if your testimony varies because the facts of the two cases are different, thereby yielding different conclusions or opinions, that should be pointed out to the questioning lawyer or jury, either by you or through questioning of the lawyer who called you to testify. Keep in mind, whether or not you are *impeached* is often in the eye of the beholder – some jurors may find your explanation credible, others may not.

3. I would like to review cases for lawyers to assess the merits of the case, but I don't like to testify. Can I do one without the other?

Yes. Lawyers often have the need for an "expert" review of a case without a commitment to testify – akin to a "curbside consult". As long as you and the lawyer have a clear understanding of what your expert role is, or will be, you should be able to provide a valuable service.

4. If I am asked to testify at trial and I show up at my scheduled time, but have to wait several hours before my one-hour testimony, how much should I charge for my time?

Often, physicians charge a half-day minimum amount, recognizing that they are likely to be called out of the office for longer than just their testimony time. It is recommended that you reach an agreement on charges in advance of your testimony. Whether you can actually be paid in advance of your testimony is not certain. Many lawyers prefer to avoid giving the opposing lawyer the opportunity to suggest that your testimony was "bought and paid for". Even if it is far from the truth, if you have been paid in advance of your testimony, rightly or wrongly, it could permit a juror to question your motive for testifying.

Whether you are paid in advance or not, expect to be questioned about what you are charging to appear at trial. For tactical reasons, you may be asked in a "friendly" manner on direct examination to deprive opposing counsel of the opportunity to bring up the subject of your compensation in an unfavorable light.

✦   ✦   ✦   ✦

14

WHY PATIENTS SUE DOCTORS - IMPROVE THE ODDS THAT YOUR'S WON'T

Thus, while lawyers may encourage or seek out cases, the contingency logic suggests that contingency fee lawyers should reject a large number of potential cases. Lawyers evaluate cases in terms of the risks involved and the potential returns associated with those risks. An attorney will reject cases that do not satisfy some risk/return criteria. Thus, contingency fee lawyers resemble portfolio managers, choosing to "invest" (their time) in risky cases hoping to obtain adequate or better returns.

81 JUDICATURE 22, *Contigency Fee Lawyers as Gatekeepers in the Civil Justice System*, Herbert M. Kritzer

Although patient claims are based on unique situations, there are patterns of complaints that emerge from broad reviews of complaints. This chapter looks at reasons commonly given by patients who want to sue their doctors. Most are variations of the same theme: "The doctor didn't care about me." Hopefully, by gaining some insight into what motivates patients to sue, physicians who need to can perhaps make minor adjustments in the way they approach their practice. Also presented is the case selection process that medical malpractice lawyers go through to decide whether a case is worth pursuing. Finally, statistics about medical malpractice claims are presented to put the realities of medical malpractice litigation in perspective.

Not all medical malpractice claims can be avoided. Some are brought for justifiable reasons – mistakes were made, someone was careless. However, more and more our culture appears to be one in which placing blame, finding fault, and denying personal responsibility are the prevailing societal sentiments. Because of this, there is more reason than ever to examine the "little things" that patients focus on in their health care expectations. Meeting those expectations can be difference between a disgruntled patient and a satisfied one.

Figure 14-1 lists reasons patients commonly give for wanting to sue their doctor. Some of the reasons listed may relate to valid reasons for subjecting a physician to a medical malpractice claim; importantly, many do not. For example, even though a patient may perceive that his doctor doesn't care about him, in fact, the doctor may provide standard or even superior medical care. On the other hand, the doctor who does not answer his patient's questions about treatment may not be obtaining informed consent, which would fairly provide a basis for a claim.

Profiles for physicians' claims experience can be broken down into three groups:

- **those whose conduct raises legitimate complaints**

- **those who get claims, but don't deserve to**

- **those who don't receive claims, and don't deserve to**

Physicians who actually provide substandard medical care cannot legitimately claim that resulting lawsuits against them are unjustified. There are other physicians who provide good medical care, but are often subject to unjustified patient claims. Yet, other physicians provide good care and are rarely faced with malpractice claims. It is those physicians in the middle group who can benefit significantly by making primarily minor adjustments in the way they practice. For even though a physician in the middle group may not deserve a particular complaint, and is ultimately vindicated by having a complaint dismissed, it is far better to avoid a baseless claim than to defend it and win. The time, effort, mental wear and tear, and cost of defending yourself, formally or informally, are not worth a good "won/lost" scorecard. Your overriding goal is not to win claims; it is to avoid them altogether.

Reasons Patients Give for Wanting To Sue Their Doctors

1. "My doctor/staff wouldn't return my phone calls."
2. "My doctor never told me he was going to do that."
3. "My doctor/staff wouldn't answer my questions."
4. "My doctor left for vacation and I didn't know who to turn to."
5. "My doctor didn't know what to do for me."
6. "My doctor/staff was rude to me."
7. "I don't think my doctor cared about me."
8. "I don't want this to happen to anyone else."
9. "I want the doctor to lose her license."
10. "The doctor billed me for things he didn't do."
11. "The doctor billed me for treatment that didn't help."
12. "I was billed for treatment I didn't expect."
13. "The doctor just gave up on me."
14. "I was treated like a number, not a person."
15. "The doctor didn't listen to what I was telling him."

Figure 14-1: Patient Complaints about Doctors

The key to minimizing patient complaints and claims is essentially a matter of meeting patient expectations. It sounds simple enough in theory, and for the most part, it is simple enough in practice. This is accomplished by:

- understanding and appreciating patient expectations

- meeting basic expectations

- avoiding the creation of expectations that you won't or can't meet

Patient Expectations

Consider that most patients have an expectation that physicians should be intelligent, caring, attentive, and devoted without distraction to their patients' well being. This expectation is probably influenced by a number of factors, including historical, cultural and social experience, and basic human idealism. Although the high esteem in which physicians are held has certainly been eroded somewhat in recent decades, patients still like to see their physicians as learned, caring, compassionate caregivers.

Patients do not always realize, or especially care, that their physicians have normal human limitations and are subject to life's typical pressures. Your patient probably doesn't think about the fact that your car gets flat tires just as easily as his; that you are at times up at home during the night with young or sick children; or that you are sometimes at the hospital all night with a patient emergency.

Patients Come First in Their Own Minds

Naturally, each patient believes his or her condition to be most important and deserving of due attention on the part of the physician. Remember that although you keep track of and treat many patients with many symptoms, for the most part, each patient thinks and worries only about his own symptoms. He will focus on those symptoms and on your treatment for them. He is not likely to forget from one visit to the next what you did, said, promised, or recommended. You, on the other hand, will have to rely on your record to do the same. This is one reason why good record keeping is an important tool for patient treatment and risk management.

Watch What You Say and How You Say It

Once you recognize that patients have certain expectations of physicians, it is important to take reasonable steps to meet those expectations. Often this means nothing more than adjusting what you say and don't say to patients. For instance, from a doctor's perspective there are times when different patients' care needs have to be prioritized.

It may be more important for you to consult a colleague about patient A's mysterious symptom presentation than to call patient B about a negative routine test result. Yet, it would usually be unwise and unnecessary to indicate to patient B that patient A's needs are more important and come first. If patient B calls to find out why she has not heard about her test, don't say or indicate that you were more concerned about patient A's more serious condition. Obviously, you and your staff should respond to patient B without referring to the needs of patient A's condition.

For similar reasons, office staff should be trained to avoid discussing the condition or treatment of one patient in front of other patients. To the extent possible, don't stand outside one patient's door and talk about the care of another. Orders, test results, and patient questions should be discussed out of the hearing of other patients. There may be instances when it is most efficient, practical, or necessary, to respond to phone calls about one patient while you are in a treatment room with another patient, but this practice should be kept to a minimum. Also, when speaking in front of other patients, remember not to violate patient confidentiality.

Return Phone Calls When Promised

You and your office should be scrupulous about returning phone calls. If your staff indicates to a patient that you will call back within a certain time, make sure you do so. If you cannot, have a staff member call and let the patient know why. Moreover, if you know you cannot return calls within 30 minutes, don't tell patients that you can.

In some non-urgent cases it may be reasonable and perfectly acceptable to a patient for you to return a phone call the next day. Yet, if your staff tells that patient to expect a call from you within 2 hours, and you don't call back until the next day, the patient would have a legitimate reason to be disappointed and perhaps annoyed. This is because your office unnecessarily created an expectation in the patient's mind, and then you didn't meet it. Of course, if a call back is indicated within 2 hours, or 10 minutes, make sure you follow through. The point is that you want to avoid creating expectations on the part of the patient that you cannot, or don't need to meet. The value of a sensible and sensitive employee to handle phone calls cannot be understated.

Keep Track of and Follow Through on Promises

If you say to a patient that you will do something on the next visit, make a note of it in the chart, and do it. If you don't do something that you said you would, be sure to explain why to the patient and document your thought process in the chart. If you are only considering a certain course of treatment, be very clear with the patient (and in the record) that it is a consideration and not a certainty.

Always keep in mind that if you document in the record that you are going to do something, and then don't, it might suggest to a subsequent fact finder that you omitted to do something you once thought important. This is why it is very important to explain to the patient and document in the chart your thought process whenever you decide upon a different plan of treatment.

If you create an expectation in the patient's mind, and don't meet it on a subsequent date, the patient may become disappointed. She will either think that you forgot to do something that you once thought was important, or she will think that you are not reliable because you did not do what you said you would. In either instance, your credibility as her physician has been damaged and her suspicions about your treatment have been raised. Both outcomes increase the risk having to defend your conduct.

Because every promise you make creates an expectation in the patient, the obvious corollary is that you should not make promises, or create expectations that you can't or won't keep. Even seemingly insignificant "promises" can lead to expectations on the part of patients. Anytime a statement or action on the part of the physician or his staff falls short of a patient's expectations, it gives rise to potential for disappointment. Patients who feel disappointed with their physicians are much less likely to excuse unexpected or poor treatment outcomes. Those are the patients who will be quicker to question whether they can "sue for their rights".

Use the Record to Help Meet Expectations

As you can see, it is to your advantage to use your medical record not only as a chronicle of the patient's care, but also as a tool to help you remember the patient, her condition, and the expectations that might have been created on previous encounters. You can then take steps to see to that you meet those expectations or to explain why you are not. Remember, though, it is simply best not to create unnecessary expectations in the first place.

Bedside Manner

Doctors who receive very few or no complaints from patients tend to be those who relate well to their patients. Interpersonal skills may have little to do with the technical practice of medicine, but it seems that they have very much to do with patient satisfaction. On the other hand, doctors who lack the skills, or for other reasons don't relate well to patients are more often subject to patient complaints. The complaints are most apt to be from patients who perceive (justly or not) that their physician, their physician's staff, or their physician group, doesn't appear to care about them or their needs. The patients' perceptions could be based on ongoing physician contacts, or a single encounter with the physician's office.

Quite often the caring attitude patients expect is associated with the concept of "bed-side manner". A physician's bedside manner is in great part influenced by one's personality. For some physicians being comforting and "warm" comes naturally. For others, it does not. Yet, even for those physicians who are not necessarily talkative or expressive, there are many ways to convey to patients that you do care about them.

Most importantly, whatever your innate demeanor, you should always be sincere in your approach to patients. Whether you are naturally outgoing, taciturn, or easy-going, doesn't necessarily matter. What really does matter is that whatever your natural personality, you ought to sincerely convey to the patient that you are striving to provide good care. If you truly care about your patient's wellbeing, and you should, the best way to show that is to ensure that you take enough time for them. More specifically, it is more a matter of quality rather than quantity of time.

Give Patients "Quality" Time

Although you may have a very busy schedule on a given day, each patient you see that day should feel that the time he has with you is "quality" time. Even if you are rushed, as you often will be, don't rush the patient. The patient should be made to feel that she has your undivided attention. Imagine what it is like to be the patient who has waited for an hour in your waiting room to finally see you, only to be hurried in and out of the exam. The patient is likely to feel that it was not worth the wait, and she will not be very forgiving of you. Whereas, if you give that same patient your undivided attention while she is with you, she is more likely to feel that the one-hour wait was worth it.

There is nothing wrong with explaining to a patient that you are running late because a particular (un-named) patient has had some unexpected, but important demands. That patient may be reassured to know that you would do the same for her if the need arose. On the other hand, don't use that as an excuse if it is not true. If you habitually over schedule patient appointments, it won't be long before your patients come to realize that this is a recurring theme rather than an occasional exception.

Complaints that Become Cases and those that Don't

Lawyers who handle medical malpractice cases as a regular part of their practice are able to offer some valuable insights on the question of why patients want to sue their doctors. Experienced medical malpractice lawyers could readily list the most common "complaints" of potential medical malpractice claimants. They would also tell you that many would-be claimants are often nothing more than disgruntled patients. It may be helpful to consider the typical analysis a plaintiff's medical malpractice lawyer goes through when evaluating a potential medical malpractice case.

Threshold Questions

Most experienced medical malpractice lawyers go through a fairly standard method of evaluating potential medical malpractice claims. The two threshold questions he will ask are:

> 1) does it *appear* that the doctor acted unreasonably according to medical standards of care; and
>
> 2) does it appear that the patient suffered some harm or injury as a result?

If it is obvious that the doctor did nothing wrong in terms of providing care, the matter will be rejected right away. Similarly, even if there is a strong suggestion that the doctor's care was substandard, if the patient suffered no harm as a result, there is no case. Most lawyers will tell a client right away that he believes a claim has no merit. Some may offer to refer the inquirer to another lawyer for a second opinion. It is not uncommon for lawyers to encounter patients who have "shopped" 'round and 'round" for an attorney who will take their cases. As a general rule though, lawyers shy away from lousy cases no matter how persistent the client.

Lawyers Reject the "Lousy" Cases Right Away

As mentioned previously, a surprisingly large number of patients who go to see a lawyer about suing their doctor do so because they are upset about matters that relate to poor patient management rather than to malpractice. Many patients think they can sue their doctor for not returning a phone call, for a billing misunderstanding, for "not seeming to care", or for not communicating well about treatment. Simply put, they are mad and want to do something about it.

Seasoned malpractice lawyers can readily spot a client who is simply "put out" by his doctor and attempt to persuade the would-be client that litigation is not an appropriate remedy. If it seems merited, the lawyer might also suggest that the patient file a complaint with the governing regulatory board. Such a complaint may ultimately have an impact the doctor's license, but will rarely yield a monetary recovery for the complaining patient other than a possible refund of some or all of the doctor's charges.

Preliminary Lawyer Interest – Is this be a Good Case?

If the threshold questions are answered in the affirmative, the next step for the lawyer will be to consider a more rigorous analysis of the merits of the potential claim. If there is an appearance of potentially substandard care, the lawyer will consult a person with medical knowledge for a formal or informal evaluation. The person consulted could be an in-house nurse consultant, a physician friend, a renowned expert in the field, or anyone else who is qualified to evaluate whether the doctor in question complied with the standard of medical care.

Sometimes several medical-legal consultations are sought if the conduct in question or the standard of care in question is subject to an honest difference of opinion.

This second level of screening will again weed out a large number of claims. Most plaintiff's lawyers rely very heavily on the formal or informal evaluations of consultants and will go no further with a case investigation unless a qualified expert opines that malpractice did, or arguably did, occur.

What are the Case Economics?

While evaluating the factual merits of a case, at the same time, the lawyer is evaluating the economics of the case. She is attempting to determine whether the potential dollar value of the harm to the patient is enough to justify the cost of bringing a suit, and the risk of losing the case. Because plaintiff's lawyers almost always take malpractice cases on a contingency fee basis, meaning they will only be paid if there is a recovery for the client, they are very cautious about taking a marginal case. No lawyer wants to put in scores of hours of work on a case that has a low likelihood of success. Even in those cases where liability can more than likely be established, if the dollar value of the case is low, the experienced malpractice lawyer will likely pass on the case.

The "Good" Malpractice Case

The type of case that every malpractice lawyer is willing to work hard on is one in which there is compelling evidence of substandard care on the part of the physician, and evidence that the substandard care caused significant demonstrable harm to the patient. It is worth it for the lawyer and his firm to commit the time and resources to a case that more than likely will generate a reasonable fee for the firm.

Often times, decisions to take or reject cases are not so clearly and easily made. In general, lawyers tend to be quite selective about the medical malpractice cases they are willing to take. This is because medical malpractice cases are usually complex, don't settle readily, and require a significant commitment of time, money, and other firm resources to pursue. Considering that the cost of taking poor cases is so great, lawyers are generally very cautious about accepting and pursuing medical malpractice cases.

Lawyers take the medical malpractice case selection process very seriously. Articles, book, chapters, and seminars all provide instruction telling lawyers who handle malpractice cases that the key is "selection, selection, selection".

The Good, the Bad, the Rejected

One simplified way to look at the universe of potential cases is on a continuum. On one end of the continuum of potential cases are those that are rejected because there is an absence of, or weak case of, substandard care with little or no harm to the patient. On the other end is the case with strong evidence of malpractice that produced significant harm to the patient. In the middle, are the majority of potential cases that require a lawyer's careful consideration of the overall likelihood of obtaining a successful result for the client.

Although the lawyer's selection/rejection process involves two main categories of variables, liability and damages, in actual practice, there are a number of more subtle factors that will also be considered. The lawyer will evaluate the potential parties: What kind of impression will the plaintiff make? Is she likeable and believable? Is the defendant doctor credible? Is there any indication that his records have been altered? Is he pleasant? Has he been sued before? What is his reputation among his peers?

The strength of one factor can influence the evaluation of the overall strength of the case. For instance, if the damages (dollar value) in a case are very high, a lawyer will be more willing to pursue a case where proof of the physician's malpractice is less convincing. It may be well worth it for the lawyer to commit his time and his firm's resources to the case, and take the risk of losing, as long as there is the potential for a large recovery on behalf of the patient. Likewise, even though the damages in a particular case may be small, if there is very clear evidence of substandard care, the risk of losing the case is low and it may make economic sense to proceed with the case. Different lawyers and firms may have different standards for accepting and rejecting cases. Some are more selective than others depending on firm resources and trial schedules. Even so, it is safe to say that even the busiest firm will likely make room for "the big case".

Figure 14-2 is a graphical depiction of the relative importance of both the liability (fault) and damages variables in evaluating the "strength" of a malpractice case.

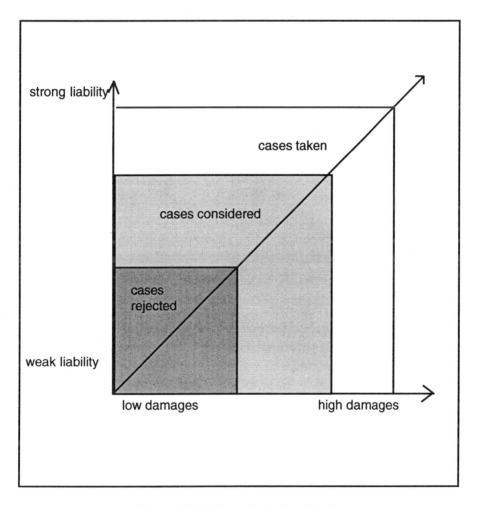

Figure 14-2: Case Selection Matrix

Is Lawsuit Phobia Justified?

For the most part, experienced medical malpractice lawyers do a fairly effective job of screening potential medical malpractice cases before they are even filed. It really is not in their economic interest to pursue groundless cases. Even so, there are the occasional horror stories that go around about outrageous cases that have been brought.

As with many "rumor mills", sometimes the outrageous nature of a case has been exaggerated or misunderstood. In other instances, the case may have had a very short life span in the court system, which did its job of weeding out frivolous cases. Admittedly though, there are instances of seemingly outlandish claims that somehow succeed. It is these truly rare cases that catch our attention. For some, these types of cases precipitate undue feelings of dread and fear of being the victim of a frivolous awsuit.

Are such feelings of gloom and doom justified? Probably not. As mentioned, notorious cases more often than not fit into the "oddball case" category - unusual cases that receive inordinate amounts of attention and notoriety, and become almost legendary within certain professional groups. Typically though, there was more to the "story" than what is rumored.

What is often unappreciated by those claiming or fearing that everyone is out to get a doctor, is that by one method or another an extremely high percentage of would-be claims are screened out of the system. Apart from those cases weeded out by plaintiff's lawyers, among the cases that are actually filed, a large majority do not make it to a jury trial. They are dismissed along the way. Just because a case is filed, doesn't mean it will progress to a trial.

The fact-finding function of the litigation process serves to screen out a number of unworthy cases. During the course of litigation, upon written request of the defense attorney, and briefing by both parties, a judge can make a preliminary determination as to whether there is a legal basis for maintaining a suit. If it appears that a lawsuit is unmeritorious, the judge is obligated to dismiss the case.

All of these different mechanisms in the process render the likelihood of pursuing a frivolous or specious case an exception rather than the rule. So, are there sensational cases that slip through the screening process? Undoubtedly, yes. Are they lurking behind every exam room? In reality, no.

Lawsuit Statistics

Having discussed why patients are often motivated to sue, what you can do to minimize unwarranted claims against you, and what makes a good case, a look at the big picture of medical malpractice claims helps put things in perspective. Data on medical negligence claims are kept by a number of different entities. One of the most comprehensive databases of medical malpractice statistics was collected by the Physician Insurers Association of America, reported in *Medical Malpractice Law*, September, 1988.

PIAA is a trade association of physician-owned or physician-controlled professional liability carriers – those that provide professional malpractice insurance to physicians. PIAA collated data reported by 18 insurers throughout the country over a 13 year period. Here are some results that might be of interest:

- Nearly 63% of cases brought are dropped or dismissed with no payout to the plaintiff.

- About 30% of cases brought are settled with a payout to the plaintiff.

- 5.4% of cases brought proceed to trial and result in a verdict for the defendant physician and no payout.

- 1.3% of cases brought proceed to trial result in a verdict (payout) for the plaintiff.

- Malpractice claims originate more than twice as often in hospitals as compared to practitioners' offices.

T

- Within hospitals, just over a third of claims arise in the operating room setting.

- The types of procedures most often giving rise to medical malpractice claims include: diagnostic interviews, evaluations, and consults; medical prescriptions; diagnostic radiology (excluding CT scans); joint surgery (excluding spinal fusion); and the absence of care.

It is interesting to see that of all the cases brought, less than 32% result in a payout to the plaintiff. Also, note that of those malpractice cases that proceed to trial, defense verdicts are returned nearly 5 times as often as verdicts for the plaintiff. To look at it another way, of all medical malpractice cases brought, just 1.3% result in a trial verdict or for the plaintiff. Keep in mind that this includes even very small awards to plaintiffs. Statistically speaking, physicians fare rather well overall in medical malpractice statistics.

Next

Not all medical negligences claims are avoidable. With that in mind, in the next chapter the stages of a medical malpractice case are covered from beginning to end.

FAQ:

1. Isn't it a good idea to overtreat patients to minimize the likelihood of claims against me?

If the term "overtreat" is used to mean the practice of providing treatment beyond what is truly necessary, the answer is "no". It is very tempting in these litigious times to practice what is considered by some to be *defensive medicine* — by ordering tests or referrals that aren't really indicated or necessary. The preferred approach is to practice medicine the common sense way – that is, by keeping the patient's best interest in mind, by giving the patient enough information to permit him to make informed decisions about his care, and by erring on the side of due caution. The legal yardstick by which your conduct will be measured is that of the "reasonable physician in the same or similar situation" standard. You will not be measured against the "ultra-conservative", "overly cautious", or "extremely aggressive" standard.

2. Why would a lawyer want to take an "iffy" case.

Most of the time, he wouldn't. For most lawyers, there are very few reasons to take difficult cases. A lawyer might take a difficult case with very serious damages, but would have little interest in taking a case of small economic value. There are some lawyers who will take "small" cases on principle, but they are very few in number. Another reason to take a difficult case is that it might bring notoriety to the lawyer. This happens rarely. For most lawyers, it is a bottom line type of analysis that determines what cases will be taken.

3. Based on news stories of outrageous verdicts it seems that the legal system is not working very well. Does the system work well?

This question would be answered differently by 10 different persons. It calls for a subjective assessment. However, most would admit that although our system of resolving disputes is probably the fairest in the world, it is not perfect. If you look at the statistics for medical malpractice claims, you might conclude that the system works pretty well. If you consider only media reports of sensational cases, your view of the system is likely to be jaundiced.

4. I sometimes have the sense that patients and lawyers are out to get doctors. Is this feeling justified?

Although there may be a few patients and a few lawyers who can't wait to file that next malpractice claim, most patients and lawyers are simply looking out for their own interest. Most potential cases are screened by lawyers who are trying to earn a living. Lawyers quickly learn that it is not profitable to take small or risky cases. Granted, we do live in a litigious culture but statistically speaking, medical malpractice cases are among those with lowest success rates for patients and their lawyers.

✦   ✦   ✦   ✦

15

A MEDICAL MALPRACTICE CASE FROM BEGINNING TO END

"We the jury, duly empaneled, upon our oaths do find for . . ."

The purpose of this chapter is to outline in chronological order the events of a medical malpractice case as it progresses from an initial claim through to a trial and appeal. A number of the concepts introduced and discussed throughout this book are mentioned here once again. It is hoped that seeing these concepts and terms in the context of a medical malpractice case will provide added understanding of their significance.

Overview

Although the facts of every medical negligence case are different, nearly all cases will progress through a fairly standard legal process. Figure 15-1 depicts the track that a typical case will take through litigation and trial. The various stages are then explained in greater detail.

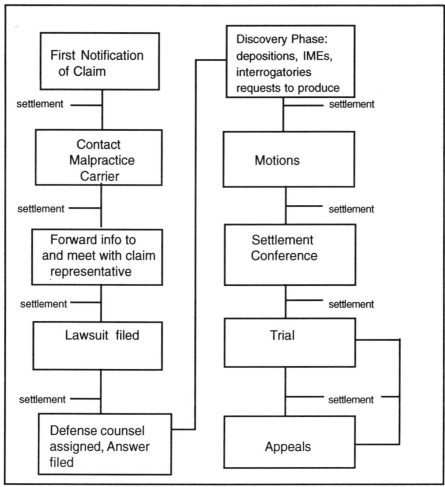

Figure 15-1: Litigation Process

Notification of Claim

The initial notification to a physician that a patient intends to bring a claim is often a letter from the patient's lawyer. The standard claim letter usually informs the physician that the lawyer has been retained to represent the patient in bringing a claim against the physician ". . . arising out of . . . such and such treatment . . ." See Figure 15-2. A typical letter will also ask that the physician forward a copy of the letter to his malpractice carrier for further handling.

Law Offices of Larry Lawyer
123 Complaint Court
Anchorage, Alaska 12345

Dear Doctor Cautious,

We have been retained to represent Phil Phinicky in connection with a medical negligence claim arising out of your treatment beginning on April 1, 1999. Please forward a copy of this letter to your malpractice insurance carrier at your earliest convenience.

Please have your insurance representative contact me so that we can discuss in detail the nature of this claim and the possibility of settlement.

Thank you for your cooperation and attention to this matter.

Sincerely,

Larry Lawyer

Figure 15-2: Claim Notification Letter

Although a claim notice letter from an attorney may be the first "official" notification of a claim to the physician, certain activity that precedes such a letter should alert the physician to the likelihood of a claim. Anytime a patient expresses dissatisfaction, verbal or written, with the care or treatment provided (or not provided), the physician should anticipate that the patient may attempt to bring a claim.

Whether or not a patient's dissatisfaction is justified, the physician should not be surprised by further action from such a patient. Action may take the form of demanding letters in which free services or refunds are requested, or letters in which threats of exposing or reporting the "incident" are made. It is also possible that the patient will ask for a copy of his records to have them reviewed by an attorney.

The physician's response in this situation should be carefully thought out. Although the knee jerk reaction may be to respond in kind with a "nasty" letter back to the patient, it is best not to do so. For requests for records, respond as you would ordinarily. Whether or not to respond to demanding and threatening letters may depend on the situation. If it is clear from the patient's letter that he is acting under a misunderstanding or misimpression, it may be all right to respond by calmly correcting the patient's misunderstanding. However, the best approach for the physician is to notify his malpractice carrier about the situation. He will then be advised on how to proceed. In any event, the physician should always be sure to keep copies of any letters from or to a patient.

It is very important to keep in mind that most malpractice policies require as a condition of coverage that prompt notification of claims be provided to the carrier. What this means is that if the physician does not provide timely notice of a claim, he may not be covered by the policy for that particular claim. What is considered to be "timely" is usually defined in the policy. Do not wait for a lawsuit to be filed before notifying your carrier. Waiting could not only decrease the opportunity for settling pre-suit, it could jeopardize your coverage as well. When in doubt, contact the carrier.

It is better to notify and have a false alarm than it is to not notify and have a wild fire.

Settlement

Notice in the overview diagram that between or at each stage of the malpractice case process, there is a *settlement* option. The diagram is attempting to depict the reality that malpractice cases can and do settle at every stage of the litigation process. Sometimes cases settle before suit is filed; a number settle as a result of formal and informal settlement conferences; at times cases settle during trial; and cases can even settle during or after an appeal.

Forward Claim to Insurance Carrier

In the event that you receive notice of a claim from or on behalf of a patient, contact your malpractice carrier right away. Your claim will be assigned to an experienced claims handler or adjuster. As mentioned previously, timely notification of a claim or potential claim is critically important to receiving all the benefits of your insurance protection. Moreover, you will receive advice and instruction on what to do, and what not to do, in connection with the patient's claim.

It is important to remember that your malpractice carrier and its employees are very experienced in handling and resolving claims. You should take some comfort in knowing that your interests will be well-served by your carrier and adjuster. To get the most out of your policy, be willing to develop a good working relationship with the carrier's representatives.

Provide Information to Medical Malpractice Carrier

Once you notify your carrier of a claim or potential claim, a claim representative will want information from you about the patient and the claim. It is likely that you will be asked to provide a complete copy of the chart and any other pertinent documents. You may also be asked to prepare a written summary detailing the events giving rise to the claim. Also, expect to have a face-to-face meeting with the claim representative to fill in details and answer questions.

The information you provide to the claim representative will be used to evaluate the claim. First, the representative will make an assessment of whether or not you are at fault, i.e., whether it is likely that you committed malpractice. Second, the claim representative will try to evaluate the nature and extent of the damages to the patient. If it appears to the adjuster that a jury is likely to conclude that the physician was negligent, he may try to settle the claim with the patient.

Some policies require that the physician provide consent to settle; others do not. If your policy requires that you give consent, the representative will not attempt to negotiate a settlement unless you have given consent. However, once consent has been provided, it is up to the insurance company to negotiate the amount of the settlement.

If it is clear from a review of the records and the information initially gathered that the physician was not negligent, then no settlement offers are likely to be made to the claimant by the claim representative. At that point, it is up to the patient to decide whether or not he wants to file a formal suit against the physician. If he does, the insurance company will retain a medical malpractice defense attorney to represent the physician.

Suit is Filed

Many would-be medical malpractice plaintiffs lose interest in pursuing a claim once the insurance company tells them that no settlement offers will be made. This is often the case with claimants who *are not* represented by counsel. For those claimants who have retained counsel, it is much more likely that they will proceed with a lawsuit. This frequently reflects the fact that an experienced malpractice lawyer has evaluated the case, and has already retained a supportive expert witness.

Sometimes the first notification of a claim a physician will receive is when he is formally served with a lawsuit by a process server. If this happens, be absolutely sure to contact your carrier at once and forward all the documents that you were served with. Once a defendant has been served with a lawsuit, certain court filing deadlines begin to run and the failure to meet those deadlines could result in loss of the case on a technicality rather than on the merits. Also, the failure to notify and forward documents to the carrier could result in a loss of malpractice insurance coverage for the claim.

Once the patient has filed suit, the case is said to be in "litigation". By virtue of filing the formal Complaint, the patient has become a "plaintiff", and the physician has become a "defendant". If there are multiple plaintiffs, each one will be identified in the caption of the case as a plaintiff. In some states it is standard practice to also name the spouse of the patient as a plaintiff, especially if consortium damages are claimed.

If there are multiple defendants, as there are likely to be, each co-defendant will also be identified in the caption, whether he or she is an individual, a partnership, or a corporate entity, such as a hospital or HMO. In many states, such as community property states, it is also common practice to name each defendant's spouse as a defendant as well. This is done so that assets of the marital community may be sought to satisfy a judgment if one is entered in favor of the plaintiff.

It is also common to see "John and Jane Does" and "Black and White Corporations" named as defendants in a medical malpractice suit. These are fictitious defendants whose identities may not be known by the plaintiff at the time of filing the suit. The use of fictitious defendants is often seen when a patient has been treated by a number of physicians, nurses, and others in a hospital. It may not be clear from the records which persons or entities were responsible for allegedly injuring a patient. If in the course of the discovery phase of the case it becomes clear, subject to court rules and approval, the plaintiff may want to substitute the subsequently identified defendant in place of the Doe defendant.

In Figure 15-3 a typical case caption is shown for a case brought against several individual physicians, a health care entity, and Doe defendants.

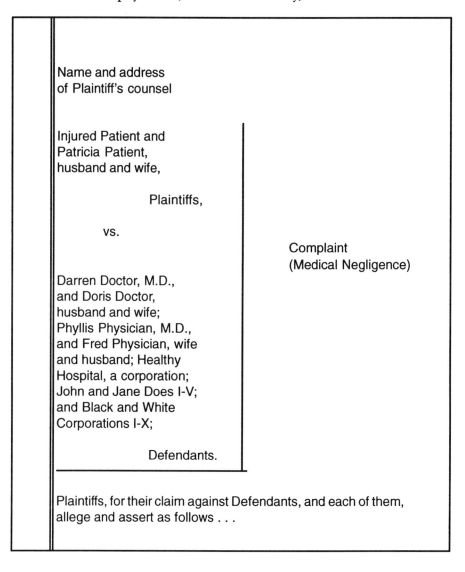

Name and address
of Plaintiff's counsel

Injured Patient and
Patricia Patient,
husband and wife,

        Plaintiffs,

  vs.

                            Complaint
                        (Medical Negligence)

Darren Doctor, M.D.,
and Doris Doctor,
husband and wife;
Phyllis Physician, M.D.,
and Fred Physician, wife
and husband; Healthy
Hospital, a corporation;
John and Jane Does I-V;
and Black and White
Corporations I-X;

        Defendants.

Plaintiffs, for their claim against Defendants, and each of them, allege and assert as follows . . .

Figure 15-3: Case Caption

Defense Counsel Assigned – Answer Filed

Once a medical malpractice case has been filed, your insurance company will select, retain, and pay for a malpractice defense attorney to represent you. (If, for some reason, you do not have coverage, you must hire and pay an attorney to represent you.) Once the attorney has been retained, he will want to review all pertinent documents, and will want to meet with you before preparing and filing an Answer on your behalf.

The Complaint is likely to allege certain facts and claims against you and your lawyer will need your assistance to determine how best to respond to each charge brought against you and other defendants. The Answer is your formal response to each allegation of the Complaint. Certain allegations may be admitted, such as those relating to background information, but most likely the allegations of malpractice will be denied.

Discovery Phase

Once the Complaint and Answer have been filed, both parties engage in a process to develop their own evidence and "discover" what they can about their opponent's case. The rules of engagement so to speak, vary from jurisdiction to jurisdiction. In many states, statutes and court rules require that each party disclose all theories, potential witnesses, and potential exhibits to the opposing party. A party's failure to make timely disclosures can lead to sanctions, including preclusion of claims and evidence, or monetary sanctions. In other states, the parties are obligated only to respond to requests for disclosure, rather than to affirmatively disclose information. Within such jurisdictions, for the most part, there is no obligation to disclose information in the absence of a request.

Interrogatories

Regardless of the jurisdiction, the methods by which the parties conduct *discovery* are fairly standard, and are used in a fairly standard sequence. Initially each side is likely to submit a set of written interrogatories to the opposing party. Interrogatories are written questions that are to be answered by a party. If the party is a corporation, such as a hospital, one or more representatives of the corporation may provide answers, but one corporate representative will ultimately verify that the answers are those of the corporation.

If you are a defendant in a medical malpractice case, expect your lawyer to contact you once the plaintiff has submitted interrogatories. Standard interrogatories typically include the following categories of questions:

- biographical questions about you

- questions about your education and training

- questions about witnesses and exhibits

- questions about your insurance

- questions about your defenses to the claims

- questions about your treatment of the plaintiff

When your attorney contacts you about the interrogatories you will probably be asked to answer those that you can, and to then meet to go over those remaining. Then all answers will be put into final form. Your lawyer will have submitted interrogatories to the plaintiff seeking similar types of information. Appendix 2 contains a sample set of medical malpractice interrogatories.

Requests for Production

Either along with interrogatories, or separately, any party may submit *a request for production* to another party. A request for production is a discovery tool that is used when a party wants an opposing party to produce tangible items for inspection or copying. Requests for production could include requests for originals or copies of such things as:

- all pertinent records • diagnostic studies

- pathology samples
- correspondence
- billing statements
- exhibits

- photographs
- policies and procedures
- materials given to experts
- curriculum vitae of experts

If the plaintiff submits a request for production, you may be asked to help obtain originals or copies of many of the requested items.

Depositions

Often before, but usually after interrogatories and requests for production have been propounded, it is likely that the parties will take depositions of the opposing parties, important factual witnesses, and the experts. The order of taking depositions is determined by the lawyers for the parties. There is no standard order, except that usually experts' depositions are taken after the parties and fact witnesses have been deposed. This is because the experts often rely on information that is developed in these other depositions.

For the medical malpractice defendant, being deposed by the plaintiff's attorney is a key event in the case. Yet most defendant physicians approach the deposition experience with a sense of dread and loathing. This is a completely understandable reaction. Going through a lawsuit, especially one in which one's professional competencies are called into question, is a very stressful and unsettling event.

It is at this stage of the litigation proceedings that defense counsel should take great pains to ensure that his physician-client fully understands the case and is well-prepared to be questioned by opposing counsel. If you are a medical malpractice defendant, expect your lawyer to sit down with you and prepare you for your deposition. Your lawyer is likely to be a skilled defense lawyer so you should take his counsel to heart. If you are at all uncomfortable before going in to the deposition, let him know so that useless anxiety can be avoided.

When you meet with your lawyer to prepare for your deposition, you should expect that he or she will do the following:

- explain the procedural aspects of the case to you in understandable terms

- go through each allegation brought against you, including its meaning and its probable merits

- discuss the strengths and weaknesses of the case

- discuss anticipated key questions

- explain the deposition procedure

- explain how the deposition transcript can be used at trial

- explain how to respond to questions

- go through all pertinent medical records, studies, and legal documents

- explain how to handle objections

You should not go into a deposition with the expectation that you will destroy the plaintiff's case by outperforming the plaintiff's attorney. This is an unwise strategy because it is unrealistic. The plaintiff's lawyer is likely to be skilled, prepared, and knowledgeable about the case, and in particular, knowledgeable about you and your care. A good plaintiff's lawyer will have pored over the records (perhaps with an expert), your licensing file, your answers to interrogatories, any articles you have written, and any depositions you might have given in other cases.

You and your lawyer should anticipate the preparation of the plaintiff's lawyer and thereby prepare for questioning in all the areas likely to be covered. Be sure to review the legal pleadings (Answer, answers to inter-rogatories, and responses to requests for production) as well as the medical documents in the case. If there are weaknesses in your case, anticipate that the plaintiff's lawyer will surely delve into aspects of vulnerability. Have your lawyer anticipate specific questions and prepare so that you are able to answer them.

As for the mechanics of answering deposition questions, it is very important that you listen closely to each question asked. Answer only what is asked. Generally, refrain from volunteering information. If you do not know the answer to a question, indicate that and explain why if appropriate. For instance, you may not know the answer to a question because you have not memorized the patient's chart. If you know where to find the answer, you may want to respond by saying that you are able to answer the question by referring to your chart. If you are asked a question to which you truly don't know the answer, simply state that you don't know the answer. Beware however, that it is foolish to use the "I don't know" response as an excuse for giving a damaging, yet honest answer. It will quickly become apparent if you consistently avoid answering the tough questions. You will lose credibility, which can do more damage to your case than providing honest yet unfavorable answers.

It is important for you to realize that the plaintiff's lawyer is assessing your demeanor during the deposition. If you are obnoxious, argumentative, or condescending in attitude, your professionalism and credibility will be called into question. Maintain a professional approach even if it appears that the plaintiff's lawyer is hostile. Although it is always appropriate to stand your ground, be sure to do so in a calm and collected way.

There is no doubt that being deposed as a medical malpractice defendant is a very unpleasant experience. But, if you are well-prepared and respond to questions sincerely, you will have done the best you can in mounting your defense. Remember, you cannot control the evidence in the case. The best you can do is be honest. Your lawyer and insurance carrier will provide you with the best defense possible based on all the evidence gathered.

Independent Medical Examinations

One of the other discovery tools sometimes used in medical malpractice cases is the *independent medical exam,* or *IME*. When the physical or mental condition of the plaintiff is an issue in a case, as it usually is, the defendant may request an IME for the purpose of evaluating the physical or mental status of the plaintiff. As an example, a defendant would be likely to request an IME of a plaintiff in a case where the plaintiff claimed that the defendant's negligence caused a physical limitation that prevented him from working at his occupation.

By use of the IME, a defense lawyer can arrange for the plaintiff to be "independently" tested and evaluated by a qualified expert. The expert who conducts the evaluation is required by court rule to provide a written summary or report of his findings and conclusions. Use of an IME allows the defense an opportunity to either confirm, but in most instances, rebut, a plaintiff's claim of injury or disability.

Motions

In essence, a *motion* is a petition to the court made by one or more of the parties to a lawsuit. Just as when following parliamentary procedure, motions are made to take a certain action. However, in litigation parties most often file *written* motions when they want the judge assigned to their case to take certain action with respect to the case. For instance, if a defendant (and his attorney) believe that all, or part of the suit filed against him is completely without merit, the attorney may file a motion asking the judge to dismiss those claims.

Although the flow chart places this section on **Motions** after the **Discovery Phase**, various types of motions can be, and often are, filed throughout the course of the litigation. Motions may be filed during the discovery phase if the parties disagree on the type or extent of the discovery the parties can conduct. To resolve the disputes that arise, one, or sometimes both of the parties may file motions with the court either asking permission to conduct certain discovery or asking that the opposing party be precluded from conducting certain discovery.

Each time a motion is filed by a party, the opposing party is nearly always given an opportunity to file a response. In most instances, the moving party is then given an opportunity to file a reply. The judge may rule based solely on the written briefs filed by the parties, or after a hearing at which the parties orally attempt to persuade the judge of the correctness of their positions.

Two of the most significant types of motions that are sometimes filed in cases are *motions to dismiss* and *motions for summary judgment*. In these motions, parties seek to persuade the judge to rule on an issue, claim, or the entire case, without waiting to submit the case to the jury. When a judge has granted a motion for summary judgment, it means that the judge concluded that based on undisputed facts, the law is clear as to which side should prevail. If a motion for summary judgment is denied, it usually means that there are material facts that are in dispute, or that based on the facts presented by the parties, it is not clear from the law which party should prevail.

Motions are often supported by factual evidence developed in the case and it is not unusual for attorneys to present facts to the court via affidavits of witnesses or parties. If you are asked to provide an affidavit, it will typically cover a very specific topic and your knowledge of it. The effect of providing a notarized affidavit is the same as if providing sworn testimony.

Settlement Conferences

With increasing frequency, jurisdictions are requiring that medical malpractice litigants (and in many instances litigants in all types of civil claims) participate in a formal settlement conference before proceeding to trial. The timing of the settlement conference varies, but most often they are scheduled by the court at a point when the parties have gathered enough information to evaluate the strengths and weaknesses of the case. In medical malpractice cases, this is often rather late in the process once the experts have been deposed.

Settlement Conference Goals

The decision of when to set a settlement conference is based on several competing factors. One of the goals of conducting a settlement conference is economically based – that is, to resolve the case early on in the process thereby saving money and resources of the litigants and the court. However, in complex cases, which medical negligence cases usually are, each of the parties needs to conduct enough discovery (interrogatories, IMEs, and depositions) to evaluate just how strong, or weak, his case is. That often means that nearly all of the discovery will be completed before the parties can realistically be prepared to discuss settlement. By that time, the goal of saving the time and cost of litigation has been nearly eclipsed by the parties' need for information.

Even though saving the cost of litigation is not often a practical goal for holding settlement conferences in medical malpractice cases, there are still several other goals that make settlement conferences worthwhile. First, there is the opportunity to save the time, effort, and cost of going through a trial. Second, there is the opportunity for certainty. Settlements are a sure thing, whereas going to trial has been likened by some to a form of legalized gambling.

Settlements are Final

Settlements are non-appealable and therefore provide each party with finality. At trial, there is no guarantee as to how or when a matter will be concluded. A successful outcome at trial nearly always means that the losing party will appeal. The appeals process can result in an adverse decision after several years of time and fees. In many instances, appellate courts can order that cases be retried. That may mean that the parties have to endure another several years of litigation and re-trial before resolving the case.

Settlement Conference Mechanics

As for the actual mechanics of a settlement conference, there are a number of variations, but some general comments apply. Most often, conferences are conducted by a judge other than the one who will preside at the trial. This is the preference of most trial judges, as they wish to avoid the appearance of improper influence and the chance that they may subconsciously exert any undue pressure on the parties.

In some cases, the parties are permitted to select a mutually agreeable third person, often a retired judge or respected lawyer, to conduct the settlement conference.

The attendance of all parties and their insurance representatives is required by most courts. It is thought that the efforts to settle will be more earnest if all parties are present. It also provides an opportunity for the judge to address his comments to both parties and it may be the first time since the litigation began that all parties meet face-to-face.

Should You Settle?

It is most likely that your malpractice carrier will decide whether to settle, and for how much. The adjusters know the legal climates (caliber of judges, juror values, and local attitudes) in the communities where cases are tried and have access to statistical data about the outcomes of similar cases. If the claim specialist recommends that you settle, you should give that opinion great weight. On the other hand, if your claim specialist recommends against settlement, you should consider that the recommendation is most likely the result of the collective wisdom of several experienced specialists (or even a committee) who work for your malpractice carrier.

Settlement "Psychology"

Lawyers, sociologists, psychologists, and others who study human behavior have all developed theories about the best way to encourage parties to settle their claims. Some recommend giving each side an opportunity to "present" their case to the other side in the form of a mini opening statement by the lawyers. Others recommend that the judge should take a very active role and point out to each side the strengths and weaknesses of the case. Some even suggest that soothing background music can put the parties in a conciliatory mood.

Whatever trend or school of thought the judge follows, the physician should view and attend the settlement conference as a good faith effort to see whether settlement is possible. Sometimes both parties have "dug in their heels" and know in advance that settlement is not possible. If so, this will quickly become apparent to the judge and the settlement conference will end shortly. Other times, the parties will have made some preliminary efforts to settle and may truly benefit from attending the settlement conference.

In some cases the extra "push" provided by a settlement judge is all it takes to make a case settle. It may be that the judge points out some weaknesses in the case that were not obvious to the party or his lawyer. Or it may that the opposing side has improved its settlement offer just enough to make it more reasonable to "meet half-way". For these, and a number of other reasons, settlement conferences are often successful at doing what they are designed to do – settling cases.

For those litigants who are unable to settle, or who do not want to settle, their cases will proceed to trial or in some jurisdictions, to a pre-trial screening method.

Medical Malpractice Case Screening

A number of jurisdictions have special procedural mechanisms to screen medical malpractice cases before they proceed to trial. In some states the screening procedures are mandatory; in others, they are optional. The most commonly seen screening methods are medical malpractice arbitrations, medical malpractice mediations, and medical liability review panels. The details of the various screening devices are set forth in Appendix 3.

Trial

The trial stage of litigation is accurately perceived by most as the pinnacle of the case (although it is not necessarily the end of the case). Stated poetically, it is the crucible in which the drama of the case will be played out. Going through a trial as a litigant is an exercise in tension and patience. It seems as though one is riding on an emotional roller coaster. More than likely you will feel "up" after your opening statement, "down" after your opponent's, "up" after direct examination of your witnesses, "down" after cross examination of their witnesses, and so on until closing arguments at the end of the case.

In addition, there will be rulings on major and minor objections, evidentiary matters, and motions throughout each day, and many are likely to produce an internal reaction - pleasant or unpleasant. In short, during the course of any given day at trial, a litigant and his lawyer are likely to experience euphoria at the "wins" and dismay at the "losses". A daily diet of such highs and lows over the course of several weeks (or more) can take its toll on even the most confident litigant.

For those whose exposure to trial proceedings comes from watching televised court cases – celebrated, mundane, or fictional – their view of how a typical trial proceeds may be jaundiced, inaccurate, or incomplete. Here is an overview of the components of a typical trial.

Pretrial Motions

Pretrial motions deal with those issues that the parties believe are critical to resolve before the start of the trial. Often such motions are brought to establish what can or cannot be introduced as evidence during the trial. It is likely that the judge will hear argument on the motions and decide the merits of each party's position at a pre-trial conference. In some ways, pretrial motions have the effect of fashioning the landscape for the trial. The claims, facts, issues, and evidence lists (witnesses and exhibits) are often pared or streamlined as a result of the judge's rulings on pretrial motions.

Pretrial Conference

Shortly before the start of trial, the judge and lawyers for all parties meet for the purpose of going over administrative matters – the judge's daily and weekly trial schedule, the anticipated length of the trial, time limits placed by the judge on the parties' presentations, and the judge's approach to jury selection. It is also the time when the judge rules on pretrial motions and any other outstanding disputes that must be decided before the start of trial.

Jury Selection

Once the ground rules for the trial have been established and all preliminary issues have been resolved, the first order of business is for the parties to select a jury. (As discussed a bit later, jurors are not actually "selected".) In order for a party to obtain a "fair and impartial jury of one's peers", courts provide panels of prospective jurors by summoning citizens who are qualified to sit as jurors.

Summoning Jurors

In most courts in which medical malpractice claims are tried, prospective jurors are summoned on a county-wide basis. On any given day, a court's jury commissioner will summon prospective jurors based on the number of trials scheduled to begin that day. In large urban court systems or in celebrated cases this could involve calling hundreds of citizens to appear in court. In the courts of smaller rural counties and in simple cases the need for veniremen (a rarely used term for prospective jurors) might be met by summoning a score of citizens from the corners of the county's boundaries.

Size of Jury

The size of the jury in a case will depend on several factors. The size of juries to be used in civil and criminal cases may differ, depending on the statutes and court rules of each state. It is not unusual for a jurisdiction to require eight jurors to sit on civil cases and twelve jurors for criminal cases. It is likely that the jury in a medical negligence case will consist of eight jurors. Depending on the length of a trial, alternate jurors will also be allowed to sit on the jury in the event that a regular juror cannot attend for the duration of the trial.

Jury Selection Process

It is somewhat of a misnomer to speak of juror "selection". It is actually more accurate to state that jurors for any given case are obtained by a process of "de-selection". That is to say that unwanted jurors are stricken, and those who remain will comprise the jury for a particular case. The *de-selection* of unsuitable jurors is accomplished after a process known as *voir dire*, which in French means "to speak the truth".

Voir Dire

Usually the start of a trial begins with a brief introduction of the case by the judge or lawyers to the panel of prospective jurors. A voir dire examination is then conducted by the judge, and if permitted, the lawyers for each party may follow up with questioning of the panel as a whole or of individual veniremen. Beginning with voir dire, and throughout the trial, the parties take turns at everything, with the plaintiff always going first. Thus, the plaintiff will conduct voir dire first, will make an opening statement first, will present witnesses first, and will make closing argument first at the end of the trial.

In theory, the purpose of voir dire is to identify jurors who are unsuited to sit on a particular case because of bias, or the potential for bias. In practice, each party attempts to identify and retain jurors who will be favorably inclined to his position in the case. Juror attitudes and biases are determined through questioning designed to reveal (directly or indirectly) how jurors are likely to react to certain issues or facts in the case. Consultants are often used to assist in "reading" jurors and their attitudes.

Those panelists who have either an obvious bias, or a valid reason for being unable to participate, will be excused by the judge. All who remain are subject to further questioning by the judge and/or lawyers. At the conclusion of voir dire, each of the parties will have in some fashion "rated" the prospective jurors as being favorable, unfavorable, or somewhere in between. This rating comes in to play when the parties take turns exercising "strikes" on veniremen they do not want to sit on their jury.

The process of eliminating unwanted jurors is achieved by having the parties take turns exercising their allotted strikes. Out of the presence of the jury, the plaintiff's lawyer is given a list of the eligible jurors, a strike is exercised, and the list is passed to the defendant's lawyer. The defense lawyer then reviews the list, strikes a name off the list of those remaining, and then passes the list back to the plaintiff's lawyer. Once the lawyers have used their pre-determined allotment of strikes, the number of jurors remaining equals the number of trial jurors plus the alternates.

Assuming that each party is given five strikes, in order to end up with a jury of eight plus two alternates, there must be *at least* twenty veniremen on the final panel [20 − 10 (5 plaintiff strikes and 5 defendant strikes)]; 10 = 8 jurors plus two alternates).

The end result of the strike process is that the parties tend to eliminate panelists who are obviously extreme in terms of their desirability as jurors. As might be expected, a person thought to be a "good" plaintiff's juror, is likely to have been rated "bad" by the defense, and will therefore will be struck by the defense. The plaintiff likewise often strikes those jurors most desired by the defense. The remaining panelists (eight plus the alternates) are usually those whom both sides had the least strenuous objections to. Keep in mind however that lawyers and their consultants often "guess wrong" about juror attitudes. Lawyers are sometimes quite surprised when they talk to jurors at the end of a case and find out how wrong they were.

The process of voir dire and "jury selection" can take as little as an hour or as much as several days, depending on the complexities of a case. In most instances, voir dire and jury selection are accomplished in less than a day.

Opening Statements

Once the jurors have been seated and sworn in, the lawyers for each of the parties are permitted to make opening statements. The theoretical purpose of an opening statement is to introduce one's side of the case to the jury – that is, to describe the claims, defenses, the evidence (witness testimony and exhibits) and "what the lawyers believe the evidence will show". Strictly speaking, lawyers are not permitted to "argue" their case during opening statements. In practice, lawyers make an effort to be as persuasive as they possibly can be in describing the strengths of their case and the weaknesses of their adversary's.

The length of an opening statement varies with each case and each lawyer. Generally though, the longer the trial, the longer the time needed to describe the anticipated evidence and its significance in the case. Some trial attorneys have been known to use the "hour/week" standard. That means that for every week of expected trial time it will require approximately an hour of time in opening statement. Thus, in a trial expected to last two weeks, one lawyer's opening statement may last approximately two hours.

In some cases the length of opening statements is limited by judicially imposed restrictions. Some judges very actively control the "scheduling" of a trial by allotting a certain amount of time not only for opening statement, but also for presentation of each party's entire case.

Plaintiff's Case in Chief

At the conclusion of opening statements, the plaintiff's case begins with the calling of the first witness. Generally, for each witness called in the plaintiff's case, the plaintiff's lawyer will conduct a direct examination, followed by cross-examination by each of the defense lawyers. The plaintiff's lawyer may then follow up with re-direct.

The presentation of the plaintiff's case consists of the testimony of witnesses and the introduction of exhibits. Because the plaintiff has the "burden of proof", he or she is obligated to present certain types of evidence in order to proceed with the case. The failure to present required evidence will likely prompt the defense lawyer to make a motion for directed verdict. If in fact, essential evidence has not been presented by the conclusion of the plaintiff's case in chief, the judge will grant a motion for directed verdict in favor of the defense.

In every medical malpractice case, the standard by which the defendant's conduct will be measured is known as the "standard of care". Failure to meet or comply with the standard of care is deemed malpractice, or medical negligence. This element of proof must be established by expert testimony.

The term "standard of care" refers to the level or type of care required or expected of a reasonable physician in the same or similar situation. The actual standard of care at issue in each case will vary from case to case depending on the facts and situation of each case. In order to satisfy his burden of proof in a medical negligence case, the plaintiff must adduce evidence at trial from an expert who must:

- be qualified to testify about the standard of care applicable to the defendant

- testify what the standard of care actually required the defendant to do

- testify that the defendant did not comply with the standard of care

Another aspect of the plaintiff's burden of proof is the requirement that he or she present *competent* evidence that the defendant's deviation from the standard of care *caused* injury to the plaintiff. If it appears from the evidence that the plaintiff's condition was caused by something other than the defendant's negligence, the plaintiff's claim will fail. It is not unusual to see medical negligence cases where the issue of causation is *the* pivotal issue in the case. In those cases, the parties are likely to present expert testimony to explain how particular negligent conduct either caused or did not cause the plaintiff's injury. In some cases negligence is admitted, and the key defense is that the negligence did not cause plaintiff any harm.

"Burden of Proof" Equals Burden of Persuasion

The burden of proof in civil cases differs from the burden of proof in criminal cases. In criminal cases the state must prove its allegations against the defendant "beyond a reasonable doubt". That means that jurors must convict a criminal defendant if they have no reasonable doubt about the truth of the state's allegations.

In civil cases, the plaintiff's burden is to prove that his allegations are more probably true than not true. Many trial lawyers explain this burden by referring to an evenly balanced scale. If the evidence presented by the plaintiff tips the scale ever so slightly in favor of the plaintiff, he has met his burden of proof. Thus, to find in favor of the plaintiff in a civil case, a juror must be persuaded by the evidence that the plaintiff's claims are more probably true than not.

Defendant's Case in Chief

Once the plaintiff has "rested", each defendant presents his case in turn. A defendant does not have a burden of proof. This means that he or she is not *required* to present any particular types of evidence. However, it is usual for a defendant to call witnesses and introduce exhibits that cast doubt on the credibility of the plaintiff's claims, or otherwise support his defense.

Plaintiff's Rebuttal Case

At the conclusion of the defendant's case, the plaintiff has the option to present rebuttal evidence as long as it is limited to rebutting evidence presented by a defendant. The plaintiff cannot introduce evidence totally unrelated to testimony or exhibits presented in the defendant's case.

Closing Arguments

At the conclusion of the presentation of evidence by both sides, the lawyers are permitted to present their "arguments" to the jury about what the evidence has shown. In addition to reviewing the testimony of the witnesses and the significance of the exhibits, the plaintiff's lawyer will "ask" the jury to make a monetary award to compensate the plaintiff for her damages. There could be several categories of damages, such as:

- past and future pain and suffering
- loss of earnings
- past and future medical expenses
- punitive damages

The defense attorney will also outline the evidence, and "argue" to the jury why the plaintiff's claims should rejected. In cases where liability is disputed, the defense lawyer will attempt to persuade the jury that the evidence compels a complete defense verdict. In some cases where the fault of a defendant is conceded, the defense lawyer will argue that the damages claimed by the plaintiff are unsupported by the evidence. The defense lawyer will argue for a much lower amount, and may suggest a figure to counter the plaintiff's demand.

After the defendant's closing argument the plaintiff is permitted to make a final closing argument to rebut arguments raised by defense counsel. No new arguments are to be made.

Importance of Opening Statements and Closing Arguments

Closing arguments, like opening statements, are important for several reasons. Primarily, they are opportunities for the lawyers to present their cases in an organized, coherent fashion. Due to scheduling constraints of witnesses, trial strategies, or both, the actual presentation of evidence is often not chronological or complete. It may take the testimony of several witnesses testifying on different days, or during different weeks, to establish a key element of a case. The lawyers' statements and arguments are designed to pull together bits of evidence that may have been presented in piecemeal fashion throughout the case.

Lawyers often refer to their case as a puzzle that is built piece by piece throughout the case. They tell jurors that the testimony of each witness and introduction of each exhibit represent a piece of the puzzle, that may not become clear until all the pieces have been put together at the end of the case. In opening statements lawyers attempt to give a preview of the completed puzzle. In closing arguments lawyers explain the meaning of the puzzle and how the pieces fit together – or a defendant may argue that metaphorical pieces are missing or don't fit together.

As an aside, remember to keep straight the difference between opening statements (given at the beginning of a case) and closing arguments (given at the conclusion of the case). Despite frequent confusion of the two by those in the media, they are not interchangeable. You may really impress your trial lawyer friends if you remember that the plaintiff's arguments at the end of the case are referred to as opening and closing *arguments*.

Jury Instructions and Deliberations

When the lawyers have concluded their closing arguments the trial judge "instructs" the jurors on the law they are to apply in the case. The jury instructions used in a case are determined by the judge based on the type of case and particular issues raised. Each party may submit proposed jury instructions on issues presented in the case, but it is the judge who actually decides how the jury will be instructed.

There are standard jury instructions, and those that vary depending on the issues in the case. Essentially, the instructions explain:

- which party has the burden of proof

- what the burden of proof is

- the number of claims of each party

- the requirements of proving each claim or defense

- the law that pertains to any particular issue

- the types of damages that may be awarded, if any

- the forms of verdicts that may be used

After the judge has instructed the jury, the bailiff conducts the jurors to the room where they will deliberate. The court clerk transfers all the exhibits that have been admitted into evidence to the jury room. At that point the jurors begin their deliberations. Usually, one of the first tasks addressed by the jurors is the selection of a foreperson. The foreperson is often seen by other jurors as a leader who moderates the deliberations.

All the deliberations of the jurors are confidential. No one is permitted in the jury deliberation room other than the jurors. If a juror has a question or concern, it is communicated in writing to the bailiff, who then conveys it to the judge. If appropriate, the judge will respond to the inquiry in writing after consulting the lawyers.

The duration of juror deliberations is unpredictable. Sometimes juries can reach a verdict in less than an hour. In some cases it may take days of deliberations. For litigants and their lawyers it is a nerve-wracking experience to wait for a verdict.

"We Have a Verdict"

When a jury has reached a verdict the lawyers and parties are notified and may return to court to "take the verdict". When the judge, parties, and lawyers have assembled in the courtroom, the jury is brought from the jury room to the courtroom by the bailiff. The judge will ask the foreman, whose identity may be unknown until then, whether they have reached a verdict. If the foreman responds in the affirmative, the bailiff brings the verdict form from the foreman to the judge, who reads it silently. The judge then hands the verdict to the clerk to read aloud. This is an agonizing moment of truth for the parties and lawyers – one that has been anxiously and nervously awaited.

As the verdict is announced, the parties transform into victor and vanquished, with all their attendant emotions. One side will feel completely vindicated; the other will feel utter disappointment. In an ordeal of "ups and downs", each side has at this point experienced the ultimate "up" or "down".

Post-trial Motions

Although many believe that the end of a trial marks the end of a case, in practice it rarely does. It is not unusual for a party who is dissatisfied with the outcome of a trial to file motions with the judge asking for relief from the verdict. In response to post trial motions, the judge may adjust the amount of the verdict (rarely), grant a new trial (rarely), or deny the motions (frequently).

Appeals

In any case of consequence, it is likely that the losing party will appeal the outcome. In medical malpractice cases, which are almost always cases of consequences, it is usually a given that the losing party will file an appeal. As noted in Chapter 2, the basis for filing an appeal is error in the trial court proceeding. A party who files an appeal must demonstrate in a brief to the appellate court that the trial judge misapplied the law, erroneously admitted or excluded certain evidence, or erroneously instructed the jury on the law.

It would not be uncommon for an appeal to an intermediate review court to take several years from beginning to end — written briefing, oral argument, appellate decision. Once a decision on the appeal has finally been reached, the parties find out whether the intermediate appellate court decided to uphold or overturn the verdict, in whole or in part.

Any party who "loses" on appeal at the intermediate level may then appeal to the highest state court of review, referred to in most states as state supreme court. The higher court may accept or decline review of the case depending on its interest in re-deciding the issues presented in the appeal. If the appeal is accepted, it may be several years again before a decision is issued. If the trial court verdict is ultimately upheld, the case is finally over. If the trial court verdict is ultimately overturned, the parties head back to trial court for a new trial.

Because the appellate process is lengthy and the outcome is unpredictable, parties often become motivated to settle during a pending appeal. Often a settlement is reached when the winning party agrees to accept a discounted amount of the jury verdict. Just how much of a discount it is will depend on the negotiating strengths of the parties, which is usually a function of the relative strength of their positions on the appeal. This is more apparent in some cases than in others.

Next

It is important for physicians to understand the basics of their medical malpractice insurance coverage. In the next chapter you will learn what types of protections and benefits are provided by your policy.

FAQ:

1. May interrogatories be submitted to anyone in the case?

A party may only submit interrogatories to an opposing party. They cannot be submitted to witnesses or potential witnesses.

2. If I am sued and the case goes to trial do I have to be present during the entire trial?

It is very likely that your lawyer will want you to be present during the entire trial. Your attendance at the trial impresses upon the jury the fact that you take the case, and allegations against you very seriously. It is important to remember that the jurors are required to take time away from their work and families in order to listen to and decide your case.

3. If I attend a settlement conference but have no interest in settling, can the judge make me settle?

No. Although some judges may try to exert pressure to settle, they cannot (and should not try to) make you settle. Keep in mind however that your professional malpractice carrier, through its claim representative may decide to settle the claim brought against you. So, unless your policy has a "consent to settle" clause, it is up to the carrier to decide when to settle and how much to pay. See further discussion on this in the next chapter.

4. When a case goes to trial, who decides the amount of an award, if any?

It depends on whether the trial is a jury trial or a bench trial. If all parties agree to have their case decided by a judge, the case will be presented to and decided by a judge. The judge will decide all issues in the case including questions or law, questions of fact, liability, and damages. In a jury trial, questions of law are decided by the judge; questions of fact are decided by the jury and it is the jury that will decide issues of liability and damages, if any.

5. What causes a mistrial?

A mistrial can be declared by a judge for a variety of reasons. Usually mistrials are declared based on the misconduct of a witness, lawyer, or juror that causes the proceeding to be unfair. In the event that a mistrial is declared, the case is re-scheduled and tried again.

✦　✦　✦　✦

16

MEDICAL MALPRACTICE INSURANCE BASICS

In interpreting an insurance policy we apply the general principle that doubts as to meaning must be resolved against the insurer and that any exception to the performance of the basic underlying obligation must be so stated as clearly to apprise the insured of its effect.

Gray v. Zurich Insurance Company, 65 Cal.2d 263, 269, 419 P.2d 168, 171 (1966)

Professional malpractice insurance for physicians typically protects against several types of liabilities and risks that may be encountered during the course of one's practice. It is commonly understood that malpractice insurance provides protection against liability for medical malpractice claims. In addition, most policies typically provide other benefits that are important for the practitioner to understand. Basic policy coverages, typical exclusions, and important terms are outlined in this chapter.

Nature and Purpose of Insurance

Stated simply, the function of insurance is to spread risk among groups or pools of similarly situated people — people who are engaged in like activities with an interest to protect, or those with a similar property interest to protect. Automobile liability insurance spreads the risk, or cost of liability for damage and injury among automobile drivers. Property insurance spreads the risk of damage to property among property owners. Life insurance spreads the risk of financial consequences from death among persons of similar age. Professional malpractice insurance primarily protects professionals – lawyers, physicians, accountants, and others – from the consequences of liability for malpractice.

The basic premise upon which insurance operates is that premiums are collected from a group at large, to pay for the liabilities of a few in the group. People and entities need and purchase insurance protection when they do not have absolute control over whether or not they will be among the "few". When it is impossible as a practical matter to guarantee that one will not be subject to any given risk or liability, insurance may be purchased to protect against that risk or liability. The premiums paid by all those within the defined interest group are used to fund payments for those within the group who actually experience the risk protected against.

Since any given property owner cannot be absolutely certain that he will never suffer property damage, he might be inclined to protect his interest in a property by purchasing insurance. In the same way, it is sensible for automobile drivers to purchase auto insurance because no driver can say with certainty that he will never suffer damage to his car or cause an accident. Even though a driver can drive and operate his vehicle in a way so as to minimize the likelihood of causing an accident, even the best driver can at times be inattentive, careless, or otherwise suffer a lapse of judgment. To protect against the potentially devastating financial consequences of such an event, most drivers appreciate the benefit of insurance protection. Physicians need malpractice insurance primarily to protect against the risk of being careless, and against the risk of claims by patients.

Medical Malpractice Insurance Policy Basics

It is helpful to remember that your medical malpractice insurance policy is a contract. In order to receive the benefits of the contract, each party (physician and insurer) agrees to perform certain obligations. For instance, the physician agrees to submit an honest application and pay premiums; in return, the insurer agrees to provide a policy of insurance. The policy itself is the contract that sets forth the obligations and promises of each party to the contract. It defines the meaning of certain terms and phrases in order to avoid misunderstandings. It sets forth the coverages that are provided, and it sets forth exclusions to coverages. Insurers make every effort to avoid ambiguities in policy language because under standard insurance law, in most instances courts will interpret ambiguities in favor of insureds.

Next is a look at the standard features and sections of a professional liability insurance contract.

Declarations Page

Attached to or provided with every malpractice policy is a one or two page document that provides important information about the coverages provided to a specific insured. This is referred to as the *declarations page*. A standard declarations page is represented in Figure 16-1. Declaration pages will vary from insured to insured, along with standard insurance policy language. In other words, variations between similar type insureds are reflected in the declaration page rather than in the standard policy language.

The declarations page is very useful because it provides a summary of information specific to your particular policy. It shows who the named insured is (you), the effective dates of your policy (start and end dates), the types of coverage you may have, and the dollar amounts, or limits, of each type of coverage. The declarations page is where you will want to look for this type of information because it does not typically appear in the policy portion itself.

DECLARATIONS PAGE

Name and Address   Policy No.
of Insured Physician

Effective Date of Policy: Policy End Date:

Retroactive Date (if any):

Limits of Liability

Part I – Liability for Diagnosis and Treatment of Patients	
Each occurrence: $ x,xxx,xxx	Aggregate: $ x,xxx,xxx
Part II – Liability for: Injuries to Patients and Third Persons	
Each occurrence: $ xxx,xxx	Aggregate: $ xxx,xxx
Part III – Persons Physically Harmed by Operation of Premises	
Each occurrence: $xxx,xxx	Aggregate: $ xxx,xxx

Coverage Descriptions

Part I and II – type of specialty

Part III – location of professional premises

Insurance Company

_____
Company Representative

Figure 16-1: Policy Declaration Page

Although policy formats vary from insurer to insurer, most policies include fairly standard sections and terms:

Introduction or "Features"

Most policies include a section toward the beginning of the policy that describes important features of the policy and the layout or format of the policy. It may provide a narrative summary that describes the type of policy, important obligations of the insured under the policy, peculiar features of the policy, and what endorsements are available.

Definitions

Terms that have special or significant meanings are defined in the policy to minimize the opportunity for ambiguity. You may find that commonly understood terms have more unique meanings in the context of the policy. Some terms may be used more narrowly than the commonly understood meaning.

Insuring Agreements

For each type of coverage provided in a malpractice policy there will be a statement that specifies what benefits are provided under the policy. These statements are referred to as "insuring agreements". Two of the most common and important protections provided by standard malpractice insurance policies include:

- the insurer's promise to **defend** you in actions brought by your patients (defense)

- the insurer's promise to **pay** sums which you be come legally obligated to pay as damages to patients (indemnity).

If ever a malpractice claim is brought against you, these insuring agreements are the ones that will provide and pay for your defense, and pay any damage awards that are a result of settlement or trial.

Rights and Responsibilities

This type of section goes by various names or headings but essentially describes in detail the rights of the insurance company, the responsibilities of the insured, what conditions can affect the parties' rights and responsibilities, and how they are affected. Topics often covered in this section are:

- Expiration of coverage for non-payment of premiums

- Cancellation of the policy for good cause

- Circumstances that void coverage (material misrepresentations or omissions in the insurance application)

- Termination of coverage upon revocation or suspension of license

- Physician's duty to *promptly* report occurrences, claims, and suits

- Requirement of cooperation with defense counsel chosen by insurer

- Non-assignability of policy

- Eligibility to purchase tail coverage

- Relationship to other sources of coverage

- Explanations of limits of liability (per occurrence, aggregate)

- Exclusions from coverage

Policy Exclusions

The section of the policy that sets forth acts and events which are excluded from coverage (defense and indemnity) should be carefully read and contrasted with the insuring agreement portion of the policy. Read together, this should provide you with a fairly good understanding of what is, and is not, covered by your policy. There are several common exclusions that are especially important to note.

Malpractice policies do not provide coverage for you when you are acting outside the course and scope of your duties as a physician, or for your employees acting outside the course or scope of their employment. This means that a surgeon who negligently injures his pal with a knife while on a fishing trip will have a hard time persuading his malpractice carrier to defend or pay if the pal brings a claim against the surgeon.

Another important standard coverage exclusion relates to health care provided outside the state in which you are licensed and ordinarily practice. This exclusion typically applies *unless* there is an emergency situation, or you have prior written approval from your insurance carrier.

If you lecture, write professional articles or books, speak on radio or television broadcasts, or advertise with respect to your medical practice, chances are good that your standard malpractice policy will not apply to liabilities arising out of such activities. Keep in mind that if you lecture or write articles in which you give medical advice or recommend treatment that subjects you to a claim from an aggrieved listener or reader, your malpractice insurer is not likely to defend you against or pay damages on your behalf to the claimant.

Liability Limits

The terms "per occurrence" and "aggregate" that appear in the definition section are usually explained in more detail in the section on liability limits. Both terms also appear on the declarations page where corresponding dollar values are listed.

The term "per occurrence" limit refers to the maximum amount payable for each covered event or occurrence. "Occurrence" is usually construed to mean an event or related series of events that give rise to a single claim or suit. Most policies state that all damages arising from a continuing course of treatment, a series of related events, or repeated exposure to substantially the same general conditions arise from a single "occurrence".

The question of whether a series of arguably related events constitutes a single occurrence or separate occurrences has on occasion given rise to an insurance dispute between physician and insurer. In situations that can be argued either way, the insurer will want to take the position that related events are part of a single "occurrence" because the per occurrence limit of liability will apply to the series of related events. On the other hand, the physician is better off when each event is treated as a separate occurrence because then the per occurrence limit applies to each event. This means more protection against a claim with a high dollar value.

Consider a scenario in which a physician sees as a patient, a famous artist with classic symptoms of a disease that leads to blindness. The physician negligently fails to make the sight-saving diagnosis and sends the patient away. Six months later the patient returns, and again the physician neglects to make the obvious diagnosis. After another six months the patient is seen yet again and still the physician misses the diagnosis. Ultimately, the patient-artist succumbs to the disease and loses sight in both eyes. Thereafter the artist brings suit against the physician for his negligent treatment and seeks $1,500,000 in damages.

For the sake of our example, we will say that the physician has a malpractice policy with a per occurrence liability limit of $500,000. This means that the insurer will pay a maximum of $500,000 for each occurrence involving the physician. If the three visits of the artist to the physician are considered to be arising from a continuing course of treatment and therefore constitute a single "occurrence", then the maximum amount the malpractice insurer is obligated to pay under the policy is $500,000. In that event, the physician may be significantly under-insured for this particular claim. However, if the three different visits are viewed as being unrelated, and thus considered to be separate occurrences, the physician would have coverage of $500,000 for each occasion on which he negligently missed the diagnosis.

In actuality, the physician in this hypothetical case might have a difficult time convincing his insurer, or a judge, that the three separate visits should be viewed as separate occurrences. Since most policies make it fairly clear that a continuing course of treatment (non-treatment in this instance) is viewed under the policy as a single occurrence, the likelihood of successfully arguing that separate patient visits for the same condition or symptoms are *unrelated* is slim.

The term "aggregate" refers to the maximum amount the insurer will pay during the policy period regardless of the number of patients or persons who make claims or bring suits against you. Once the limit is reached, the insurer will not make any more payments on your behalf for that policy period. After the aggregate limit is reached, whether or not the insurer will continue to pay for defense costs depends on the type of policy.

Most policies state that defense costs will not be deducted from the limits of liability. However, under the terms of some policies, known as "wasting policies", the costs of providing a defense for claims are deducted from the liability limits. Because the defense costs in a case that proceeds through litigation can be significant, wasting policies often leave physicians with relatively low effective liability limits.

Defense attorneys who are hired to represent physicians by insurers that write wasting policies are often in the uncomfortable position of knowing that the more time and money spent defending the physician-client, the less money left under the policy to indemnify the client-physician. Such policies are uncommon, but you should make sure to read your policy to find out whether it is a wasting policy.

Consent to Settle

A provision somewhat unique to medical malpractice insurance policies, is known as a *consent to settle* clause. If this provision is found in one of the policy coverages (usually liability coverage relating to diagnosis and treatment of patients), then the insurer will not settle a claim on your behalf without your written consent. The insurer still controls the amount to be offered or paid under a settlement agreement. The physician's consent relates only to the question of whether or not to settle.

Once written consent to settle is provided by the physician, the insurer may negotiate and settle without further consent of the insured physician. The policy may except certain situations from the consent requirement, such as settlements after judgments or arbitration awards have been entered.

Defense of Claims under the Policy

In addition to the indemnity protection provided by malpractice insurance, one of the most important benefits your policy provides is the actual defense against liability asserted by your patients. What this means is that your insurer will both provide and pay for a defense against claims brought against you. As a practical matter this also means that your insurer will maintain most of the control over your legal defense. In fact, most policies state that the insurer has the right to control the physician's defense.

Insurer Controls Defense

Control is exercised by the insurance company in a number of ways. For instance, it is the insurer, not you, who selects your defense attorney in the event you need one. Even if your best friend is a premier lawyer, *you* will not be able to pick him or her to represent you under the policy.

Even though the malpractice lawyer is selected and paid for by the insurance company, the lawyer is ethically obligated to represent you, and to put your interests first and foremost. That means that even if there is a conflict between your best interest and the insurance company's best interest, the lawyer retained for you must represent your interest, and yours alone.

Most malpractice insurance companies have working relationships with lawyers and law firms that specialize in medical malpractice defense. Based on the particulars of your situation, the insurer will retain a lawyer or firm that it knows is qualified to handle your case.

Right to Retain Own Counsel

On the infrequent occasions when the physician's best interest and the insurance company's interest do not conform, the insurance company may retain its own separate counsel to represent its interest. The usual context in which the issue of separate counsel arises is when there is a dispute over interpretation of obligations or benefits due under the insurance contract (policy).

Keep in mind that even though the insurance company has the right to select your defense counsel under the policy, you are always free to consult or retain your own lawyer. If you do so, it will be at your own expense. If you do hire or consult your own personal lawyer, the insurance company is still obligated to pay for and provide you with a lawyer of its choice. It is not often that this situation occurs, but if you are ever in doubt about your rights under the insurance policy, you might consider the option of consulting a lawyer at your expense.

Insured's Duty of Cooperation

Assuming the more typical situation in which your interests are well represented by insurer selected counsel, most policies contain language requiring you to cooperate and assist in your defense. This usually means that if asked, you must help obtain evidence, assist in obtaining the attendance of witnesses, appear for a deposition, attend hearings, assist in settlement, and testify at trial. This also means that for occurrences covered under the policy, you are not permitted to provide information about the occurrence to anyone but your insurer and legal counsel. Nor are you allowed to volunteer to make any payment in settlement of a covered claim or otherwise assume any obligations.

Not only because policy language precludes it, but also as a practical matter, it is critically important that you never withhold or hide pertinent information or records from your carrier or lawyer. If you have done something, or written something, or failed to do something that puts you in a bad light (whether deserved or not), overcome the temptation to hide it.

Chances are good that the litigation process will reveal any attempted cover-up. Not only will your lawyer be unpleasantly surprised and angry, but also any judge or jurors who are called upon to evaluate your integrity and reliability will surely hold it against you.

Under most policies, in the event that you violate the requirement of assistance and cooperation with your insurer or lawyer, keep in mind that you also risk losing your coverage. It is far better to be honest and open with your malpractice carrier and lawyer so that the case, with all its blemishes, can be properly prepared and evaluated.

Trust the Carrier

In the event that you find yourself in need of the benefits of your policy, bear in mind that in the vast majority of cases both you, your insurer, and your insurer selected lawyer will have a strong mutual interest in obtaining a favorable result for you. You are likely to find that the insurance company's claim representative and your lawyer are experienced and highly skilled at their respective jobs, and both are strongly committed to your interests.

It is sometimes nice to remember that what you bargained for when you paid for your malpractice policy was protection. In the event that a claim is brought against you, whether justified or not, it should be at least a bit comforting to know that your insurance claim representative and your lawyer will work hard for you to provide that protection.

Insurance Carrier and Risk Management

One of the often-overlooked benefits of having malpractice insurance is the indirect benefit of access to expertise in the area of risk management. Risk management is a term used to describe efforts taken to reduce the likelihood of incidents, occurrences, and claims before and after they occur. Medical malpractice insurers are experts at helping you practice medicine and operate your office in such ways that claims are less likely to arise.

Many insurers have developed and provide practice/specialty specific handbooks that offer detailed guidelines on a wide range of issues and topics likely to be encountered within a given type of practice. Many handbooks include samples and forms for such as: patient letters, patient follow-up reminders, laboratory and diagnostic follow up reminders, official reporting letters, informed consent forms, telephone message forms, medication records, office memos, and chart entries. Not only are the forms developed to meet national standards of care, but many are also designed to ensure compliance with applicable national, state, and local statutes.

If in doubt about whether your conduct or practice complies with the law, check with your malpractice insurance carrier. You are quite likely to receive very sound recommendations.

If you have a question or concern about a particular incident or patient that gives you discomfort or causes you to be concerned about a potential claim, rather than waiting to see what or if anything happens, you should consider contacting your malpractice carrier. This is especially true if you see a potential problem patient on an ongoing basis. An insurance representative may give you recommendations for dealing with the patient that would not have otherwise occurred to you. Because the insurance company and its employees are experts at managing risk, you may find that the assistance they provide helps keep risk molehills from becoming risk mountains.

Reporting Malpractice Claims

State Requirements

It is the law of most states that medical malpractice insurers are required to report claims made against their insureds to the state's professional licensing board. This means that each time a claim is brought by a patient and reported to your malpractice carrier, the licensing board will be notified by the carrier. This doesn't necessarily mean that all patient claims result in board proceedings as well.

The confidential reports made to medical boards typically are required to include:

- the insured physician's name and address

- policy number

- dates of occurrence, claim, and lawsuit

- the *claimant's* summary of the occurrence

Whether or not the board takes any immediate action is likely to depend on the nature of the claim brought by the patient. If the matter raised by the claim appears to be quite serious, the board may institute proceedings to investigate. If it does so, you will be notified.

If resolution of a medical malpractice claim involves payment of a settlement or judgment, statutes also require that the insurer make a report to the board.

In addition to information provided to the board by the insurer, some states' statutes also require that plaintiff's attorneys provide information whenever suit is filed. Plaintiffs' attorneys are typically required to send a copy of any complaint filed against a physician, along with a report which provides the names and addresses of all parties, and the date, nature, and location of the event giving rise to the claim.

If you have reason to believe that the board has an inaccurate picture of what has occurred, you may want to consider consulting with your insurer about contacting the board to see whether you could provide your own statement.

Federal Requirements

There are also federal regulations that impose reporting obligations on insurers. The Health Care Quality Improvement Act, 42 U.S.C. §§ 11101 *et seq.*, and the regulations promulgated under the Act require an insurer to report to the National Practitioner Data Bank whenever it makes a payment to settle or satisfy all or part of a claim or judgment against a physician. Details of the information to be provided, who is required to provide the information, and who may request information, are set forth in the regulations. Appendix 4 contains the reporting code and regulations for your reference.

Next

In the final section of the book are additional references, resources, and information that includes selected statutes, regulations, and a glossary of medical-legal terms.

FAQ:

1. Do I have any say under my professional liability policy as whether a case should be settle, and if so, for what amount?

Generally, it is the insurer that has the final say unless you have a "consent to settle" clause. If your policy contains such a clause, the insurer will not negotiate a settlement without your consent. However, once consent has been provided, the insurer decides whether a case should be settled and for what amount.

2. I understand that if I am sued for medical malpractice my insurance company will select and hire a lawyer. What if I do not like the lawyer selected?

You are free to hire your own lawyer at your own expense. However this would be a rather extreme approach to the situation. If you simply have a personality conflict you may want to talk to your insurer about the problem. If you question the qualifications or approach the lawyer is taking, contact your claim representative. Your disatisfaction may be due to a misunderstanding that can be cleared up. It is the very rare occasion that a physician and insurer-selected attorney have significant problems working together.

3. If I am sued for the mistake of my nurse, does my professional malpractice policy cover her mistake?

In most instances your policy will defend actions against you based on the acts and omissions of employees who are acting within the course and scope of their employment with you.

4. If a medical malpractice case brought against me goes to trial, am I required to attend the trial every day?

Nearly all professional malpractice policies require that you cooperate with your defense counsel. Your defense counsel will definitely want you to attend the trial. Most policies include a provision that the insurer will pay a set amount for time lost from work for attending court proceedings.

✦   ✦   ✦   ✦

APPENDIX 1

State Code References Relating to Medical Malpractice

APPENDIX 2

Sample Medical Malpractice Interrogatories

APPENDIX 3

Statutory Case Screening Methods

APPENDIX 4

Federal Code and Regulations for Database Reporting

SECTION FIVE

APPENDICES

APPENDIX 1

STATE CODE REFERENCES RELATING TO MEDICAL MALPRACTICE

Each state has its own system of nomenclature for referring to statutory code laws. For instance, in Alaska state statutes are referenced as "ALASKA STATUTES" and abbreviated "AS". In Nebraska, statutes are referred to as "NEBRASKA REVISED STATUTES" – abbreviated as "NEB.REV.ST." The numbering of specific statutes is also different. Overall, there tends to be great variation from state to state. For those with general or specific interest in looking up statutes in their own or any other state, here are state statute references. The numbers cited refer to some aspect of medical malpractice law in each state. The § symbol means "section". Generally, the specific statutes selected for illustrative purposes are those that define medical malpractice action terms, statutes of limitation, or general procedures.

Alabama	Ala. Code 1975 § 6-5-481
Alaska	AS 09.55.540
Arizona	A.R.S. § 12-561

Arkansas	ACA § 16-114-201
California	West's Ann. CAL.CIV.CODE § 3333.1
Colorado	C.R.S.A. 13-20-602
Connecticut	C.G.S.A. § 52-184c
Delaware	18 Del. C. § 6801
Florida	West's F.S.A. § 766.102
Georgia	Code 51-1-27
Hawaii	HRS § 671-1
Idaho	I.C. § 6-1012
Illinois	735 ILCS 5/2-1704
Indiana	IC 34-18-2-14
Iowa	I.C.A. § 147.136
Kansas	K.S.A. § 60-3401
Kentucky	K.R.S. § 413.140
Louisiana	LSA – R.S. 37:1262
Maine	24 M.R.S.A. § 2851
Maryland	MD CTS & JUD PRO § 3-2A-04

Massachusetts	M.G.L.A. 111 § 203
Michigan	M.C.L.A. 600.2912A
Minnesota	M.S.A. § 144.693
Mississippi	Code 1972, § 15-1-36
Missouri	V.A.M.S. 516.105
Montana	MCA 27-6-103
Nebraska	Neb.Rev.St. § 44-2828
Nevada	N.R.S. 41A.009
New Hampshire	R.S.A. § 507-C:2
New Jersey	N.J.S.A. 45-9-19.8
New Mexico	NMSA 1978, § 41-5-3
New York	McKinney's CPLR§3012-a
North Carolina	G.S. § 90-21.11
North Dakota	NDCC, 28-01-46
Ohio	R.C. § 4731.244
Oklahoma	12 Okl.St.Ann. § 96
Oregon	O.R.S. § 742.400
Pennsylvania	40 P.S. § 1301.821-A

Rhode Island	Gen.Laws 1956, § 5-37-1
South Dakota	SDCL § 21-3-11
Tennessee	T.C.A. § 29-26-115
Texas	Vernon's Ann. Texas Civ.St.Art. 4495b
Utah	U.C.A. 1953 § 78-14-2
Vermont	12 V.S.A. § 521
Virginia	Code 1950, § 8.01-581.1
Washington	West's RCWA 7.70.100
West Virginia	Code, § 30-3-14
Wisconsin	W.S.A. 655.42
Wyoming	W.S. 1977 § 9-2-1506

✦   ✦   ✦   ✦

APPENDIX 2

SAMPLE MEDICAL MALPRACTICE INTERROGATORIES

Interrogatories are one of several types of tools used to discover facts, theories, claims, or defenses advanced by an opposing party. Interrogatories, or written questions, are very commonly used in medical malpractice cases – indeed, it would be the rare case in which one or all of the parties involved did not use them. If you are involved in a medical malpractice case as a defendant, it is likely that interrogatories will be propounded to you fairly early on in the litigation, and nearly always before the plaintiff's lawyer requests your deposition. Anticipate that your lawyer will work with you to prepare your formal interrogatory responses.

In personal injury cases, interrogatories tend to cover areas that are common to most cases, including medical negligence cases. These categories include biographical questions, questions pertaining to the records, questions about investigations, questions regarding witnesses and exhibits, and questions regarding damages. Within these broad categories of inquiry there are variations that depend upon the claims alleged.

In some states, uniform or model interrogatories have been developed and set forth within rules of procedure for medical negligence cases. Arizona is one such state. Reviewing its uniform interrogatories will give you a feel for how interrogatories are worded, what types of information are sought, and how comprehensive interrogatories can be. Keep in mind though that parties are not required to use uniform interrogatories, nor are they precluded from using additional interrogatories.

UNIFORM INTERROGATORIES FOR USE IN MEDICAL MALPRACTICE CASES

SET A. PLAINTIFF TO DEFENDANT INDIVIDUAL HEALTH CARE PROVIDER

I. GENERAL INFORMATION

Interrogatory No. 1: Please state:

A. Your full name.
B. Any and all other names you have used or by which you have been known.
C. Date of your birth.
D. Full name of you spouse, if one.
E. Your residence and office addresses.
F. The name of your professional association or corporation, if any.

Interrogatory No. 2:

A. Which of the following is your present marital status: single, married, separated, widowed or divorced? _____
B. State the name and last known address of your spouse and every former spouse.
C. State the date of each such marriage.
D. As to previous marriages, please give the date, place and manner of each termination.

Interrogatory No. 3: Please state:

A. The name and location of each university or college you have attended, the dates of such attendance and any degrees you have received.
B. The name and location of each medical school you attended and the dates of attendance.
C. The name and location of each institution where you served as an intern and the dates of such internship.
D. The name and location of each institution where you were a medical resident or resident physician, the dates of each residency and the medical specialty which you studied during each residency.
E. The name and location of each institution where you have done a medical fellowship or other advanced study, the dates of such fellowship or study and the medical specialty which you studied.

Interrogatory No. 4: List each state in which you are, or have been, licensed to practice medicine, and in each instance, give:

A. The date on which you first received your license.
B. The name of the board or official body which issues such license.
C. The current status of each license.
D. If no longer licensed by any such state, the termination date and reason for termination.

Interrogatory No. 5: Have you ever held yourself out to the public or to the members of the medical profession as being specially qualified in any field of health care? _____ If so, please state:

A. The name of the specialty.
B. The date you first held yourself out as a specialist.
C. Whether you are board certified in such specialty.
D. The board which certified you.
E. The date you first became board certified.

F. The date you qualified to take the board certification examination.
G. The number of times you took the oral and written exams and the dates thereof.

Interrogatory No. 6: Have you ever been connected in a teaching capacity with any medical institution? _____ If so, please state:

A. The name and address of the institution.
B. What position you held and the dates that you held each teaching position.
C. The name of each subject taught by you.

Interrogatory No. 7: Have you ever written or collaborated in writing any treatises, papers or articles on any phase of medical practice or treatment? _____ If so, please state:

A. The title of each writing.
B. The citation for each writing.

Interrogatory No. 8: List the name of every professional society or organization in which you have held membership, the inclusive dates of your membership, any positions which you have held, and the dates such positions were held.

Interrogatory No. 9: List the names of each hospital where you have had staff privileges in the last five years, any limitations on your privileges, any hospital staff or committee memberships that you have held, and the dates thereof.

Interrogatory No. 10: Have you ever testified in deposition or in court in a malpractice or professional negligence lawsuit? _____ If so, please state:

A. The name of the plaintiff.

B. The name of any and all defendants.
C. The cause number and court where filed.
D. The names of the lawyers for the parties.
E. The subject matter of your testimony (e.g., standard of care, causation, damages).
F. The allegations of negligence in the suit.
G. The name and address of the person presently having possession of each deposition or any copy thereof.

II. RECORDS OF HEALTH CARE

Interrogatory No. 11: With regard to each occasion on which Defendant saw _____ in his office, please state the following:

A. Any history taken.
B. The precise physical examination performed and a detailed listing of all findings upon this physical examination.
C. Any other diagnostic aids employed.
D. Any other diagnoses or diagnostic impressions which were reached.
E. Any modalities of treatment selected.
F. Any and all conversations with _____ .

Interrogatory No. 12: With regard to each occasion on which Defendant saw _____ in the hospital, please state the following:

G. A. Any history taken.
H. The precise physical examination performed and a detailed listing of all findings upon this physical examination.
I. Any other diagnostic aids employed.
J. Any other diagnoses or diagnostic impressions which were reached.
K. Any modalities of treatment selected.
L. Any and all conversations with _____ .

Interrogatory No. 13: Please state whether the Defendant ever indicated or suggested to anyone that _____ was an unsatisfactory patient, or made any other critical representations concerning _____ . If the answer to the foregoing is in the affirmative, please state the following with respect to each such representation.

A. A general description of the representation.
B. The date and place where it was made.
C. The name and address of each person to whom this representation was made.

Interrogatory No. 14: Do you contend that any entries in the answering Defendant's medical/hospital records are incorrect or inaccurate? _____ If so, state:

A. The precise entry(ies) that you think are incorrect.
B. What you contend the correct or accurate entry(ies) should have been.
C. The name, address and employer of each and every person who has knowledge pertaining to A and B.
D. A description, including the author and title, of each and every document that you claim supports your answer to A and B.
E. The name, address and telephone number of each and every person you intend to call as a witness in support of your contention.

Interrogatory No. 15: Are you aware of any medical records, reports or letters from health care providers, or other written or recorded information or photographs concerning the medical, mental or physical condition of the Plaintiff(s) prior to the incident in question? _____ If so, state:

A. The nature and subject of each such item.
B. The date each item was prepared.
C. The name and last known address of the person or persons preparing each item.

D. The name and last known address of the person who presently has custody or control of each item.

E. Whether you are in possession of copies of each or any item.

III. INVESTIGATION

Interrogatory No. 16: Are you aware of the existence of any oral, written or recorded statement or admission made or claimed to have been made by any party or witness? _____ If so, state:

A. The name of the person making the statement or admission.

B. The date of the statement or admission.

C. The name, employer, occupation, and last known address of the person or persons taking or hearing the statement or admission.

D. The name and last known address of the person now in possession of a written or recorded statement or admission.

Interrogatory No. 17: Have any drawings, diagrams, photographs, motion pictures, or video-tapes been prepared or taken of any object or person involved in the incident? _____ If so, state:

A. What is depicted by each drawing, diagram, photograph, motion picture and/or video-tape.

B. The date on which each drawing, diagram, photograph, motion picture and/or video-tape was taken.

C. The name and address of the person preparing the drawing or diagram and/or the photographer of each photograph motion picture or video-tape.

D. The name and address of the person who now has custody of the drawing, diagram, photograph, motion picture and/or video-tape.

Interrogatory No. 18: Please state whether any meetings or hearings were held by any hospital committee, or any other committee or organization, at which _____ or any of the occurrences complained of in this case were discussed. _____ If the answer to the foregoing is in the affirmative, please state the following with respect to each such meeting or hearing:

A. The date and place where it was held.
B. The name of each person present.
C. Whether any written memoranda or minutes were made of the meeting.
D. Please list each written or documentary item submitted to the committee or organization.
E. As to each item set forth in D above, please state whether you contend the item is privileged (i.e., not subject to discovery).

IV. WITNESSES AND EXHIBITS

Interrogatory No. 19: Are you aware of any person you may call as a witness at the trial of this action who may have or claims to have any information concerning the medical, mental, or physical condition of the Plaintiff(s) prior to the incident in question? _____ If so, state:

A. The name and last known address of each such person and your means of ascertaining the present whereabouts of each such person.
B. The occupation and employer of each such person.
C. The subject and substance of the information each such person claims to have.

Interrogatory No. 20: Other than as disclosed above, are you aware of any person who may have or claims to have knowledge of the history or background of the Plaintiff(s) whom you may call as a witness in this action? (The "history or background of Plaintiff(s)" as used in this interrogatory is intended to have the broadest possible reference to the Plaintiff(s) background, including, but not limited to any of the following that may apply: Plaintiff(s)' personal, employment, academic, military, criminal, financial, religious, social or marital background) _____ If so, state:

A. The name and address of each person.
B. The occupation and employer of each person.
C. The nature and substance of the information concerning the Plaintiff(s) of which each person has knowledge.

Interrogatory No. 21: Other than as described above, are you aware of any written or recorded information relating to the history or background of the Plaintiff(s) (as defined in the previous interrogatory) which you may offer as exhibits in this action? _____ If so, state:

A. The nature of each such item of written or recorded information with sufficient particularity to identify it.
B. The date of each such item.
C. The name and address of the author or preparer of each such item.
D. The name and address of the person presently having possession of each such item or any copy thereof.

Interrogatory No. 22: List the names, addresses, official titles, if any, and other information of all persons, not previously identified, who:

A. Were known to be present at the events in question;
B. Claimed to have information concerning the events in question;
C. Were reported to have inform ration concerning the events in question;
D. Have knowledge of any pre-existing medical problems or medical treatment received by Plaintiff(s) prior to the events in question;
E. Have knowledge of the medical problems or medical treatment received by Plaintiff(s) from the events in question up to the present time;
F. Participated in any investigation concerning this incident in question of any party or witness thereto;

G. Participated in any surveillance of the Plaintiff(s). As to each such person, please state:
1. Name.
2. Present or last known address.
3. Present or last known address of employer.
4. Please set forth the subject and substance of the information each such person claims to have.
5. The present whereabouts of such person and the telephone number.

Interrogatory No. 23: Do you know of any person who is skilled in any particular field or science who you may call as a witness at trial of this action and who has expressed an opinion on any issue of this action? _____ If so, state:

A. The name and address of each person.
B. The field or science in which each such person is sufficiently skilled to enable him (or her) to express opinion evidence in this action.
C. A complete list of all medical malpractice actions in which each person has rendered an opinion, whether by written report, deposition testimony or trial testimony, including:
1. The name of the case.
2. The court in which it was filed.
3. The docket number assigned.
4. Whether each person rendered his (or her) opinion by written report, deposition testimony, trial testimony or a combination thereof.
D. Whether such person will base his (or her) opinion:
1. In whole or in part upon the facts acquired personally by him (or her) in the course of an investigation or examination of any of the issues of this case, or
2. Solely upon information as to facts provided him (or her) by others.

E. If your answer to D (above) discloses that any such person has made a personal investigation or examination relating to any of the issues of this case, please state the nature and dates of such investigation or examination.

F. Each and every fact, and each and every document, item, photograph or other tangible object supplied or made available to such person.

G. The general subject upon which each such person may express an opinion.

H. The substance of the facts and opinions to which such person is expected to testify.

I. Whether such persons have rendered written reports. _____ If so, state:
   1. The dates of each report.
   2. The name and address of the custodian of such reports.

Interrogatory No. 24: With respect to every lay witness whom you intend to or may call to testify, please state:

A. The name, address, occupation and employer of each such person.

B. What information or facts such person has provided or communicated to you.

C. What knowledge or information you believe the witness has with respect to the matters which are at issue in this lawsuit.

D. The subject about which such witness will or may testify, i.e., liability, damages, injuries, etc.

E. The substance of the testimony of each witness.

Interrogatory No. 25: List specifically and in detail each and every exhibit you propose to utilize at trial in this matter. This interrogatory is directed both to exhibits you intend to use at trial and to exhibits you may use.

Interrogatory No. 26: At the time of trial, do you intend to use or refer to any medical textbook, periodical or other medical publication during direct examination of your witness? _____ If your answer is in the affirmative, provide the citation for any text or periodical you intend to use.

V. MISCELLANEOUS

Interrogatory No. 27: Is it your contention that the Plaintiff(s)' injuries were caused in whole or in part by the fault of some person or persons other than yourself, whether named as a defendant in this action or not, or that some such other person or persons may have or share in the legal responsibility for the injuries set forth in Plaintiff(s)' Complaint _____ If so, state:

A. The name and present address of each such person or entity.
B. Each act or omission by which you contend such person is at fault for causing the Plaintiff(s)' injuries.
C. The relationship of each person or entity, if any, to you or to any other party in this action.

Interrogatory No. 28: Has this answering Defendant entered into any agreement or covenant with any other person or entity in any way compromising, settling, and/or limiting the liability or potential liability for any party to the claim arising out of the occurrence alleged in Plaintiff(s)' Complaint? _____ If so, please set forth the following:

A. The name and last known address of each person or entity with whom such agreement or covenant was made.
B. The date of each such agreement or covenant.
C. Is the agreement or covenant in writing? _____ If so, state the name and address of the individual who has custody and control of a copy of each such agreement or covenant.
D. The terms of each such agreement or covenant.
E. The consideration paid for each such agreement or covenant.

Interrogatory No. 29: As to any affirmative defenses you allege, state the factual basis of and describe each such affirmative defense, the evidence which will be offered at trial concerning any such alleged affirmative defense, including the names of any witnesses who will testify in support thereof, and the description of any exhibits which will be offered to establish each such affirmative defense.

Interrogatory No. 30: Have you ever been sued for malpractice or professional negligence? _____ If so, please state:

A. The name of the Plaintiff.
B. The name of any and all other Defendants.
C. The cause number and court where filed.
D. The name of the lawyer representing the Plaintiff, if any.
E. The name of the lawyer representing you, if any.
F. The allegations of negligence made against you.
G. The manner in which the claim was resolved.

Interrogatory No. 31: Please state the name of any insurance company or any person carrying on any insurance business who might be liable to satisfy part or all of a judgment which may be entered in favor of Plaintiff, or to indemnify or reimburse for payments made to satisfy the judgment. With respect to each such insurance company or person carrying on any insurance business listed above, please state the following:

A. The date on which the policy was issued.
B. The period for which the policy was issued.
C. The policy limits for bodily injury liability and medical pay coverage.
D. Whether any policy defenses are claimed to be applicable with regard to any claim made by Plaintiff.
E. Whether any claim made by Plaintiff is being defended under a reservation of rights.

F. If any policy of insurance is being defended under a reservation of rights, each and every factual basis for the insurance company's defense under a reservation of rights.

G. If any policy of insurance is being defended under a reservation of rights, the exact language of the policy which provided the basis for the insurance company's reservation of rights or attach a copy of the policy language in question.

H. If more than one insurance company is listed, state which company carries the primary coverage, and which company or companies carry the secondary coverage.

Taken from Arizona's UNIFORM RULES OF PRACTICE FOR MEDICAL MALPRACTICE CASES

APPENDIX 3

STATUTORY MEDICAL MALPRACTICE CASE SCREENING METHODS

For a variety of reasons, all which relate in some fashion to the goal of screening out un-meritorious medical malpractice cases, a number of states have set up pretrial procedural requirements that apply specifically to medical malpractice cases. In some states a medical malpractice plaintiff must present his case to a review panel before being allowed to take his case to trial. In other states, either party may ask for a professional review of the merits of the case. In some states these procedures are mandatory; in others they are permissive. Here are examples of four types of screening mechanisms used in four different states. If your state is one in which some form of screening is used, chances are good that it will be a variation of one of these.

Method I – Mediation of Health Care Claims

In Washington, mediation of health care claims is mandatory per statute, RCWA 7.70.100:

Mandatory mediation of health care claims – Procedures

(1) All causes of action, whether based in tort, contract, or otherwise, for damages arising from injury occurring as a result of health care provided after July 1, 1993, shall be subject to mandatory mediation prior to trial.

(2) The supreme court shall by rule adopt procedures to implement mandatory mediation of actions under this chapter. The rules shall address, at a minimum:

(a) Procedures for the appointment of, and qualifications of, mediators. A mediator shall have experience or expertise related to actions arising from injury occurring as a result of health care, and be a member of the state bar association who has been admitted to the bar for a minimum of five years or who is a retired judge. The parties may stipulate to a non-lawyer mediator. The court may prescribe additional qualifications of mediators;

(b) Appropriate limits on the amount or manner of compensation of mediators;

(c) The number of days following the filing of a claim under this chapter within which a mediator must be selected;

(d) The method by which a mediator is selected. The rule shall provide for designation of a mediator by the superior court if the parties are unable to agree upon a mediator;

(e) The number of days following the selection of a mediator within which a mediation conference must be held;

(f) A means by which mediation of an action under this chapter may be waived by a mediator who has determined that the claim is not appropriate for mediation; and

(g) Any other matters deemed necessary by the court.

(3) Mediators shall not impose discovery schedules upon the parties.

Method 2 – Medical Liability Review Panels

In Wyoming, medical malpractice plaintiffs must first present their claims to a review panel before filing suit in court. Here is the Wyoming statute, W.S. 1977 § 9-2-1506:

Claims to be reviewed by panel; prohibition on filing claims in court; tolling of statute of limitation; immunity of panel and witnesses; administration.

(a) The panel shall review all malpractice claims against health care providers filed with the panel except those claims subject to a valid arbitration agreement allowed by law or upon which suit has been filed prior to July 1, 1986. No complaint alleging malpractice shall be filed in any court against a health care provider before a claim is made to the panel and its decision is rendered. The running of the applicable limitation period in a malpractice action is tolled upon receipt by the director of the application for review and does not begin again until thirty (30) days after the panel's final decision is served upon the claimant.

(b) Panel members and witnesses are absolutely immune from civil liability for all acts in the course and scope of the duties under this act, including but not limited to communications, findings, opinions and conclusions.

(c) The panel may provide for the administration of oaths, the receipt of claims filed, the promulgation of forms required under this act, the issuance of subpoenas in connection with the administration of this act, and the performance of all other acts required to fairly and effectively administer this act. A party requesting a subpoena shall bear all costs of mileage and witness fees.

Method 3 – Medical Malpractice Screening Panels

Under the law of Connecticut, the parties to a medical malpractice action may stipulate to present the claim to a review panel – C.G.S.A. § 38a-33.

Selection of panel to screen malpractice claim

Whenever all parties to a claim for malpractice agree, they may request the Insurance Commissioner or his designee to select a panel composed of two physicians and one attorney from the Malpractice Screening Panel established under section 38a-32. None of the members of the panel, insofar as possible, shall be from the same community of practice of either the physician involved or the attorneys for the parties. At least one of the physicians shall be from the same specialty as the physician against whom such claim is filed and the attorney shall have experience in the trial of personal injury cases. The attorney so designated shall act as chairman.

Method 4 – Court-Ordered Arbitration

Florida's approach to processing medical negligence cases permits parties to requrest arbitration of claims before proceeding to trial. See West's F.S.A. § 766.107:

Court-ordered arbitration

(1) In an action for recovery of damages based on the death or personal injury of any person in which it is alleged that such death or injury resulted from the negligence of a health care provider as defined in § 768.50(2), the court may require, upon motion by either party, that the claim be submitted to nonbinding arbitration. Within 10 days after the court determines the matter will be submitted to arbitration, the court shall submit to the attorneys for each party the appropriate list of arbitrators prepared pursuant to subsection (2) and shall notify the attorneys of the date by which their selection of an arbitrator must be received by the court.

(2)(a) The chief judge of the judicial circuit shall prepare three lists of prospective arbitrators. A claimant's list shall consist of attorneys with experience in handling negligence actions who principally represent plaintiffs and who are eligible and qualified to serve as arbitrators. A defendant's list shall consist of health care practitioners, and attorneys who principally handle the defense of negligence actions, who are eligible and qualified to serve as arbitrators. A third list shall consist of attorneys who are experienced in trial matters but who do not devote a majority of their practice either to the defense or to the representation of plaintiffs in medical negligence matters. The chief judge shall appoint an advisory committee made up of equal numbers of at least three members of the defense bar and three members of the plaintiff's bar, which shall approve the qualifications of the persons on the claimant's list and the persons on the defendant's list. The advisory committee shall assist the chief judge in screening applicants and aiding in the formulation and application of standards for selection of arbitrators. Each committee shall meet at least once a year.

(b) A person may be certified to serve as an attorney arbitrator if the person has been a member of The Florida Bar for at least 5 years and the chief judge determines that he or she is competent to serve as an arbitrator. A person may be certified as a health care practitioner arbitrator if the person has been licensed to practice his or her profession in this state for at least 5 years and the chief judge determines that he or she is competent to serve as an arbitrator. Current lists of all persons certified as arbitrators shall be maintained in the office of the clerk of the circuit court and shall be open to public inspection. An attorney may not be disqualified from appearing and acting as counsel in a case pending before the court because he or she is serving as an arbitrator in another case.

(c) The plaintiff or plaintiffs shall select one arbitrator from the claimant's list and the defendant or defendants shall select one arbitrator from the defendant's list, and each shall notify the chief judge of such selection. If a party does not select his or her arbitrator within 20 days, the party's right to select an arbitrator is waived and the chief judge shall proceed with the selection of an arbitrator from the appropriate list. The two arbitrators selected shall, within 10 days after their selection, select a third arbitrator from the third list. If the arbitrators have not selected the third arbitrator within such 10-day period, the chief judge shall submit three names from the third list to the two arbitrators. Each arbitrator shall strike one name from the list, and the person whose name remains shall be the third arbitrator. No person may serve as an arbitrator in any arbitration in which he or she has a financial or personal interest. The third arbitrator shall disclose any circumstances likely to create a presumption of bias which might disqualify him or her as an impartial arbitrator. Either party may advise the chief judge why an arbitrator should be disqualified from serving. If the third arbitrator resigns, is disqualified, or is unable to perform his or her duties, the chief judge shall appoint a replacement. If an arbitrator selected by one of the parties is unable to serve, that party shall select a replacement arbitrator, unless he or she has waived such right, in which case the replacement shall be selected by the chief judge. The chief judge shall designate one panel member as chair.

(3)(a) Immediately upon the selection of the arbitrators, the clerk of the circuit court shall communicate with the parties and the arbitrators in an effort to ascertain a mutually convenient date for a hearing and shall then schedule and give notice of the date and time of the arbitration hearing. The hearing shall be scheduled within 60 days after the date of the selection and designation of the arbitrators, provided that there has been at least 20 days notice to the parties. Thereafter, the chief judge may for good cause shown grant a continuance of the hearing, provided that the hearing is rescheduled within 90 days after the date of the selection and designation of the arbitrators.

(b) The panel shall consider all relevant evidence and decide the issues of liability, amount of damages, and apportionment of responsibility among the parties. Punitive damages any not be awarded by the arbitration panel.

(c) The arbitration hearing may proceed in the absence of a party who, after due notice, fails to be present, but an award of damages shall not be based solely on the absence of a party.

(d) At least 10 days prior to the date of the arbitration hearing, each party shall furnish every other party with a list of witnesses, if any, and copies or photographs of all exhibits to be offered at the hearing. The arbitrators may refuse to hear any witness or to consider any exhibit which has not been disclosed.

(e) The hearing shall be conducted informally. The Florida Rules of Evidence shall be a guide, but shall not be binding. It is contemplated that the presentation of testimony shall be kept to a minimum and that cases shall be presented to the arbitrators primarily through the statements and arguments of counsel.

(f) The arbitrators may receive and consider the evidence of witnesses by affidavit, but shall give it only such weight as the arbitrators deem it is entitled to after consideration of any objections made to its admission.

(g) Any party may have a recording and transcript of the arbitration hearing made at his or her own expense.

(h) The members of the arbitration panel shall be paid $100 each for each day or portion of a day of service on the arbitration panel. The court shall assess each party equally for such payments.

(i) No member of the arbitration panel shall be liable in damages for any action taken or recommendation made by such member in the performance of his or her duties as a member of the arbitration panel.

(j) The decision of the arbitrators shall be rendered promptly and not later than 30 days after the date of the close of the hearings. The award of the arbitrators shall be immediately provided in writing to the parties. The award shall state the result reached by arbitrators without necessity of factual findings or legal conclusions. A majority determination shall control the award.

(4) The decision of the arbitration panel shall not be binding. If all parties accept the decision of the arbitration panel, that decision shall be deemed a settlement of the case and it shall be dismissed with prejudice. After the arbitration award is rendered, any party may demand a trial de novo in the circuit court by filing with the clerk of the circuit court and all parties such notice as is required by rules adopted by the Supreme Court.

(5) At the trial de novo, the court shall not admit evidence that there has been an arbitration proceeding, the nature or the amount of the award, or any other matter concerning the conduct of the arbitration proceeding, except that testimony given at an arbitration hearing may be used for the purposes otherwise permitted by the Florida Rules of Evidence or the Florida Rules of Civil Procedure. The trial on the merits shall be conducted without any reference to insurance, insurance coverage, or joinder of the insurer as codefendant in the suit. Panel members may not be called to testify as to the merits of the case.

(6) The Supreme Court may adopt rules to supplement the provisions of this section.

(7) This section shall apply only to actions filed at least 90 days after October 1, 1985.

✦　　✦　　✦　　✦

APPENDIX 4

FEDERAL CODE AND REGULATIONS FOR DATABASE REPORTING

In the first section is a partial listing of federal code sections that relate to reporting requirements involving actions against physicians and their licenses. These laws are found in the Health Care Quality Improvement Care Act of 1986, and found in 42 U.S.C. §§ 11101 *et seq.*

The second section contains the National Practitioner Data Bank Regulations, found at C.F.R. §§ 60.1 *et seq.* These regulations implement the federal code sections.

Health Care Quality Improvement Care Act of 1986

§ 11101. Findings

The Congress finds the following:

(1) The increasing occurrence of medical malpractice and the need to improve the quality of medical care have become nationwide problems that warrant greater efforts than those that can be undertaken by any individual State.

(2) There is a national need to restrict the ability of incompetent physicians to move from State to State without disclosure or discovery of the physician's previous damaging or incompetent performance.

(3) This nationwide problem can be remedied through effective professional peer review.

(4) The threat of private money damage liability under Federal laws, including treble damage liability under Federal antitrust law, unreasonably discourages physicians from participating in effective professional peer review.

(5) There is an overriding national need to provide incentive and protection for physicians engaging in effective professional peer review.

§ 11131. Requiring reports on medical malpractice payments

(a) In general

Each entity (including an insurance company) which makes payment under a policy of insurance, self-insurance, or otherwise in settlement (or partial settlement) of, or in satisfaction of a judgment in, a medical malpractice action or claim shall report, in accordance with § 11134 of this title, information respecting the payment and circumstances thereof.

(b) Information to be reported

The information to be reported under subsection (a) of this section includes–

(1) the name of any physician or licensed health care practitioner for whose benefit the payment is made,

(2) the amount of the payment,

(3) the name (if known) of any hospital with which the physician or practitioner is affiliated or associated,

(4) a description of the acts or omissions and injuries or illnesses upon which the action or claim was based, and

(5) such other information as the Secretary determines is required for appropriate interpretation of information reported under this section.

(c) Sanctions for failure to report

Any entity that fails to report information on a payment required to be reported under this section shall be subject to a civil money penalty of not more than $10,000 for each such payment involved. Such penalty shall be imposed and collected in the same manner as civil money penalties under subsection (a) of § 1320a-7a of this title are imposed and collected under that section.

(d) Report on treatment of small payments

The Secretary shall study and report to Congress, not later than two years after November 14, 1986, on whether information respecting small payments should continue to be required to be reported under subsection (a) of this section and whether information respecting all claims made concerning a medical malpractice action should be required to be reported under such subsection.

§ 11132. Reporting of sanctions taken by boards of medical examiners

(a) In general

(1) Actions subject to reporting

Each Board of Medical Examiners –

(A) which revokes or suspends (or otherwise restricts) a physician's license or censures, reprimands, or places on probation a physician, for reasons relating to the physician's professional competence or professional conduct, or

(B) to which a physician's license is surrendered,

shall report, in accordance with § 11134 of this title, the information described in paragraph (2).

(2) Information to be reported

The information to be reported under paragraph (1) is –

(A) the name of the physician involved,

(B) a description of the acts or omissions or other reasons (if known) for the revocation, suspension, or surrender of license, and

(C) such other information respecting the circumstances of the action or surrender as the Secretary deems appropriate.

(b) Failure to report

If, after notice of noncompliance and providing opportunity to correct non-compliance, the Secretary determines that a Board of Medical Examiners has failed to report information in accordance with subsection (a) of this section, the Secretary shall designate another qualified entity for the reporting of information under § 11133 of this title.

§ 11133. Reporting of certain professional review actions taken by health care entities

(a) Reporting by health care entities

(1) On physicians

Each health care entity which–

(A) takes a professional review action that adversely affects the clinical privileges of a physician for a period longer than 30 days;

(B) accepts the surrender of clinical privileges of a physician—

(i) while the physician is under an investigation by the entity relating to possible incompetence or improper professional conduct, or

(ii) in return for not conducting such an investigation or proceeding; or

(C) in the case of such an entity which is a professional society, takes a professional review action which adversely affects the membership of a physician in the society,

shall report to the Board of Medical Examiners, in accordance with § 11134(a) of this title, the information described in paragraph (3).

(2) Permissive reporting on other licensed health care practitioners

A health care entity may report to the Board of Medical Examiners, in accordance with § 11134(a) of this title, the information described in paragraph (3) in the case of a licensed health care practitioner who is not a physician, if the entity would be required to report such information under paragraph (1) with respect to the practitioner if the practitioner were a physician.

(3) Information to be reported

The information to be reported under this subsection is–

(A) the name of the physician or practitioner involved,

(B) a description of the acts or omissions or other reasons for the action or, if known, for the surrender, and

(C) such other information respecting the circumstances of the action or surrender as the Secretary deems appropriate.

(b) Reporting by Board of Medical Examiners

Each Board of Medical Examiners shall report, in accordance with § 11134 of this title, the information reported to it under subsection (a) of this section and known instances of a health care entity's failure to report information under subsection (a)(1) of this section.

(c) Sanctions

(1) Health care entities

A health care entity that fails substantially to meet the requirement of subsection (a)(1) of this section shall lose the protections of § 11111(a)(1) of this title if the Secretary publishes the name of the entity under § 11111(b) of this title.

(2) Board of Medical Examiners

If, after notice of noncompliance and providing an opportunity to correct noncompliance, the Secretary determines that a Board of Medical Examiners has failed to report information in accordance with subsection (b) of this section, the Secretary shall designate another qualified entity for the reporting of information under subsection (b) of this section.

(d) References to Board of Medical Examiners

Any reference in this subchapter to a Board of Medical Examiners includes, in the case of a Board in a State that fails to meet the reporting requirements of § 11132(a) of this title or subsection (b) of this section, a reference to such other qualified entity as the Secretary designates.

§ 11134. Form of reporting

(a) Timing and form

The information required to be reported under §§ 11131, 11132(a), and 11133 of this title shall be reported regularly (but not less often than monthly) and in such form and manner as the Secretary prescribes. Such information shall first be required to be reported on a date (not later than one year after November 14, 1986) specified by the Secretary.

(b) To whom reported

The information required to be reported under §§ 11131, 11132(a), and 11133(b) of this title shall be reported to the Secretary, or, in the Secretary's discretion, to an appropriate private or public agency which has made suitable arrangements with the Secretary with respect to receipt, storage, protection of confidentiality, and dissemination of the information under this subchapter.

(c) Reporting to State licensing boards

(1) Malpractice payments

Information required to be reported under § 11131 of this title shall also be reported to the appropriate State licensing board (or boards) in the State in which the medical malpractice claim arose.

(2) Reporting to other licensing boards

Information required to be reported under § 11133(b) of this title shall also be reported to the appropriate State licensing board in the State in which the health care entity is located if it is not otherwise reported to such board under subsection (b) of this section.

§ 11135. Duty of hospitals to obtain information

(a) In general

It is the duty of each hospital to request from the Secretary (or the agency designated under § 11134(b) of this title), on and after the date information is first required to be reported under § 11134(a) of this title) –

(1) at the time a physician or licensed health care practitioner applies to be on the medical staff (courtesy or otherwise) of, or for clinical privileges at, the hospital, information reported under this subchapter concerning the physician or practitioner, and

(2) once every 2 years information reported under this subchapter concerning any physician or such practitioner who is on the medical staff (courtesy or otherwise) of, or has been granted clinical privileges at, the hospital.

A hospital may request such information at other times.

(b) Failure to obtain information

With respect to a medical malpractice action, a hospital which does not request information respecting a physician or practitioner as required under subsection (a) of this section is presumed to have knowledge of any information reported under this subchapter to the Secretary with respect to the physician or practitioner.

(c) Reliance on information provided

Each hospital may rely upon information provided to the hospital under this chapter and shall not be held liable for such reliance in the absence of the hospital's knowledge that the information provided was false.

§ 11136. Disclosure and correction of information

With respect to the information reported to the Secretary (or the agency designated under § 11134(b) of this title) under this subchapter respecting a physician or other licensed health care practitioner, the Secretary shall, by regulation, provide for—

(1) disclosure of the information, upon request, to the physician or practitioner, and

(2) procedures in the case of disputed accuracy of the information.

§ 11137. Miscellaneous provisions

(a) Providing licensing boards and other health care entities with access to information

The Secretary (or the agency designated under § 11134(b) of this title) shall, upon request, provide information reported under this subchapter with respect to a physician or other licensed health care practitioner to State licensing boards, to hospitals, and to other health care entities (including health maintenance organizations) that have entered (or may be entering) into an employment or affiliation relationship with the physician or practitioner or to which the physician or practitioner has applied for clinical privileges or appointment to the medical staff.

(b) Confidentiality of information

(1) In general

Information reported under this subchapter is considered confidential and shall not be disclosed (other than to the physician or practitioner involved) except with respect to professional review activity, as necessary to carry out subsections (b) and (c) of § 11135 of this title (as specified in regulations by the Secretary), or in accordance with regulations of the Secretary promulgated pursuant to subsection (a) of this section. Nothing in this subsection shall prevent the disclosure of such information by a party which is otherwise authorized, under applicable State law, to make such disclosure. Information reported under this subchapter that is in a form that does not permit the identification of any particular health care entity, physician, other health care practitioner, or patient shall not be considered confidential. The Secretary (or the agency designated under § 11134(b) of this title), on application by any person, shall prepare such information in such form and shall disclose such information in such form.

(2) Penalty for violations

Any person who violates paragraph (1) shall be subject to a civil money penalty of not more than $10,000 for each such violation involved. Such penalty shall be imposed and collected in the same manner as civil money penalties under subsection (a) of § 1320a-7a of this title are imposed and collected under that section.

(3) Use of information

Subject to paragraph (1), information provided under § 11135 of this title and subsection (a) of this section is intended to be used solely with respect to activities in the furtherance of the quality of health care.

(4) Fees

The Secretary may establish or approve reasonable fees for the disclosure of information under this section or § 11136 of this title. The amount of such a fee may not exceed the costs of processing the requests for disclosure and of providing such information. Such fees shall be available to the Secretary (or, in the Secretary's discretion, to the agency designated under § 11134(b) of this title) to cover such costs.

(c) Relief from liability for reporting

No person or entity (including the agency designated under § 11134(b) of this title) shall be held liable in any civil action with respect to any report made under this subchapter (including information provided under subsection (a) of this section without knowledge of the falsity of the information contained in the report.

(d) Interpretation of information

In interpreting information reported under this subchapter, a payment in settlement of a medical malpractice action or claim shall not be construed as creating a presumption that medical malpractice has occurred.

National Practitioner Data Bank Regulations, 45 C.F.R. §§ 60.1 *et seq.*

§ 60.1 The National Practitioner Data Bank.

The Health Care Quality Improvement Act of 1986 (the Act), title IV of Pub.L. 99-660, as amended, authorizes the Secretary to establish (either directly or by contract) a National Practitioner Data Bank to collect and release certain information relating to the professional competence and conduct of physicians, dentists and other health care practitioners. These regulations set forth the reporting and disclosure requirements for the National Practitioner Data Bank.

§ 60.2 Applicability of these regulations.

The regulations in this part establish reporting requirements applicable to hospitals; health care entities; Boards of Medical Examiners; professional societies of physicians, dentists or other health care practitioners which take adverse licensure of professional review actions; and entities (including insurance companies) making payments as a result of medical malpractice actions or claims. They also establish procedures to enable individuals or entities to obtain information from the National Practitioner Data Bank or to dispute the accuracy of National Practitioner Data Bank information.

§ 60.3 Definitions.

Act means the Health Care Quality Improvement Act of 1986, title IV of Pub.L. 99-660, as amended.

Adversely affecting means reducing, restricting, suspending, revoking, or denying clinical privileges or membership in a health care entity.

Board of Medical Examiners, or *"Board,"* means a body or subdivision of such body which is designated by a State for the purpose of licensing, monitoring and disciplining physicians or dentists. This term includes a Board of Osteopathic Examiners or its subdivision, a Board of Dentistry or its subdivision, or an equivalent body as determined by the State. Where the Secretary, pursuant to section 423(c)(2) of the Act, has designated an alternate entity to carry out the reporting activities of S 60.9 due to a Board's failure to comply with § 60.8, the term "Board of Medical Examiners" or "Board" refers to this alternate entity.

Clinical privileges means the authorization by a health care entity to a physician, dentist or other health care practitioner for the provision of health care services, including privileges and membership on the medical staff.

Dentist means a doctor of dental surgery, doctor of dental medicine, or the equivalent who is legally authorized to practice dentistry by a State (or who, without authority, holds himself or herself out to be so authorized).

Formal peer review process means the conduct of professional review activities through formally adopted written procedures which provide for adequate notice and an opportunity for a hearing.

Health care entity means:

(a) A hospital;

(b) An entity that provides health care services, and engages in professional review activity through a formal peer review process for the purpose of furthering quality health care, or a committee of that entity; or

(c) A professional society or a committee or agent thereof, including those at the national, State, or local level, of physicians, dentists, or other health care practitioners that engages in professional review activity through a formal peer review process, for the purpose of furthering quality health care.

For purposes of paragraph (b) of this definition, an entity includes: a health maintenance organization which is licensed by a State or determined to be qualified as such by the Department of Health and Human Services; and any group or prepaid medical or dental practice which meets the criteria of paragraph (b).

Health care practitioner means an individual other than a physician or dentist, who is licensed or otherwise authorized by a State to provide health care services.

Hospital means an entity described in paragraphs (1) and (7) of section 1861(e) of the Social Security Act.

Medical malpractice action or claim means a written complaint or claim demanding payment based on a physician's, dentists or other health care practitioner's provision of or failure to provide health care services, and includes the filing of a cause of action based on the law of tort, brought in any State or Federal Court or other adjudicative body.

Physician means a doctor of medicine or osteopathy legally authorized to practice medicine or surgery by a State (or who, without authority, holds himself or herself out to be so authorized).

Professional review action means an action or recommendation of a health care entity:

(a) Taken in the course of professional review activity;

(b) Based on the professional competence or professional conduct of an individual physician, dentist or other health care practitioner which affects or could affect adversely the health or welfare of a patient or patients; and

(c) Which adversely affects or may adversely affect the clinical privileges or membership in a professional society of the physician, dentist or other health care practitioner.

(d) This term excludes actions which are primarily based on:

(1) The physician's, dentist's or other health care practitioner's association, or lack of association, with a professional society or association;

(2) The physician's, dentist's or other health care practitioner's fees or the physician's, dentist's or other health care practitioner's advertising or engaging in other competitive acts intended to solicit or retain business;

(3) The physician's, dentist's or other health care practitioner's participation in prepaid group health plans, salaried employment, or any other manner of delivering health services whether on a fee-for-service or other basis;

(4) A physician's, dentist's or other health care practitioner's association with, delegation of authority to, support for, training of, or participation in a private group practice with, a member or members of a particular class of health care practitioner or professional; or

(5) Any other matter that does not relate to the competence or professional conduct of a physician, dentist or other health care practitioner.

Professional review activity means an activity of a health care entity with respect to an individual physician, dentist or other health care practitioner:

(a) To determine whether the physician, dentist or other health care practitioner may have clinical privileges with respect to, or membership in, the entity;

(b) To determine the scope or conditions of such privileges or membership; or

(c) To change or modify such privileges or membership.

Secretary means the Secretary of Health and Human Services and any other officer or employee of the Department of Health and Human Services to whom the authority involved has been delegated.

State means the fifty States, the District of Columbia, Puerto Rico, the Virgin Islands, Guam, American Samoa, and the Northern Mariana Islands.

§ 60.4 How information must be reported.

Information must be reported to the Data Bank or to a Board of Medical Examiners as required under §§ 60.7, 60.8, and 60.9 in such form and manner as the Secretary may prescribe.

§ 60.5 When information must be reported.

Information required under §§ 60.7, 60.8, and 60.9 must be submitted to the Data Bank within 30 days following the action to be reported, beginning with actions occurring on or after September 1, 1990, as follows:

(a) *Malpractice Payments* (§ 60.7). Persons or entities must submit information to the Data Bank within 30 days from the date that a payment, as described in § 60.7, is made. If required under § 60.7, this information must be submitted simultaneously to the appropriate State licensing board.

(b) *Licensure Actions* (§ 60.8). The Board must submit information within 30 days from the date the licensure action was taken.

(c) *Adverse Actions* (§ 60.9). A health care entity must report an adverse action to the Board within 15 days from the date the adverse action was taken. The Board must submit the information received from a health care entity within 15 days from the date on which it received this information. If required under § 60.9, this information must be submitted by the Board simultaneously to the appropriate State licensing board in the State in which the health care entity is located, if the Board is not such licensing Board.

§ 60.6 Reporting errors, omissions, and revisions.

(a) Persons and entities are responsible for the accuracy of information which they report to the Data Bank. If errors or omissions are found after information has been reported, the person or entity which reported it must send an addition or correction to the Data Bank or, in the case of reports made under § 60.9, to the Board of Medical Examiners, as soon as possible.

(b) An individual or entity which reports information on licensure or clinical privileges under §§ 60.8 or 60.9 must also report any revision of the action originally reported. Revisions include reversal of a professional review action or reinstatement of a license. Revisions are subject to the same time constraints and procedures of §§ 60.5, 60.8, and 60.9, as applicable to the original action which was reported.

§ 60.7 Reporting medical malpractice payments.

(a) *Who must report.* Each entity, including an insurance company, which makes a payment under an insurance policy, self-insurance, or otherwise, for the benefit of a physician, dentist or other health care practitioner in settlement of or in satisfaction in whole or in part of a claim or a judgment against such physician, dentist, or other health care practitioner for medical malpractice, must report information as set forth in paragraph (b) to the Data Bank and to the appropriate State licensing board(s) in the State in which the act or omission upon which the medical malpractice claim was based. For purposes of this section, the waiver of an outstanding debt is not construed as a "payment" and is not required to be reported.

(b) *What information must be reported.* Entities described in paragraph (a) must report the following information:

(1) With respect to the physician, dentist or other health care practitioner for whose benefit the payment is made–

(i) Name,

(ii) Work address,

(iii) Home address, if known,

(iv) Social Security number, if known, and if obtained in accordance with section 7 of the Privacy Act of 1974,

(v) Date of birth,

(vi) Name of each professional school attended and year of graduation,

(vii) For each professional license: the license number, the field of licensure, and the name of the State or Territory in which the license is held,

(viii) Drug Enforcement Administration registration number, if known,

(ix) Name of each hospital with which he or she is affiliated, if known;

(2) With respect to the reporting entity—

(i) Name and address of the entity making the payment,

(ii) Name, title, and telephone number of the responsible official submitting the report on behalf of the entity, and

(iii) Relationship of the reporting entity of the physician, dentists, or other health care practitioner for whose benefit the payment is made;

(3) With respect to the judgment or settlement resulting in the payment—

(i) Where an action or claim has been filed with an adjudicative body, identification of the adjudicative body and the case number,

(ii) Date or dates on which the act(s) or omission(s) which gave rise to the action or claim occurred,

(iii) Date of judgment or settlement,

(iv) Amount paid, date of payment, and whether payment is for a judgment or a settlement,

(v) Description and amount of judgment or settlement and any conditions attached thereto, including terms of payment,

(vi) A description of the acts or omissions and injuries or illnesses upon which the action or claim was based,

(vii) Classification of the acts or omissions in accordance with a reporting code adopted by the Secretary, and

(viii) Other information as required by the Secretary from time to time after publication in the Federal Register and after an opportunity for public comment.

(c) *Sanctions.* Any entity that fails to report information on a payment required to be reported under this section is subject to a civil money penalty of up to $10,000 for each such payment involved. This penalty will be imposed pursuant to procedures at 42 CFR part 1003.

(d) *Interpretation of information.* A payment in settlement of a medical malpractice action or claim shall not be construed as creating a presumption that medical malpractice has occurred.

§ 60.8 Reporting licensure actions taken by Boards of Medical Examiners.

(a) *What actions must be reported.* Each Board of Medical Examiners must report to the Data Bank any action based on reasons relating to a physician's or dentist's professional competence or professional conduct—

(1) Which revokes or suspends (or otherwise restricts) a physician's or dentist's license,

(2) Which censures, reprimands, or places on probation a physician or dentist, or

(3) Under which a physician's or dentist's license is surrendered.

(b) *Information that must be reported.* The Board must report the following information for each action:

(1) The physician's or dentist's name,

(2) The physician's or dentist's work address,

(3) The physician's or dentist's home address, if known,

(4) The physician's or dentist's Social Security number, if known, and if obtained in accordance with section 7 of the Privacy Act of 1974,

(5) The physician's or dentist's date of birth,

(6) Name of each professional school attended by the physician or dentist and year of graduation,

(7) For each professional license, the physician's or dentist's license number, the field of licensure and the name of the State or Territory in which the license is held,

(8) The physician's or dentist's Drug Enforcement Administration registration number, if known,

(9) A description of the acts or omissions or other reasons for the action taken,

(10) A description of the Board action, the date the action was taken, and its effective date,

(11) Classification of the action in accordance with a reporting code adopted by the Secretary, and

(12) Other information as required by the Secretary from time to time after publication in the Federal Register and after an opportunity for public comment.

(c) *Sanctions.* If, after notice of noncompliance and providing opportunity to correct noncompliance, the Secretary determines that a Board has failed to submit a report as required by this section, the Secretary will designate another qualified entity for the reporting of information under § 60.9.

§ 60.9 Reporting adverse actions on clinical privileges.

(a) *Reporting to the Board of Medical Examiners. –*

(1) *Actions that must be reported and to whom the report must be made.* Each health care entity must report to the Board of Medical Examiners in the State in which the health care entity is located the following actions:

(i) Any professional review action that adversely affects the clinical privileges of a physician or dentist for a period longer than 30 days;

(ii) Acceptance of the surrender of clinical privileges or any restriction of such privileges by a physician or dentist –

(A) While the physician or dentist is under investigation by the health care entity relating to possible incompetence or improper professional conduct, or

(B) In return for not conducting such an investigation or proceeding; or

(iii) In the case of a health care entity which is a professional society, when it takes a professional review action concerning a physician or dentist.

(2) *Voluntary reporting on other health care practitioners.* A health care entity may report to the Board of Medical Examiners information as described in paragraph (a)(3) of this section concerning actions described in paragraph (a)(1) in this section with respect to other health care practitioners.

(3) *What information must be reported.* The health care entity must report the following information concerning actions described in paragraph (a)(1) of this section with respect to the physician or dentist:

(i) Name,

(ii) Work address,

(iii) Home address, if known,

(iv) Social Security number, if known, and if obtained in accordance with section 7 of the Privacy Act of 1974,

(v) Date of birth,

(vi) Name of each professional school attended and year of graduation,

(vii) For each professional license: the license number, the field of licensure, and the name of the State or Territory in which the license is held,

(viii) Drug Enforcement Administration registration number, if known,

(ix) A description of the acts or omissions or other reasons for privilege loss, or, if known, for surrender,

(x) Action taken, date the action was taken, and effective date of the action, and

(xi) Other information as required by the Secretary from time to time after publication in the Federal Register and after an opportunity for public comment.

(b) *Reporting by the Board of Medical Examiners to the National Practitioner Data Bank.* Each Board must report, in accordance with §§ 60.4 and 60.5, the information reported to it by a health care entity and any known instances of a health car entity's failure to report information as required under paragraph (a)(1) of this section. In addition, each Board must simultaneously report this information to the appropriate State licensing board in the State in which the health care entity is located, if the Board is not such licensing board.

(c) *Sanctions —*

(1) *Health care entities.* If the Secretary has reason to believe that a health care entity has substantially failed to report information in accordance with § 60.9, the Secretary will conduct an investigation. If the investigation shows that the health care entity has not complied with § 60.9, the Secretary will provide the entity with a written notice describing the noncompliance, giving the health care entity an opportunity to correct the noncompliance, and stating that the entity may request, within 30 days after receipt of such notice, a hearing with respect to the noncompliance. The request for a hearing must contain a statement of the material factual is sues in dispute to demonstrate that there is cause for a hearing. These issues must be both substantive and relevant. The hearing will be held in the Washington, D.C., metropolitan area. The Secretary will deny a hearing if:

(i) The request for a hearing is untimely,

(ii) The health care entity does not provide a statement of material factual issues in dispute, or

(iii) The statement of factual issues in dispute is frivolous or inconsequential.

In the event that the Secretary denies a hearing, the Secretary will send a written denial to the health care entity setting forth the reasons for denial. If a hearing is denied, or if as a result of the hearing the entity is found to be in noncompliance, the Secretary will publish the name of the health care entity in the Federal Register. In such case, the immunity protections provided under section 411(a) of the Act will not apply to the health care entity for professional review activities that occur during the 3-year period beginning 30 days after the date of publication of the entity's name in the Federal Register.

(2) *Board of Medical Examiners.* If, after notice of noncompliance and providing opportunity to correct noncompliance, the Secretary determines that a Board has failed to report information in accordance with paragraph (b) of this section, the Secretary will designate another qualified entity for the reporting of this information.

§ 60.10 Information which hospitals must request from the National Practitioner Data Bank.

(a) When information must be requested. Each hospital, either directly or through an authorized agent, must request information from the Data Bank concerning a physician, dentist or other health care practitioner as follows:

(1) At the time a physician, dentist or other health care practitioner applies for a position on its medical staff (courtesy or otherwise), or for clinical privileges at the hospital; and

(2) Every 2 years concerning any physician, dentist, or other health care practitioner who is on its medical staff (courtesy or otherwise), or has clinical privileges at the hospital.

(b) *Failure to request information.* Any hospital which does not request the information as required in paragraph (a) of this section is presumed to have knowledge of any information reported to the Data Bank concerning this physician, dentist or other health care practitioner.

(c) *Reliance on the obtained information.* Each hospital may rely upon the information provided by the Data Bank to the hospital. A hospital shall not be held liable for this reliance unless the hospital has knowledge that the information provided was false.

§ 60.11 Requesting information from the National Practitioner Data Bank.

(a) *Who may request information and what information may be available.* Information in the Data Bank will be available, upon request, to the persons or entities, or their authorized agents, as described below:

(1) A hospital that requests information concerning a physician, dentist or other health care practitioner who is on its medical staff (courtesy or otherwise) or has clinical privileges at the hospital,

(2) A physician, dentist, or other health care practitioner who requests information concerning himself or herself,

(3) Boards of Medical Examiners or other State licensing boards,

(4) Health care entities which have entered or may be entering employment or affiliation relationships with a physician, dentist or other health care practitioner, or to which the physician, dentist or other health care practitioner has applied for clinical privileges or appointment to the medical staff,

(5) An attorney, or individual representing himself or herself, who has filed a medical malpractice action or claim in a State or Federal court or other adjudicative body against a hospital, and

who requests information regarding a specific physician, dentist, or other health care practitioner who is also named in the action or claim. Provided, that this information will be disclosed only upon the submission of evidence that the hospital failed to request in formation from the Data Bank as required by § 60.10(a), and may be used solely with respect to litigation resulting from the action or claim against the hospital.

(6) A health care entity with respect to professional review activity, and

(7) A person or entity who requests information in a form which does not permit the identification of any particular health care entity, physician, dentist, or other health care practitioner.

(b) *Procedures for obtaining National Practitioner Data Bank information.* Persons and entities may obtain information from the Data Bank by submitting a request in such form and manner as the Secretary may prescribe. These requests are subject to fees as described in § 60.12

§ 60.12 Fees applicable to requests for information.

(a) *Policy on Fees.* The fees described in this section apply to all requests for information from the Data Bank, other than those of individuals for information concerning themselves. These fees are authorized by section 427(b)(4) of the Health Care Quality Improvement Act of 1986 (42 U.S.C. 11137). They reflect the costs of processing requests for disclosure and of providing such information. The actual fees will be announced by the Secretary in periodic notices in the Federal Register.

(b) *Criteria for determining the fee.* The amount of each fee will be determined based on the following criteria:

(1) Use of electronic data processing equipment to obtain information—the actual cost for the service, including computer search time, runs, printouts, and time of computer programmers and operators, or other employees,

(2) Photocopying or other forms of reproduction, such as magnetic tapes— actual cost of the operator's time, plus the cost of the machine time and the materials used,

(3) Postage—actual cost, and

(4) Sending information by special methods requested by the applicant, such as express mail or electronic transfer—the actual cost of the special service.

(c) *Assessing and collecting fees.* The Secretary will announce through notice in the Federal Register from time to time the methods of payment of Data Bank fees. In determining these methods, the Secretary will consider efficiency, effectiveness, and convenience for the Data Bank users and the Department. Methods may include: credit card; electronic fund transfer; check; and money order.

§ 60.13 Confidentiality of National Practitioner Data Bank information.

(a) *Limitations on disclosure.* Information reported to the Data Bank is considered confidential and shall not be disclosed outside the Department of Health and Human Services, except as specified in § 60.10, § 60.11 and § 60.14. Persons and entities which receive information from the Data Bank either directly or from another party must use it solely with respect to the purpose for which it was provided. Nothing in this paragraph shall prevent the disclosure of information by a party which is authorized under applicable State law to make such disclosure.

(b) *Penalty for violations.* Any person who violates paragraph (a) shall be subject to a civil money penalty of up to $10,000 for each violation. This penalty will be imposed pursuant to procedures at 42 CFR part 1003.

§ 60.14 How to dispute the accuracy of National Practitioner Data Bank information.

(a) *Who may dispute National Practitioner Data Bank information.* Any physician, dentist or other health care practitioner may dispute the accuracy of information in the Data Bank concerning himself or herself. The Secretary will routinely mail a copy of any report filed in the Data Bank to the subject individual.

(b) *Procedures for filing a dispute.* A physician, dentist or other health care practitioner has 60 days from the date on which the Secretary mails the report in question to him or her in which to dispute the accuracy of the report. The procedures for disputing a report are:

(1) Informing the Secretary and the reporting entity, in writing, of the disagreement, and the basis for it,

(2) Requesting simultaneously that the disputed information be entered into a "disputed" status and be reported to inquirers as being in a "disputed" status, and

(3) Attempting to enter into discussion with the reporting entity to resolve the dispute.

(c) *Procedures for revising disputed information.*

(1) If the reporting entity revises the information originally submitted to the Data Bank, the Secretary will notify all entities to whom reports have been sent that the original information has been revised.

(2) If the reporting entity does not revise the reported information, the Secretary will, upon request, review the written information submitted by both parties (the physician, dentist or other health care practitioner), and the reporting entity. After review, the Secretary will either—

(i) If the Secretary concludes that the information is accurate, include a brief statement by the physician, dentist or other health care practitioner describing the disagreement concerning the information, and an explanation of the basis for the decision that it is accurate, or

(ii) If the Secretary concludes that the information was incorrect, send corrected information to previous inquirers.

✦   ✦   ✦   ✦

GLOSSARY

A

ADR – see alternative dispute resolution.

Affidavit – a written declaration or statement of facts that is affirmed by an oath taken before an authorized officer, usually a notary.

Affirm – the holding of an appellate court that upholds a lower court determination.

Alteration – an improper change, deletion, or addition to a medical record.

Alternative Dispute Resolution – methods of resolving civil cases other than through the traditional litigation and trial process; see arbitration and mediation.

Answer – the formal document by which a defendant responds to a Plaintiff's Complaint.

Appeal – resort to an upper court for review of rulings, judgment, or verdict in a lower court.

Arbitration – a form of alternative dispute resolution involving the submission of a civil case to a neutral third person (or panel) for decision.

Associates – generally, attorney members of a law firm who are employees of the firm as distinguished from partners, who customarily have a financial stake or interest in the firm.

B

Bailiff – a courtroom staff person to whom is given care of jurors during a trial.

Bar – a body of attorneys or members of the legal profession; in English courts it is the partition behind which those other than solicitors must stand.

Bar Exam – the professional licensing examination given in each state which law students must pass to be eligible to practice law within a state.

Bench – a body of judicial officers or judges.

Bill of Rights – the first ten amendments to the United States Constitution.

Brief – a written document prepared by counsel in which a party's position, arguments, and support are presented to a court, most often to an appellate court.

Burden of Proof – a evidentiary duty to produce evidence; the duty to establish the truth by a "preponderance of evidence" in civil cases and "beyond reasonable doubt" in criminal cases. In civil cases, the burden of proof is often described as the burden of persuading the fact finder that a claim is "more probable than not".

C

Capitation agreement – a feature of some managed care plans in which contracting physicians or physician groups are paid a set amount per patient per period regardless of the actual medical care needs of the patient.

Case law – law that is developed on a case-by-case basis by judicial interpretation of the law; also known as common law.

Causation – a necessary legal element which must be established in order to prove liability; in order to establish liability it must be proven that a defendant's negligence was a proximate cause of plaintiff's damages.

Citation – reference to a legal authority, which is usually a statute or case.

Civil case – a case involving a legal dispute between citizens (including business and government entities) in which one seeks redress for a wrong other than a criminal wrong; a civil case verdict is not required to be unanimous.

Clerk – a court room staff person who is the independent record keeper of court proceedings.

Code law – enacted law, also known as statutory law.

Common law – law that is developed on a case-by-case basis as a consequence of judicial rulings.

Complaint – the formal document by which a plaintiff sets forth his or her civil claims against another at the start of litigation.

Confidentiality – an obligation imposed by law with respect to communications regarding one's medical condition made by a patient to his physician.

Consent – voluntarily yielding, acquiescing, or conforming one's will to another; see informed consent.

Conservator – one who has been legally appointed to oversee and manage the financial affairs of another; as distinguished from guardians, generally conservators cannot provide consent to treatment on behalf of their wards.

Contingent fee – a method of payment for legal representation whereby the lawyer is paid a percentage of the recovery obtained for the client. The fee is contingent upon the outcome of the case.

Corrections – with respect to medical records, corrections are proper changes made to records to render them accurate.

Criminal case – litigation instituted by a governmental entity to enforce standards of conduct; a criminal case verdict must be unanimous.

Cross examination – the examination of a witness in deposition, hearing, or trial by a party opposed to the party who has called or produced the witness.

D

Damages – in civil actions it is monetary compensation claimed for a plaintiff's loss.

Declaration page – the page(s) of a professional liability policy on which is summarized key policy information such as the named insured, coverages, and limits of liability.

Defendant – in a civil case it is the person or entity against whom an action for damages is brought.

Deponent – a witness who gives deposition testimony.

Deposition – a pretrial discovery proceeding in which a witness is questioned under oath in the presence of all parties to the case.

Direct examination – the examination of a witness in deposition, hearing, or trial by a party on whose behalf he is called.

Discovery – the pretrial process of finding and developing evidence in support of one's own case and of opposing parties' cases.

Duty – an obligation arising from operation of the law; physicians have a duty to act in accordance with the standard of care for a reasonable and prudent physician acting in the same or similar circumstances.

E

Employee – an individual who works for another who has the right to control and direct the individual's performance of his work; see Respondeat Superior.

Equity – a general term referring to the spirit and notion of fairness and justice.

Error – this term is often used in appellate practice to describe a mistaken judgment, an incorrect belief as to facts, or a mistaken conception or application of the law. There are a number of different types of error in the appellate sense, including harmless error, fundamental error, and reversible error.

F

Fact finder – the person or persons responsible for deciding issues of fact, as distinguished from issues of law. In a jury trial, jurors are the finders of fact; the judge is responsible to decide issues of law. In cases where the parties have waived their right to a jury trial and proceed to present their case to a judge (bench trial), the judge decides both issues of fact and law.

Fault – a term that is often used to designate negligence, the failure to use due care, and liability. It is distinguished by some as encompassing negligence and causation, i.e., to find someone at fault, it must be established that conduct was unreasonable, and that such conduct was a cause of the harm to the plaintiff.

Federal – pertaining to the national government of the union of the states which is organized according to the constitution of the United States.

G

Guardian – one who is legally appointed to be responsible for taking care of another. A guardian has the authority to provide consent for treatment on behalf of a ward.

Guilty – refers to one who has been convicted of committing a crime.

H

Hearing – in a general sense, it is a semi-formal proceeding in which a party or respondent has a right to be heard and in which issues of fact or law are decided.

Hearsay – evidence that comes from the repetition of what was said by another; there is a precise legal definition of hearsay in standard rules of evidence that refers to hearsay as an out of court statement offered to prove the truth of the matter for which it is asserted.

Honorable – a title of courtesy and recognition traditionally applied to judges and other officials.

I

IME – see Independent Medical Exam

Impeach – the process of disputing, disparaging, or discrediting a witness by showing inconsistencies, erroneous assumptions, or mistaken foundations relating to his testimony.

Independent contractor – one who contracts with another to perform work according to his own methods and equipment, and without being subject to the control of the other.

Independent Medical Exam – a discovery method that may be used by a party during litigation to have the medical, physical, or psychological claim of another party evaluated by a qualified physician or psychologist.

Informed consent – consent for treatment provided by a patient after having been appropriately advised and informed about alternatives, risks, and consequences associated with the treatment.

J

Judge – an officer who presides in court and whose responsibilities include: deciding questions of law, managing flow of cases, conducting trials, and deciding questions of fact in bench trials.

Judgment – the official decision of the court at the conclusion of a proceeding or trial that sets forth the respective rights, claims, and damages of the parties.

Jurisdiction – this term has several different meanings depending on how it is applied; it may be used to refer to the geographic area that corresponds to a governmental entity; in a legal sense, there are three types of jurisdiction that a court must have: jurisdiction over the person, jurisdiction over the subject matter, and jurisdiction to render a particular judgment.

Jury – a certain number of eligible citizens who are sworn to judge the evidence presented to them and decide a case. A Grand Jury is comprised of those who are summoned to by the sheriff to evaluate complaints brought in criminal cases and return indictments upon satisfaction with the accusations brought. A Petit Jury is an ordinary jury impaneled to try both civil and criminal cases.

Jury Selection – the process by which courts and parties, through their attorneys, "strike" those who are unqualified or undesirable to serve as jurors in a particular case.

L

Liable – obligated by law for compensation to another for damages caused.

M

Managed care – a health care model in which the provision of health care services are contractually determined.

Malfeasance – conduct which is wrong or unjust.

Malpractice – professional misconduct; unreasonable professional conduct.

Master-servant – used to describe a working relationship in which the work of the servant is controlled by and done for the benefit of the master. Such a relationship gives rise to respondeat superior liability of the master for the conduct of the servant.

Mediation – an alternative dispute resolution method in which the parties to an action are aided by a neutral third person to reach a mutually agreeable out of court settlement.

Mistrial – a trial which cannot proceed due to improper conduct or irregularity on the part of a witness, party, or juror.

Motion – a request on behalf of a party, usually in writing, urging the assigned judge to take a particular action or make a particular ruling regarding the case.

Motion for summary judgment – a motion brought by a party which asks the judge to rule that based on the undisputed facts and applicable law a party is entitled to summary judgment on all or part of a case.

N

Negligence – essentially, the failure to exercise reasonable care.

Nonfeasance – the failure to act when action is required.

Notice of deposition – a document issued by a party to a witness giving notice of the witness's required appearance at a specified place and time to provide deposition testimony.

O

Objection – the act of taking exception to a question, matter, or proceeding.

Opinion – the ruling by a judge or court setting forth the court's decision and reasons therefore. Opinions are most commonly issued by appellate courts. A concurring opinion is separate from the majority opinion prepared by a judge who generally agrees with the majority decision but who wishes to express his own reasoning or views separately. A dissenting opinion is a separate opinion by a judge who disagrees with the decision of the majority.

Ordinance – this term is usually used to designate the legislative enactments of a municipality.

Overrule – in trial it refers to the decision of the judge to reject an objection made a party. A decision of a lower court is said to be overruled when a superior reviewing court decides an issue differently.

P

Partner – an attorney member of a law firm with a financial interest in the firm.

Plaintiff – the party in a civil lawsuit who brings an action against another.

Probable – when referring to the burden of proof, it means more likely than not.

Prosecutor – an attorney representing the government in pursuing charges against one for violation of criminal law.

R

"Read and sign" – the option given to a deponent of reviewing his deposition transcript to correct mistakes and sign his name indicating that he has done so.

Reasonable care – the standard applied to measure whether a defendant was negligent under the circumstances.

Remand – the action of an appellate court in sending a case back to the trial court.

Request for production – a pretrial discovery method by which a party may request that an adverse party produce documents and tangible items for inspection or copying.

Res ipsa loquitur – Latin for "the thing speaks for itself"; when applied in a negligence case it gives rise to a rebuttable presumption that the defendant was negligent on the basis that the accident in question is one that ordinarily does not occur in the absence of negligence.

Respondeat superior liability – vicarious liability of a master/principal/employer for the negligent acts of a servant/agent/employee.

Reverse – to vacate or set aside.

S

Socratic method – a method of teaching whereby students are asked a series of questions designed to lead them to the correct answers or conclusions.

Standard of care – the measure of the conduct required by an individual in a specific situation.

Statute – a written legislative enactment of law.

Subpoena – Latin for "under penalty"; a process used to command the appearance of a witness to give testimony or provide tangible items.

Sustain – to maintain; an objection that is sustained is one that is supported. When an objection to a question is sustained, the witness does not answer the question.

T

Tort – a civil wrong or injury that does not arise out of a contract; personal injury actions are generally encompassed by the term "tort".

Tortfeasor – one who commits a tort; joint tortfeasors are those who share in the responsibility for causing a civil injury to another.

V

Vicarious liability – liability imposed on one based on the conduct of another because of the relationship between the two. See also Respondeat Superior and Master-Servant.

W

"Waive signature" – the option given to a deponent who does not wish to read, correct, or sign a transcript of his deposition testimony.

INDEX

T

U

V

W

About the Author

Margaret Dean is an attorney in Phoenix, Arizona. In addition to her law degree, she has bachelor of science in nursing and is a former registered nurse. The focus of her legal practice has been personal injury litigation with a special emphasis on evaluating and litigating medical malpractice cases. She is a state bar certified specialist in personal injury and wrongful death litigation. In the past, Mrs. Dean has served as a director of the Arizona Trial Lawyers Association, a director of the Maricopa County Bar Association, a barrister member of the Sandra Day O"Connor Inn of Court, and as an associate member of the American Board of Trial Advocates. She has served on a number of committees of these organizations, and of others. Mrs. Dean has chaired and spoken at a wide variety of seminars on such topics as medical malpractice case selection, jury selection, ethics, use of medical expert witnesses, and how to spot "doctored" records.

The author is interested in comments and questions about the material presented in this book. If you would like to write to the author, please address all correspondence to her in care of the publisher at:

Legis ◆ Press
3646 E. Ray Road
Suite B16-52
Phoenix, Arizona 85044